SPANISH AMERICAN
INDEPENDENCE MOVEMENTS

THE **BROADVIEW**
SOURCES SERIES

Spanish American Independence Movements

A HISTORY IN DOCUMENTS

edited by WIM KLOOSTER

broadview press

BROADVIEW PRESS – www.broadviewpress.com
Peterborough, Ontario, Canada

Founded in 1985, Broadview Press remains a wholly independent publishing house. Broadview's focus is on academic publishing; our titles are accessible to university and college students as well as scholars and general readers. With 800 titles in print, Broadview has become a leading international publisher in the humanities, with world-wide distribution. Broadview is committed to environmentally responsible publishing and fair business practices.

Library and Archives Canada Cataloguing in Publication

Title: Spanish American independence movements : a history in documents / edited by Wim Klooster.
Names: Klooster, Wim, editor.
Series: Broadview sources series.
Description: Series statement: The Broadview sources series | Includes bibliographical references and index.
Identifiers: Canadiana (print) 20210150688 | Canadiana (ebook) 20210166681 | ISBN 9781554814565
    (softcover) | ISBN 9781770487994 (PDF) | ISBN 9781460407486 (EPUB)
Subjects: LCSH: Latin America—History—Autonomy and independence movements—Sources. | LCSH:
    Latin America—History—Wars of Independence, 1806-1830—Sources.
Classification: LCC F1412 .S63 2021 | DDC 980/.02—dc23

Broadview Press handles its own distribution in North America:
PO Box 1243, Peterborough, Ontario K9J 7H5, Canada
555 Riverwalk Parkway, Tonawanda, NY 14150, USA
Tel: (705) 743-8990; Fax: (705) 743-8353
email: customerservice@broadviewpress.com

For all territories outside of North America, distribution is handled by Eurospan Group.

 Broadview Press acknowledges the financial support of the Government of Canada for our publishing activities.

Copy-edited by Juliet Sutcliffe
Book design by Em Dash Design

PRINTED IN CANADA

CONTENTS

PART 4: FERNANDO'S RESTORATION, CONTINUED WARFARE, AND INDEPENDENCE   130

CONTENTS: DOCUMENTS SEPARATED BY REGION

INTRODUCTION

In May 1789, a funeral service was held in Caracas, Venezuela, for the Spanish King Carlos III, who had died five months earlier. Carlos IV, the new king, decreed that banners be raised in his name, the way in which a town traditionally pledged allegiance to a new monarch. During 12 days of ceremonies and festivities that December, the royal banner, embroidered with gold and silver, was blessed in Caracas's cathedral with **vespers**, a mass, and a **Te Deum**. From there, it was carried on horseback through the main streets to the Plaza Mayor and displayed on the balcony of the city hall between portraits of the Catholic monarchs, **Fernando and Isabela**. The following days saw a lot of joyful activity: games played on horseback, the enactment of comedies, bullfights involving 200 bulls, fireworks, and the presentation of a **triumphal cart** made by high school students to represent the triumph of wisdom over error, ignorance, and barbarousness.[1] At least on the surface, nothing suggested that the royal regime was entering its final stage in Spain's American provinces. But just two decades later, Caracas became one of the focal points of resistance to Spanish rule. Thus began one of the many independence movements that would ultimately put an end to Spain's presence in the mainland Americas.

BACKGROUND: ETHNICITY, CULTURE, AND POWER IN THE SPANISH TERRITORIES

Spain's American territories were divided into four **viceroyalties**: New Spain (1535–1821), made up of Mexico, Central America, and the Spanish Caribbean; Peru (1542–1824); New Granada (1739–1819), consisting of today's Colombia, Ecuador, Panama, and Venezuela; and the Río de la Plata (1776–1814), comprising today's Argentina, Bolivia, Chile, Paraguay, and Uruguay.

These territories were ethnically much more diverse than the **Iberian Peninsula**. The archbishop of Mexico wrote in 1770: "God has put two worlds in the hands of our Catholic monarch, and the New does not resemble the Old in climate, customs or native inhabitants.... In Old Spain only one caste of men is recognized, whereas in New Spain there are many different ones."[2] Indeed, ethnicity was an important organizing principle of the hierarchically structured societies of Spanish America. Whites formed the economic and political elite, although most **creoles** were poor and had no access to power. Even upper-class creoles were often excluded from high political and church offices. The highest positions of commercial, religious, military, and political control were in the hands of the much smaller group of *peninsulares*, the

vespers: An evening prayer service.

Te Deum: A liturgical hymn of praise to God, sung on special occasions.

Fernando and Isabela: King Fernando of Aragon and Queen Isabela of Castile, whose wedding in 1469 laid the foundations for the Kingdom of Spain.

triumphal cart: Cart usually on display in a procession after a military triumph.

viceroyalty: Subdivision of Spanish America, ruled by a viceroy.

Iberian Peninsula: Area in Europe made up of Spain and Portugal.

creoles: Whites of Spanish descent born in the Americas.

peninsulares: Spanish-born Spaniards who immigrated from Spain and resided in the New World.

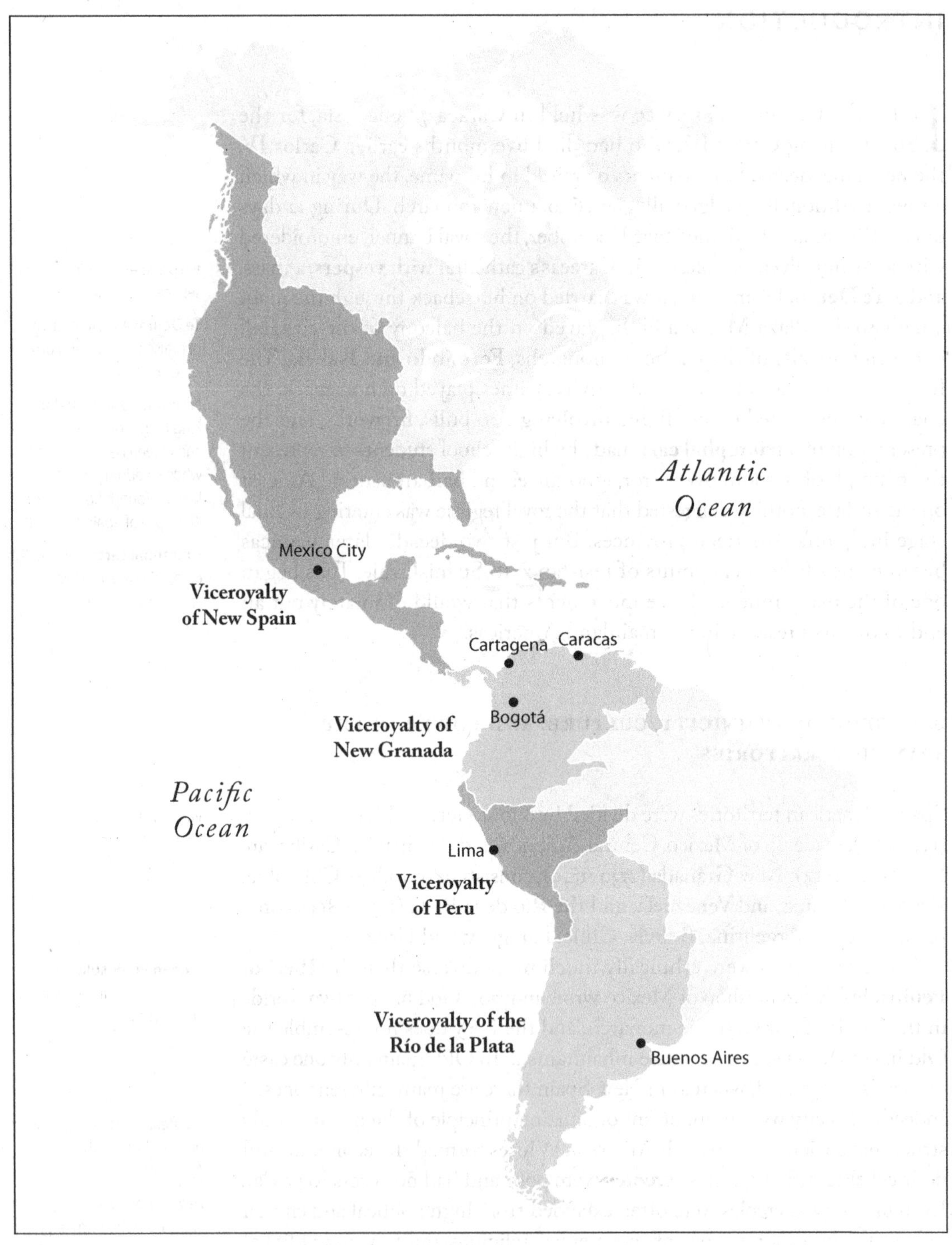

Spanish America, 1790.

merchants, military officers, and **officeholders** who hailed from Spain.[3] *Peninsulares* benefited from the fact that the import and export trades were a Spanish monopoly. The commercial system did not allow for trade with foreigners. Indigenous people, blacks, **mestizos**, and **mulattoes**—whose status was based not simply on ancestry, but also on factors such as appearance, wealth, and the people with whom they socialized—faced multiple obstacles if they aspired to climb the social ranks.[4] And yet, they did enjoy legal rights that enabled them to use legal institutions to protect their interests, often with the help of the crown. In fact, many colonial subjects—whites and nonwhites alike—conceived of their relationship with the crown as a pact rather than one of **subjugation**.[5]

Controlled by royal authorities, the colonial Catholic Church ministered to very loyal populations which were largely sheltered from the influence of other religions. Often devoted to particular saints, orders, or cults, residents of Spanish America bequeathed property in their wills to support religious activities. They also founded convents and willingly paid tithes for the upkeep of churches. In such ways, and by its participation in the market economies, the Church became enormously wealthy. It developed into the main financial institution in the colonies, and religious leaders were among the most powerful figures. The Church's religious work was supported by the **Spanish Inquisition**, which had tribunals in Mexico City, Lima, and Cartagena de Indias. The Inquisition could count on massive popular support in its chief task of identifying and prosecuting "**heretics**."

Although religiously united, the population was split along ethnic and socioeconomic lines. *Peninsulares* and creoles occupied the top two tiers of the hierarchy, respectively. The **plebeians** formed the bulk of the population and were largely nonwhite—the aforementioned Indigenous people, blacks, mestizos, and mulattoes, but also poor whites. In the Río de la Plata, most of these plebeians performed manual labor as artisans, day laborers, workers in the **provisioning trade**, washerwomen, **pressers**, peddlers, irregular workers, and beggars.[6] Popular resentment among the plebeians was often directed against the Spanish natives in their midst because of the positions they occupied in retail trade, the lighter punishments they received for crimes and misdemeanors, their role as **guild masters**—while creoles and blacks worked as **journeymen** and apprentices—and the popularity of *peninsular* males among plebeian women, who aimed to enter the ranks of respectable people by marrying them.[7]

The plebeians were excluded from a role in government. Urban governing bodies were in the hands of what may be called the "patricians." As one historian has explained, these were "the oldest and most distinguished members of the city, proud of the status of their lineage, fortune, culture and social influence. Not everyone thus described had formal noble status, but

Black and white washerwomen at work near the fort of Buenos Aires, beating clothes with wooden mallets and drying them on the grass. Emeric Essex Vidal, "Fort," from *Picturesque illustrations of Buenos Ayres and Monte Video*, 1820. Image courtesy of Wikimedia Commons

they regarded themselves—and were regarded by others—as an aristocracy."[8] Although plebeians, and even enslaved people, used the freedom they had to challenge their opponents in courts of law, they also resorted to extra-judicial action in the form of revolt. Indigenous people in (Lower) Peru and Upper Peru (present-day Bolivia), especially, expressed their discontent about issues such as rising taxes, diminished autonomy, and abuse at the hands of authorities in dozens of localized revolts throughout the early 1800s.[9] A major cause of the unrest was the *repartimiento*, a system of forced exchange in which **corregidores** and other officials monopolized the trade between Indigenous people and the world outside their districts, compelling them to sell their products at prices above their market value. The native population was also forced to accept cash and equipment to produce crops and consume commodities at inflated prices.

corregidores: District officers with local administrative and judicial powers.

Hatred of the *repartimiento* in Peru fueled the largest colonial revolt before the dawn of the independence era. Inspired by Andean **messianism** rooted in both traditional Inca beliefs and Christianity, the mestizo **muleteer** Túpac Amaru II started a rebellion in 1780 that stretched nearly 300 miles from Cuzco to Lake Titicaca and took almost two years to be suppressed. His guerrilla war, in which his wife Micaela Bastidas played a prominent role, was supported by tens of thousands of followers who helped him surround Cuzco; but after he failed to act decisively and occupy the city, probably because of the spread of dysentery, the movement began to lose ground. Spanish officials defeated his forces and had Túpac **quartered**. His legacy has been seen by some as essentially one of **pillage** and violence, whereas others have stressed his political program, which provided for the elimination of the main taxes and of large **haciendas**, and the introduction of free trade, as well as the creation of a **polity** without ethnic strife.[10]

Túpac Amaru's revolt coincided in 1781 with an uprising in New Granada against Spanish authorities that mobilized around 20,000 creoles, Indigenous people, and mestizos. Led largely by members of the landowning elite, the main goal of this ***Comuneros*** revolt was the cancelation of recent fiscal measures, such as the increase of the sales tax, and the rise of tobacco and brandy prices. Political objectives were not absent, however. Among the rebels' stated demands was, for instance, the call to give preference to American-born Spaniards (creoles) in filling local bureaucratic positions.[11] As with Túpac Amaru in Peru, an important reason for the defeat of the revolt was the clergy's opposition.

The simultaneity of these two large-scale rebellions, and the outbreak in the year 1780 of additional riots in places such as Quito (also in New Granada), and Arequipa, La Paz, Cochabamba (in the viceroyalty of Peru), was no coincidence. At this time, officials from Spain were implementing a wide-ranging reform program whose chief rationale was to restore the empire's financial health. As Britain and France had also experienced, the waging of successive wars tested the ability of Spain's ministers to pay for its troops and arms. Increasingly, they came to rely on issuing bonds and on **remittances** from American ***consulados*** and private individuals. However, expenses kept exceeding income once war with revolutionary France broke out in 1793, marking the start of a seemingly never-ending period of warfare—and of taxation to pay for it.[12]

messianism: The belief in a messiah as the savior of humankind.

muleteer: A person who drives mules.

quartered: Torn apart by four horses moving in different directions.

pillage: Collective robbery using violence, especially in wartime.

haciendas: Large estates.

polity: A politically organized unit.

Comuneros: Commoners.

remittances: Sums of money sent by mail.

consulados: Merchant guilds.

French Revolution:
Ten-year period (1789–99) during which France abolished privileges, introduced a parliamentary democracy, and exported its principles through armed invasion.

Gaceta de Lima: Lima's oldest newspaper, which began publishing in 1715.

parricide: Murdering one's father, mother, or close relative.

regicide: The killing of a king.

the Terror: Period in 1793–94 during which the French revolutionary government took extraordinary measures against its perceived enemies, resulting in massacres and numerous public executions.

Declaration of the Rights of Man and Citizen:
Human rights charter adopted by the French National Assembly in 1789, which reflected the principles of the French Revolution. It established equality before the law, freedom of speech, and the right to property.

audiencia: Royal high court, which combined the functions of administrative body, advisory board, and court of law.

Santafé de Bogotá: Capital city of the viceroyalty of New Granada.

The **French Revolution** was abhorred almost universally in Spanish America. It consisted, wrote the *Gaceta de Lima* in 1794, of murders, fires, **parricides**, and **regicide**, and threatened the basic principles on which the social, political, and religious order was built. There was no lack of information about the unbelievable chain of events in France. Peru's viceregal government used the *Gaceta* to give an account of the developments while condemning the French revolutionaries in no uncertain terms. The newspaper was especially critical of the execution of the king, the altercations between the legislature and the Catholic Church, and **the Terror**.[13] The events in France led to renewed suspicion in Peru of books by French authors, which were censored on a regular basis.

However, some intellectuals across Spanish America admired the revolutionary overthrow in France of a society based on privilege, and the authorities could not prevent the continued arrival of French books, which bypassed customs officers in cases of mother-of-pearl, hatboxes, and even in wine barrels with false bottoms sent from France.[14] In 1794, Antonio Nariño, a native of Bogotá who had worked as a tax collector, translated the **Declaration of the Rights of Man and Citizen** into Spanish and printed some copies at his own printing press, one of the few in Spanish America. The *audiencia* of **Santafé de Bogotá** accused Nariño of taking part in a perceived plot to seize power in New Granada, although no such conspiracy seems to have existed.[15] Regardless, Nariño was condemned to ten years of exile in North Africa, although he managed to escape in Spain before serving his sentence. Similarly, in 1795 authorities in Buenos Aires imagined the existence of a slave conspiracy in which leading roles were supposedly played by a French-born merchant and an Italian-born clockmaker. They arrested 31 people, used torture, and sentenced some men to live in exile, although these presumed rebels were probably completely innocent.[16]

In the main, though, news about both the French and **Haitian revolutions** created a fearful atmosphere throughout the Spanish colonies in which rumors rapidly gained currency. This was especially the case in Venezuela, where some planned slave uprisings did indeed derive inspiration from the French and Haitian revolutions. In one small port named Coro in 1795, a slave revolt broke out involving at least 400 enslaved people and free people of color who hoped, once in control, to divide the town's houses among themselves and "liberate" a long stretch of the Venezuelan **littoral**. They imagined that they were protected by a recently arrived French **privateer**, and although they destroyed several plantations and killed many white people, they ultimately lost.[17] Two years later, an unprecedentedly radical insurrection broke out in another Venezuelan port. The rebels, whose stated goals were to declare independence, abolish slavery, and introduce free trade, received open support from the republican French regime on Guadeloupe, at the eastern end of the Caribbean Sea, which provided them with a printing press to publish propaganda that could be distributed during their uprising.[18] Another two years later in 1799, a document listing **republican** principles arriving from the same island alarmed the authorities in Caracas, who arrested and expelled several foreigners.[19]

Also in 1799, "French slaves" recently acquired by the elite in the port city of Cartagena de Indias teamed up with other enslaved men and conspired to kill the governor, massacre white people, and loot the town. Before this plan could be put into practice, one *pardo* corporal betrayed the plot to the authorities.[20] This plan had some elements in common with another conspiracy that had been planned for one month later in the Venezuelan port of Maracaibo. The rebellious black people and mulattoes, to be aided by the largely black crews of two French ships at anchor, intended to kill all the white people and establish a republican government. Despite these varied uprisings, in this case and in most others the impact of the French and Haitian revolutions on Spanish America was limited to small groups of men with modest followings,[21] and while suggestive of broader unrest, their impact was minimal.

NAPOLEON'S INVASION OF SPAIN AND THE IMPERIAL CRISIS

It was actually the man who ended the French Revolution with his **coup d'état** in 1799—the French emperor Napoleon—who set in motion, albeit unintentionally, a long process that eventually encouraged revolutionary movements to spring up across Spanish America, threatening the status quo. Having subjugated a large part of continental Europe, Napoleon turned his attention to Portugal, which he punished for engaging in trade with Britain by sending an army that forced the royal family and all members of the court to pack their bags and leave for Rio de Janeiro in Brazil. In order to reach Portugal, Napoleon first needed permission from Spain's King Carlos IV to send his troops through Spanish territory. In due course, the emperor used this permission to flood Spain with French soldiers, 100,000 of which crossed the border between December 1807 and March 1808 alone. Ironically, the conquest of Spain had thus started with what amounted to an invitation from its king. This fateful misstep coincided with the bubbling over of a long-standing public **antipathy** to the prime minister Manuel Godoy, a powerful favorite of King Carlos IV. The unrest culminated in a staged uprising against Carlos in the town of Aranjuez in central Spain that forced him to abdicate the throne in favor of his son, who was subsequently proclaimed as

King Fernando VII. Carlos made it clear, however, that he had not stepped down voluntarily, and he hoped for support from Napoleon in regaining his throne. Recognizing the opportunity presented by the weakened and unstable monarchy, Napoleon moved to bring about a dynastic change in Spain.[22] He invited the old and the new kings to a castle in Bayonne in southwestern France, where he forced first Fernando and then Carlos to abdicate the throne. Napoleon then appointed his own brother Joseph, King of Naples, to fill the vacant Spanish throne, promising the Spanish people that Napoleon would allow their monarchy to make a new start.

However, Napoleon and his advisers had seriously underestimated anti-French sentiment among both the Spanish elite and the general population. In fact, a carefully orchestrated insurgency began in Madrid on 2 May 1808 that was intended to spread an anti-French revolt to the countryside. The French reacted to the uprising in brutal fashion with massive executions. Their army, which had already advanced far into the Spanish heartland, was subsequently beaten by a Spanish force, but recovered quickly and went on to conquer most of Spain despite ongoing harassment from Spanish guerrilla fighters.

As a response to the French invasion, ruling councils sprang up all over Spain in order to organize local defenses. By September 1808, these *juntas*—none of which was democratically elected—decided to join forces and form a Central Junta, a body that acted as the executive branch of the Spanish government in the absence of Fernando VII, who spent the next years in internment in a castle in central France. Significantly, in the absence of cohesive and consistent leadership, the establishment of city and regional juntas would become a hallmark of Spanish American independence movements, too.

Napoleon, meanwhile, tried hard to win the hearts and minds of Spanish Americans across the Atlantic. He had gotten wind of Britain's plans to use the crisis in the Spanish monarchy to its advantage. Britain's leadership envisioned that certain strongholds among Spain's colonies might be subsumed into the British empire, and so, within days of his abduction of Carlos and Fernando, Napoleon started to plan expeditions to Spanish America to help the residents ward off a possible British invasion. He identified the port city of Buenos Aires as a main target, to which he wanted to send an army of 12,000 men. By early June in Spain, however, entire regiments of the Spanish army had deserted, and popular resistance to Joseph (King José) and French rule had begun to fester. The Spanish rebels now appealed to Britain to form an alliance against their common French enemy, to which the British government responded positively. In this climate it was impossible for either a British or a Franco-Spanish expedition to sail to Spanish America. Napoleon, like the British, decided to concentrate on Spain itself,

juntas: Ruling councils in the absence of the king.

Caricature of King Joseph of Spain. The caption reads, "Everyone has their luck, yours is drunk to death." Echoing unfavorable public opinion, Joseph's political opponents in Spain gave him the nickname "Pepe Botella"—akin to "Joe Bottle"—to smear his character with the implication of heavy drinking, despite this being untrue.
Anonymous, *Pepe Botella*, 1808–14. Image courtesy of Wikimedia Commons

where his men would have to fight native army units and guerrilla fighters as well as soldiers from what he called **"perfidious Albion."** But he did not forget about Spanish America. He started a diplomatic offensive there by sending at least three dozen agents in all directions. Their task was to convince senior officials, parish priests, and **prelates** of Britain's misdeeds all around the world.[23] Very few were persuaded.

It took a long time for Spanish Americans to find out about Carlos and Fernando's forced abdications. The news trickled in from Spain one ship at a time, causing surprise, uncertainty, and fear, and dominating conversations among all walks of life—at the workplace, at cafés over coffee, and at home at the dinner table.[24] Many believed that the French victories in Spain could lead to the disappearance of the mother country as an independent nation.[25] Spaniards were exceedingly familiar with violent conflict. Spain had participated in a series of wars against both Britain and France over

perfidious Albion:
Negative term used to describe Great Britain, especially Britain's perceived treachery in international affairs.

prelate: High Church dignitary.

the past three decades, but none had exercised such a direct bearing on the fate of its king. The archbishop of Mexico City, Francisco Xavier de Lizana y Beaumont, delivered a message that was echoed in many parts of the Americas when he stressed the sacred duty of the king's subjects to serve King, God, and Fatherland. His colleague in Lima, archbishop Bartolomé Maria de las Heras, added that prayer was not enough. Financial help should also be offered to the poor residents of Spain affected by the war, especially widows, orphans, and families dependent on soldiers.[26]

Not only did authorities frequently order public prayers to take place in churches and convents to ask for a defeat of the French and the restoration of Fernando, but there were also countless spontaneous acts of loyalty. Throughout the Spanish empire, **cockades** or badges with Fernando's image appeared. The young king was praised as "**august**," "just," "beloved," and "desired," but also described as "unfortunate" because of his imprisonment.[27] Conversely, Napoleon was labeled an irreligious tyrant, and caricatures ridiculing him and his brother were common. Women participated fully in organizing support for the lamented king and his country, and fundraising campaigns went door to door seeking donations.[28]

In Cuba, the news about the French invasion of Spain and what was called the "enslavement" of the Spanish people created a tense situation. During the Haitian Revolution, tens of thousands of Frenchmen had moved to Cuba, where they contributed to the island's rise as a global leader in sugar production. At the same time, these Frenchmen were looked upon with suspicion by the white elites who feared the turmoil associated with France and its former colony of Saint-Domingue (Haiti). The local black population also sided with Fernando, not only because of events in Spain, but also in view of bloodshed inflicted on black insurgents during the Haitian revolution at the hands of the French. Governor Salvador de Someruelos initially ignored the call by the Central Junta in Spain to expel all Frenchmen, but to stem the tide of popular rage, he issued an order in March 1809 for all Frenchmen living in Cuba who had not been naturalized as Spanish to leave. An emissary of Napoleon was publicly hanged a year later.[29]

THE ROAD TO A CONSTITUTION

In the midst of Napoleonic rule and ongoing warfare, Spain's Central Junta issued a decree in May 1809 for representatives from its Iberian *and* American provinces to meet in the **Cortes**, which would serve as the Spanish empire's legislative body and prepare a constitution. The invitation was preceded by the Junta's remarkable statement that the American territories formed an essential part of the Spanish monarchy, and that the two parts of Spain were inextricably entwined: "There exists a union between the two hemispheres, between the Spaniards of Europe and of America, a union that can never be destroyed either by intrigue or force of tyrants because it is grounded upon the most solid bases that tie men together: a common origin, the same language, laws, customs, religion, honor to principles and sentiments, and relations and interests. These are the ties that unite."[30]

Early in 1810, when French troops moved into Seville in southwest Spain, the Central Junta dissolved itself to make way for a five-man Council of Regency for Spain and the Indies, whose task it became to organize the Cortes. It issued a call for the election of representatives to be sent to the Cortes but conspicuously bypassed viceroys and colonial *audiencias* by stipulating that only members of **ayuntamientos** could vote for candidates. Also, representatives could only be those who had been born in the province where the elections took place. Thus, only creoles in the colonies could stand for election, not *peninsulares*. Pursuant to the Council of Regency's rules, voters cast their ballots, after which one name was chosen at random from among the three candidates with the highest number of votes. Despite the exclusion of the bulk of the population from the process, the elections led to enthusiasm and optimism among the colonists about the situation back in Spain.[31]

Practical difficulties prevented some American delegates from traveling to Spain. Lack of funds delayed the voyage of a few Peruvians, while others were delayed by disease.[32] But in the end, 67 American delegates from all viceroyalties crossed the ocean to serve in the Cortes, more than half of them clergymen, and 21 of them representing New Spain. Since they would arrive in Spain after debates had already begun, it was decided that they would be substituted in the interim by Americans residing in the Iberian Peninsula.[33] When the delegates finally arrived, they found themselves in a country that was almost entirely under French occupation. The only place where the Council of Regency could still claim to hold sway was the Isla de León in the bay of Cádiz in the extreme southwestern part of the country just north of Gibraltar. The Cortes would be held on this island. On the day of its inauguration, its members proclaimed that the **sovereignty** of the monarchy resided in the nation. Since no such nation existed in reality, they had to create it themselves through political action.[34]

THE CONSTITUTION OF CÁDIZ

The Spanish Empire faced a chaotic situation. The Council of Regency claimed to be in charge of the entire empire, while juntas in Spain and the Americas ruled over their own cities or regions, and all professed to be

ayuntamientos: Town councils presided over by elite members of the population.

sovereignty: Authority of a state to govern itself.

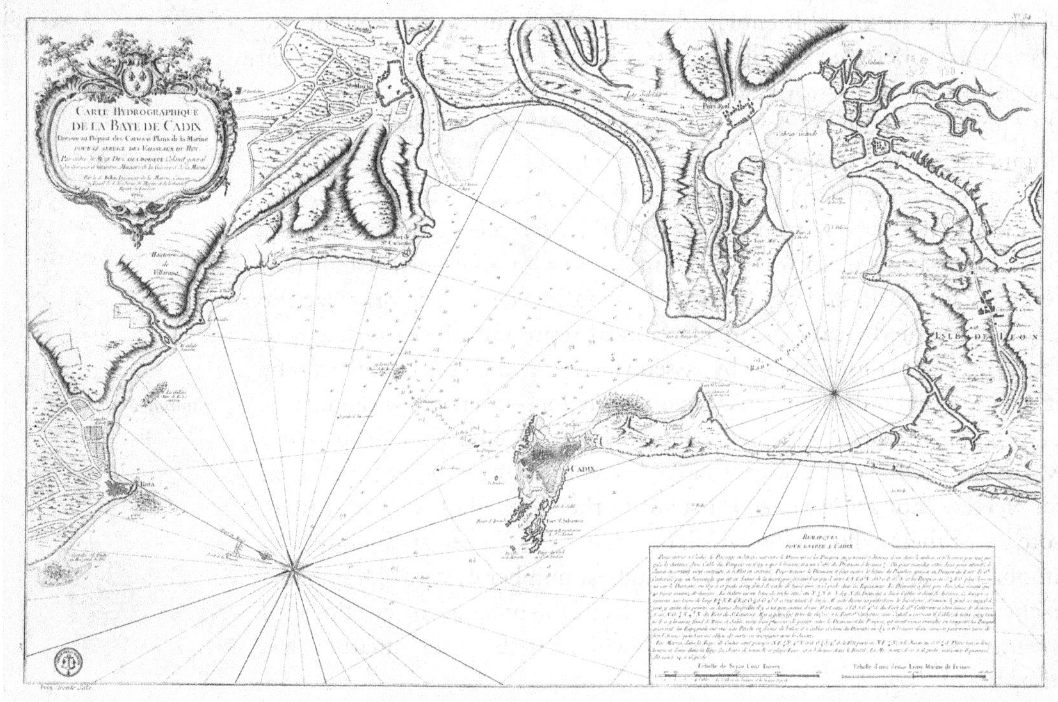

Hydrographic Map of the Bay of Cádiz.
Jacques-Nicolas Bellin, 1762. Image courtesy of the David Rumsey Map Collection

governing on behalf of the absent king. In the years that followed, residents of the colonies would be confronted with yet another, and significantly more radical, departure from monarchical rule as independence movements gained ground. Inhabitants could align themselves with these movements or remain faithful to Spanish rule. As we will see, independence was no uniform drive, but a splintering of many parts of Spanish America. And at the same time that this drive for independence began to intensify, the Cortes met in Cádiz, where Spaniards and Spanish Americans soon found themselves on opposing sides.

Nevertheless, the debates that took place in the Cortes over the next two years ended up producing one of the great constitutions of history. The Constitution of Cádiz, established on 19 March 1812, affirmed freedom of the press and free enterprise, abolished **Indian tribute** and forced labor, eliminated most privileges acquired by birth, and created a **unicameral** legislature whereby the power of aristocrats was curtailed. It located sovereignty in the people and made the king the executor of the people's will. Elections for the Cortes were to be held every two years based on a system in which a large part of the adult male population held the right to vote, including Indigenous people and mestizos.[35] However, the debates about equal rights

Indian tribute: Tax paid by Indigenous people.

unicameral: Consisting of a single legislative chamber.

for the Indigenous revealed blatant racism on the part of some delegates. José Pablo Valiente y Bravo, the representative for Seville, maintained that the Indigenous American was stupid by nature and legally a child. He contended that three centuries of colonialism had not seen any advancement: the native's intelligence was still as limited and his propensity to leisure as marked as in the days of the **Conquest**, and he did not, therefore, deserve the right to vote.[36] The argument fell flat. Indigenous men did receive suffrage.

By contrast, domestic servants and men of African birth or descent were barred from the vote, even if they were free. Suffrage for men with African backgrounds was not just important in its own right, but also relevant to the debate about the so-called American question, a question rooted in the overseas delegates' advocacy for equal representation as a natural right. Spanish American delegates held that this right derived from a decree the Cortes had adopted stressing the equality of all subjects who lived under the monarchy. In their eyes, the electoral rules used to form the current Cortes were patently unfair in that the residents of the Americas were allowed one deputy for every 100,000 inhabitants, while the people of Spain were granted one for every 50,000 residents. Given the accepted population numbers at the time for both sides of the Spanish Atlantic, parity would have given the Americans a majority in the Cortes. Spanish delegates, however, refused to count the six million *castas* as Americans. Besides, the Spaniards argued, changing the electoral rules could threaten the legitimacy of the assembly and thereby jeopardize all the work that had been accomplished. The Spanish American proposal was thus defeated.[37]

The peculiar circumstances under which the discussions took place help explain the limits of what was achieved in Cádiz. Unlike the founders of the United States, who declared war on a distant **metropole** headed by a monarch, and the French revolutionaries, who set about dismantling an old regime steeped in privileges that made an ultimate confrontation with the king inevitable, the Cádiz legislators discussed their empire's future during a foreign invasion. Since that invasion made the captive king a symbol of Spanish unity and identity, any experiment with **republicanism** was automatically ruled out.[38] The war with the French also made it hard to defend religious toleration as a principle, since those who took up arms against the invaders insisted that they did so to defend Catholicism and oppose Napoleon, who was known for championing **freedom of conscience**. Even delegates who did defend rights and freedoms were opposed to allowing any room for beliefs other than Roman Catholicism. Religious toleration was not an option for the men gathered in Cádiz, and any nod in this direction would have been thwarted by the many clergymen there, the profession most represented among delegates in the Cortes. In the end, the following article became incorporated in the Cádiz constitution: "The religion of the

A distinct genre of art created for an elite audience in eighteenth-century Mexico, casta paintings presented racial categories in a hierarchical fashion. They ceased to be produced following Mexico's independence in 1821 when casta designations were abolished.

Artist unknown, *Las Castas*, oil on canvas, eighteenth century. Image courtesy of Wikimedia Commons

Spanish Nation is and will forever be **apostolic** Roman Catholicism, the only true religion. The Nation protects it with wise and just laws and prohibits the exercise of any other." A year after the adoption of the constitution, the Cortes abolished the Inquisition, but this effected little change, since it also set up new tribunals charged with investigating heresy that could still mete out a death sentence.[39]

REVOLTS IN NEW SPAIN

Spanish American delegates argued that equal representation was the only measure that could put an end to the rebel movements that had erupted in the American colonies.[40] After news had arrived on American shores about Fernando's forced abdication, loyalty to Spain, which had initially seemed universal, quickly diminished. Spanish Americans considered the king to be the ruler of their lands, not Spain. The king's absence meant that sovereignty had reverted to the "people." But who made up "the people"?

As in Spain, it was the elites who controlled the town councils; in Spanish America, these were the *peninsulares* and creoles. They assumed power, establishing juntas of their own while claiming to rule in Fernando's name. Once they had experienced the autonomy that a junta conferred, independence often seemed just a small step away—even though conditions in Spain remained the same and some juntas were set up by elites that had no intention of breaking with the metropole.[41] Elites in Lima and Mexico City also saw no reason to go their own way, even though the old viceroyalties of Peru and New Spain exhibited the most distinct cultural identities. The revolt of Túpac Amaru in Peru still reverberated. The Peruvian viceroy, José Fernando de Abascal y Sousa (1743–1821), demonstrated an uncompromising loyalty to the captive king.[42] For many years, he would halt the march of revolution not only in Peru, but in all surrounding regions.

Abascal's counterpart in New Spain, Viceroy José de Iturrigaray, also tried to maintain the political status quo which, given the loyalty to Spain and its hidden king throughout the viceroyalty, appeared to be an easy task.[43] On the other hand, Iturrigaray planned to implement commercial reforms, and the powerful peninsular-led ***consulados*** of Mexico City and Veracruz feared that the reforms would jeopardize their wealth and power. They also had misgivings about the ties he had cultivated with the creole-led mining sector since his arrival in 1803. Remarkably, on 15 September 1808 the Mexico City *consulado* staged a coup in conjunction with members of the audiencia, the archbishop, and the Inquisitor General, rounding up the viceroy's supporters, and arresting Iturrigaray and shipping him off to Cádiz.[44]

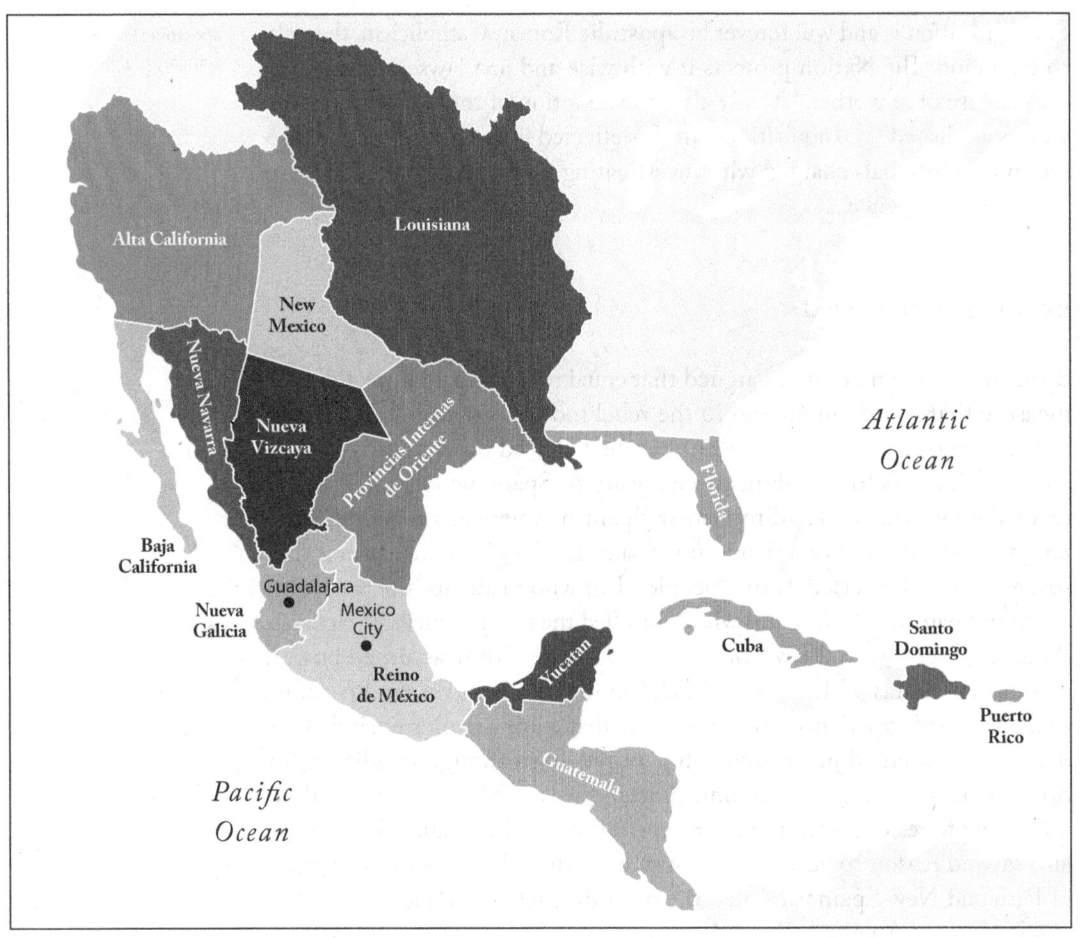

New Spain, 1795.

Ironically, the removal by Spaniards of this most senior Spanish official in order to protect their interests sowed the seeds for a movement that began to challenge the status quo and start Mexico on its long journey toward independence. In this new climate, elite creoles made themselves heard, and plebeian Mexicans of different ethnic backgrounds featured in their plans. An economic recession marked by harvest failures and unemployment was unsettling the region, although pent-up anger about preferential treatment of Spanish natives was a more widely shared complaint.[45] In late 1809 a creole revolt in the city of Valladolid west of Mexico City was nipped in the bud. Had it succeeded it would have led to the organization of a congress with delegates from towns all over New Spain. This would have ruled in the name of Fernando VII, blocking the peninsular Spaniards from turning over New Spain to Joseph, who had since been made King of Spain. The ringleaders had counted on the support of 18,000–20,000 Indigenous people and other nonwhites.

The goals of this 1809 conspiracy mirrored a second revolt in 1810 in the Bajío, an agriculturally rich region north of Mexico City that was plagued by drought, famine, and class differences between wealthy mine- and land-owners on the one hand, and the mass of Indigenous people, free blacks, and mulattoes on the other. As in Valladolid, the leaders of the revolt were upper-class creoles, among them militia officers who all resented the Spanish,[46] and some of whom may even have taken part in the 1809 revolt.

One man emerged as the pivotal figure of this uprising: Miguel Hidalgo (1753–1811), a very learned educator, priest, entrepreneur, and **bon vivant**, who had been investigated by the Inquisition a decade earlier. A man with many followers, Hidalgo gathered enthusiasts and had cannons cast in preparation for 2 October, the planned date of the insurrection. Again, as in Valladolid, the plot was discovered by the authorities, but unlike Valladolid the discovery did not doom it. Instead, Hidalgo decided to carry out the plan prematurely in Dolores, where he resided, in order not to lose time. On Sunday 16 September 1810, a market day on which many people from the surrounding countryside—and thus many potential followers—were in town, Hidalgo issued the so-called **Cry of Dolores**. His exact words are disputed, but he likely invoked the French threat, called for a revolt in the name of Fernando VII, and promised Indigenous Americans that the rebels would put an end to their tribute payments.[47]

Marching behind a banner with the image of the **Virgin of Guadalupe** that he picked up in a hamlet on the first day of the revolt, Hidalgo's army of 1,000 men grew by leaps and bounds to 80,000 by October. Most of the fighters were Indigenous men and castas who were perhaps interested in the abolition of tribute but were also motivated by the prospect of looting, in which they engaged extensively and violently. The destruction reached a climax in the mining town of Guanajuato, which they easily captured with the help of local residents and then ruthlessly sacked.[48] Hidalgo, who had dubbed his march a "reconquest," later admitted that he was ultimately responsible for the violence that had been unleashed: 60 European Spaniards in Valladolid and 350 Spaniards and creoles in Guanajuato had been executed. The sack of Guanajuato alerted Mexico's middle and upper classes, which had first viewed the revolt favorably, to the potential of a race and class war.[49]

It became clear that Hidalgo's plundering men did not constitute a real army when the first **royalist** forces—no models of discipline themselves—were sent to attack them. The royalists, however, also had to cope with autonomous guerrilla fighters who targeted commerce and haciendas, and disturbed town life,[50] and they lacked trained soldiers, making it necessary to recruit widely, especially on haciendas and ranches; Brigadier Félix Calleja, who led the royalists, consciously avoided the recruitment of plebeians, as he feared that the weapons distributed to them could in turn be used against the royalist cause. After all, plebeians formed the bulk of the insurrectionists.[51]

Helped by a propaganda campaign, the royalists reversed the losses they incurred at the hands of the guerilla fighters and put the insurgents on the defensive. In reconquered towns, authorities who had supported the rebels were replaced, and insurgent leaders and followers were publicly executed, while those who showed remorse were acquitted. In addition, some towns were burned, and a **scorched-earth policy** was applied in order to intimidate potential rebels and control rural populations.[52] On 17 January 1811, the royalists won a decisive battle outside Guadalajara, where the insurgents' military inexperience was once again exposed. Along with some other leaders, Hidalgo fled north, was betrayed, and was shot dead on 30 July. His independence movement had been a false start. Nonetheless, rebellion against colonial rule continued in other parts of Mexico. As one historian has argued, the insurgency "was a series of local rebellions following courses that sometimes crossed but never fused into a single stream."[53]

The mestizo parish priest and former mule driver José María Morelos (1765–1815) emerged as the new leader of the insurrection. Morelos had been in contact with Hidalgo in 1810 when he hoped to become his chaplain, and his achievements were due in no small part to the lessons he learned from Hidalgo's mistakes. He built support among all classes in society, imposed discipline on his soldiers and trained them extensively. He combined military action with political planning, organized a congress, and introduced a constitution. His goal was to abolish all ethnic distinctions and have all inhabitants of Mexico be known as Americans. His many military victories—most of them achieved in southern Mexico—were however followed by a string of defeats, whereupon he began to lose support, even among the insurgency's leadership. Eventually captured by a Spanish force in November 1815, he was tried and executed.

There seemed to be little hope left for an end to the royalist regime.[54] The men who followed in Morelos' footsteps as insurgent commanders were numerous, but almost all

Mestizos formed the largest casta in Mexico. This painting, one in a series, shows a Spanish male, an Indigenous female, and a mestizo child. Miguel Cabrera, *De espanol e indio, Mestizo (From Spanish and Indian, Mestizo)*, pintura de castas (caste painting), 1763. CC BY-SA 4.0, https://creativecommons.org/licenses/by-sa/4.0/

quickly disappeared from the national stage, returning to the rural settings that had produced them.[55] The only exception was Vicente Guerrero (1782–1831), a black Indigenous mule driver who would one day serve as Mexico's president. Using his close ties to the indigenous population to obtain support for his **guerrilleros**, Guerrero became the main insurgent leader in the years after 1817 and one of the leading politicians in independent Mexico.[56]

CREOLE ASCENSION IN THE RÍO DE LA PLATA

While insurgencies in New Spain **foundered**, peripheral regions of the Spanish empire with less developed cultural identities, such as the Río de la Plata and Venezuela, took the lead in the quest for sovereignty. These areas lacked the political cohesion of New Spain and were characterized instead by vast powers exercised by cities.[57] In Buenos Aires, the capital of the viceroyalty of the Río de la Plata since its establishment in 1776, a movement for autonomy began in 1806, two years before Carlos and Fernando had even arrived in Bayonne. In June 1806, the leaders of a British expeditionary force en route from the Cape of Good Hope to Europe decided to attack Buenos Aires. The attack caught the viceroy, the Marquis de Sobremonte, completely by surprise, and Spanish soldiers and local militia units could not prevent British occupation of the city, which Sobremonte had abandoned with little resistance. Consequently, the city's merchants financed an army of volunteers that took revenge for what was seen as an embarrassing surrender. They retook Buenos Aires in only 45 days. Leading the makeshift forces was the nobleman Santiago de Liniers, a French native who had made a career in the Spanish naval service and was at the time the commander of a military and naval force in the Banda Oriental (today's Uruguay). A second British invasion of Buenos Aires, now with the support of the British government, did not have the benefit of surprise. Liniers and his defenders were well-prepared. Local militia commanders, who were beginning to eclipse professional officers from Spain, recruited thousands of *porteños* from all walks of life, each one of them eager to join. This enthusiastic makeshift army confronted the British invaders in July 1807. Despite Liniers's preparedness, the British force managed to capture nearby Montevideo, in part due to new mistakes made by Viceroy Sobremonte—mistakes that prompted the town council of Buenos Aires to remove him from office. The removal, loudly supported by the city's plebeians, was revolutionary in its own right since it had not been ordered by the higher official metropolitan authorities. Under Liniers, the Buenos Aires defenders employed urban guerrilla tactics, and despite the earlier Montevideo setback they eventually routed the British and forced them to withdraw.

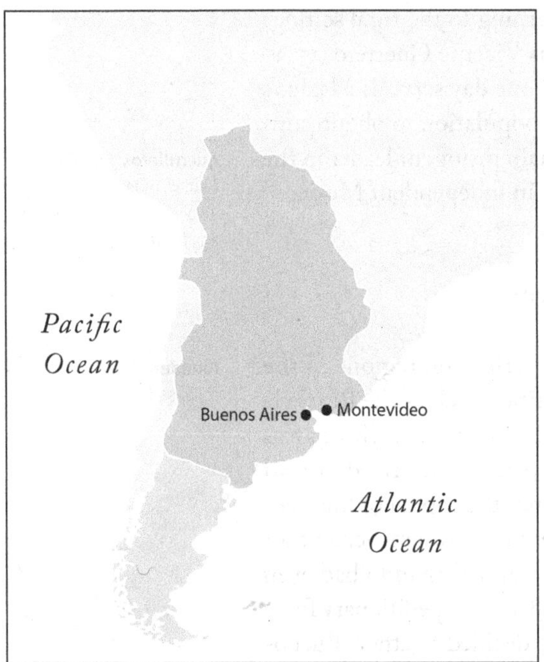

Río de la Plata, 1795.

Liniers was rewarded for his leadership with the position of interim-viceroy of the Río de la Plata, but he did not last long in his new position. His French background had been unimportant as long as France was Spain's ally, but Fernando's imprisonment and the subsequent French conquest of Spain exposed Liniers to political vulnerability. His challengers included the Spanish royalist Francisco Javier de Elío, who had served under Liniers during the second British invasion but now painted his former commander as having French interests at heart. In collusion with leading residents of Montevideo, Elío established a junta there to condemn Liniers. It was the first autonomous junta in the Spanish colonies.[58]

Spain's Central Junta back in Seville was also wary of Liniers's French background and arranged in 1809 to send the naval officer Baltasar Hidalgo de Cisneros to be Liniers's successor as viceroy. When Cisneros landed in Montevideo, Liniers gave up his government without resistance. Elío, too, accepted Cisneros, disbanded Montevideo's junta, and he again became Governor of the city; but he governed the town so inflexibly that Cisneros exiled him to Spain. The political leaders of Buenos Aires did not accept Cisneros so easily. Spain's Central Junta had been dissolved in early 1810 and the Buenos Aires leaders did not recognize the resulting Council of Regency; therefore, they held that the Council's political appointments were illegitimate. A political vacuum was thus created that led to the formation of yet another new local junta in May 1810. Cisneros served initially as a member, but the interventions of plebeians made him resign. Deposed as viceroy, he was now banished by the junta to the Canary Islands. Those bent on autonomy from Spain thus achieved a major victory, aided in large part by the passivity of the defenders of the old regime.[59] This was a momentous step in the city's history, and it was celebrated with grandeur. Twenty thousand people—one-third of the population—attended celebrations during which church bells were rung and guns were fired in salute in the illuminated city. During a solemn mass, the junta members symbolically sat where the viceroy had always been seated.[60]

Most of these 20,000 people were creoles who had benefited from the victories against the British expeditions. However, the professionalization of the army that the creole leaders set in motion met with resistance from the plebeian population in the form of both desertion and mutinies. In December 1811, plebeian sergeants, corporals, and soldiers of Buenos Aires' most prestigious regiment protested the stricter discipline required of a professional army by disobeying and throwing out their creole officers and naming commanders of their own. After prevailing in a violent battle, creole leaders disbanded the regiment and a reluctant calm was restored.[61]

Not unlike Paris during the French Revolution, Buenos Aires witnessed a feverish pace of political developments in the years after 1810. By 1812, the parading of the royal flag through the city's streets and the use of other public monarchical symbols such as the royal coat of arms were being banned.[62] Growing self-confidence among the creoles did not bode well for local peninsular Spaniards, who had been well-represented in the bureaucracy and in trade. Gradually, they became the object of everyday scorn, were taxed more heavily than creoles, and lost their social prestige. The Spaniards' response came in the form of a conspiracy that aimed at ruthlessly suppressing the creole insurgents. After the plot was discovered, 26 *peninsulares* were condemned to the gallows and hundreds of Spaniards were banished. Those who were allowed to stay could no longer ride on horseback or go out in public at night, and were expelled from the retail trade and forbidden to own stores.[63]

It was in this climate in 1812 that a native son returned from the Iberian Peninsula to the Río de la Plata. Born in a small village on the Uruguay River, José de San Martín (1778–1850) had served the Spanish military for 23 years and had recently fought in Spain against the French occupiers. After discussing the colonial rebelliousness with fellow Americans in Cádiz, San Martín resigned his army post and made his way to Buenos Aires, where he offered his services to the revolutionary creole authorities. Although they did not entirely trust this officer with experience in the Spanish army, they ordered him to set up a new branch of the local army: the cavalry. In October 1812, San Martín joined an army coup against the (creole) **triumvirate** then in charge of Buenos Aires, which was seen as authoritarian and disinclined to declare independence, after which a new triumvirate was installed.[64]

One of the new triumvirate's first acts was to issue a call for elections to form an assembly that would prepare a constitution. The resulting Constituent Assembly was also reluctant to declare independence, and started its work by stating: "Close the period of the revolution, open the era of peace and liberty." And yet, it inadvertently furthered the revolution by a series of far-reaching measures. The Assembly no longer swore allegiance to Fernando VII. It confirmed the abolition of native tribute, suppressed titles of nobility, abolished the Inquisition, prohibited torture, and introduced the gradual abolition of slavery.[65]

triumvirate: Leadership of three persons.

San Martín had already left Buenos Aires when these reforms were introduced. He had been appointed commander of the Army of the North (or the Army of Peru) and tasked with bringing Upper Peru, a northern region of the viceroyalty of Río de la Plata, in line with Buenos Aires, and to then take on Peru itself. Both of these regions remained loyal to Fernando. Upper Peru was important to Buenos Aires for several reasons: it was home to the great mining center of Potosí, and controlling its mint and collecting taxes on mining were important sources of income; Upper Peru served as a market for goods imported by Buenos Aires from Europe and for agricultural produce from other parts of the Río de la Plata; and strategically, it could block military expeditions from royalist Lima.[66] Upper Peru had been deemed defiant ever since a rebel junta had formed in La Paz in July 1809 that aimed to steer its own course, independent of both Spain and Buenos Aires. Forces sent from both Lima and Buenos Aires initially nipped this movement in the bud, but neither force could control the various bands operating there on their own, despite at times sharing interests with them. Nor were later military attempts by Buenos Aires able to bring Upper Peru to heel. One reason for their resistance was the *porteños'* pro-Indigenous policy, illustrated by the abolition of tribute—a smart decision in Buenos Aires given the demographic importance of indigenous people.[67] However, the leadership in Upper Peru was far less interested in the fight for indigenous equality.

Some groups of fighters among Upper Peru's indigenous and mestizo population sided with Buenos Aires against the royalists. One such group included the mestiza Juana Azurduy (c. 1781–1862), perhaps the most remarkable female soldier in the Spanish American wars of independence. In Spanish America's patriarchal societies, women were commonly seen as inferior to men, whose task it was to protect them. Women were supposed to live their lives inside a family or convent.[68] After the outbreak of warfare, however, soldiers' wives and other women from Mexico to the Río de la Plata prepared meals, mended clothes, took care of the sick and wounded, and carried water to the soldiers. Army leaders often viewed the female presence as an antidote to demoralization and desertion, although some commanders feared their impact on the troops' morale. In addition, women were used as spies or couriers or in attempts to "seduce" the enemy to desert and join the insurgents.[69] Women also fought on the battlefields, such as the 100 female warriors in Mexico who assaulted royalist barracks to seize arms or the royalist women who died at the battle of Ciénaga near Santa Marta (New Granada) in 1820 while keeping their husbands supplied with spare ammunition.[70] Among the women who fought at the battle of Boyacá (1819) was the New Granadan native Evangelista Tamayo, who served under Bolívar with the rank of captain.[71]

Born in Chuquisaca (Upper Peru), Juana Azurduy married Manuel Padilla, with whom she had several children. Both helped the independence struggle by collecting arms and money. Padilla also recruited 10,000 men to support an army sent from Buenos Aires in 1813. Azurduy soon distinguished herself by commanding not just her personal guard of 25 female "Amazone" fighters, but an all-male army called *Los Leales* that took part in 16 battles against royalist forces. She also joined forces with Padilla's army, suffering a devastating defeat in the battle of La Laguna (13 September 1816) that left 700 insurgents dead, including Padilla. The royalists mistakenly identified one of the Amazone fighters as Azurduy and killed and brutally dismembered this woman. Although she was wounded in the battle, Azurduy in fact escaped and lived for another 46 years, never receiving a war pension, and perishing in poverty.[72]

Claiming authority throughout Río de la Plata, the junta that had been established in Buenos Aires in May 1810, and which had defied Spain's Central Junta by banishing Cisneros from the Río de la Plata, invited deputies from all parts of the viceroyalty to a general congress. To discuss the invitation, the **governor-intendant** of Paraguay called a congress of 225 local "notables" that gathered in the provincial capital of Asunción in July. Paraguay was perhaps the most isolated of all the Spanish provinces in the Americas. Decades earlier, in 1767, the Spanish crown had expelled the Jesuits from the region, which resulted in the abandonment of their many well-functioning missions. The crown, however, subsequently neglected to help rebuild Paraguay; and the region was also more or less ignored by Spaniards migrating to the New World. The population was mostly Indigenous and mestizo, and even the white population spoke fluent Guaraní, the main native language.

The Paraguayan delegates, overwhelmingly members of the elite and residents of the capital, voted to profess loyalty to Spain's Council of Regency, thereby incurring the wrath of the *porteño* leadership in Buenos Aires, which responded in military fashion. Startlingly, the army sent from Buenos Aires was defeated twice by Paraguayan militias and forced to withdraw. With momentum on its side, the delegates meeting at a new congress decided to declare Paraguay's autonomy from Río de la Plata, while still promising to "defend the common cause of Fernando VII."[73] Although independence was in the air, it is hard to pin down a measure that could count as a declaration to that effect. The most likely candidate is the ***Reglamento*** adopted by yet another congress on 12 October 1813 in which a large part of the male population of all ethnic backgrounds took part, freely electing more than 1,000 largely lower-class delegates. The *Reglamento* omits any reference to the king, uses the term "Republic of Paraguay" for the first time, and refers to the meeting of the inhabitants in the congress as a "free and sovereign people."[74]

The government then targeted native Spaniards living on Paraguayan soil. Having failed to expel them to the adjacent province of Corrientes, Paraguay's leaders began to tax them heavily and forbade Spanish males by law to marry anyone but indigenous, black or mulatto women. Nor were they any longer allowed to act as godfathers or serve as witnesses at weddings of Paraguayans.[75] One of the leaders behind these measures was the well-educated creole lawyer Dr. José Gaspar Rodríguez de Francia, who had done much to silence local support for Buenos Aires. Emerging as the most powerful politician, Francia was made dictator for three years in 1814 and two years later for life. An outstanding micromanager, he dispensed with a legislature and virtually isolated his country from the rest of the world. Francia passed away in 1840.[76]

SOUTH AMERICA'S SOUTHERN THEATER

Meanwhile, the relationship between Buenos Aires and the **Banda Oriental** remained tense. On the one hand, both had put up resistance against the British expeditions and, in the long term, both were part of the same movement for independence.[77] On the other hand, the political turmoil in these years offered Montevideo the chance to free itself from Buenos Aires' political and commercial guidance. The chance arrival of news from Spain that France had not in fact overrun the entire Iberian peninsula—and that the Central Junta still existed—enabled royalists in Montevideo's garrison to tip the balance in favor of those who insisted on loyalty to Spain. The reappearance at this stage of Elío, whose exile to Spain was followed by his appointment as the new viceroy, could have threatened the seekers of independence in Buenos Aires, but Elío only managed to launch a weak attack on the city. He was then put on the defensive himself, as local forces supplemented by soldiers sent from Buenos Aires planned to take Montevideo.

Anti-Spanish sentiment in the Banda Oriental certainly existed; it was rooted in the recent colonization by Spaniards who had established large farms on lands claimed by small independent landowners who had no title to the land they tilled.[78] The opposition to Elío was led by José Gervasio Artigas (1764–1850), the grandson of one of the founders of Montevideo and a former member of the rural police force, who became a natural leader of the many rural workers and vagrants, many of them Indigenous people. Having barely survived an attack on the city by Artigas' men, Elío produced a trump card when he invited the Portuguese commander from the adjacent Brazilian **captaincy-general** of Rio Grande do Sul to intervene on his behalf. Fearing a permanent Portuguese takeover of the Banda Oriental, the revolutionary leadership in Buenos Aires agreed to an armistice with Elío,

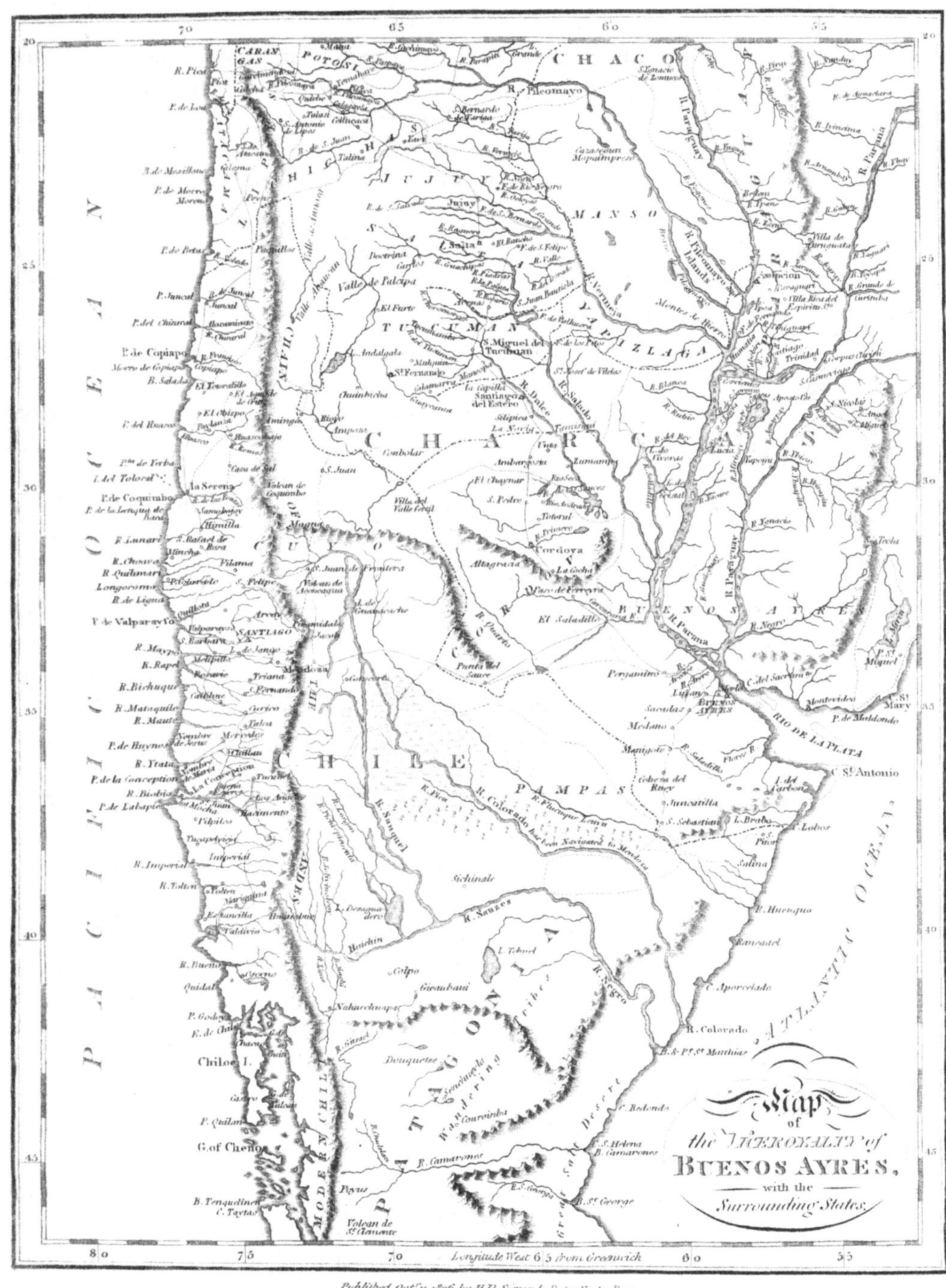

Map of the Viceroyalty of Buenos Ayres, with the Surrounding States.
Samuel Hull Wilcocke, 1806. Image courtesy of the John Carter Brown Library

allowing him to maintain his authority over the Banda Oriental. However, Artigas and his 4,000 men, accompanied by the same number of civilians, left their homes to start a guerrilla war from their new abode in Entre Ríos north of Buenos Aires. They failed to accomplish their mission. Ultimately, the embattled Artigas fled to Paraguay, where Dr. Francia granted him asylum.[79] Still, the rural anarchy that had enabled Artigas's movement to thrive did not entirely abate. The disappearance from rural areas of Spanish police and militias had allowed for the rapid increase of desertion, vagrancy, and Indigenous rebelliousness. Rural workers chased away their masters, pillaged their homes, and killed their cattle. Agricultural production almost ceased, and robbers dominated the highways.[80]

Before 1814, Spanish control of Montevideo had been integral to Spain's chances of survival in South America. Not only could soldiers from Spain disembark in the port, but the forces defending the city could team up with royalists in Peru in an attempt to crush the revolt in Buenos Aires from two directions. Peruvian Viceroy Abascal's hope for such an alliance would not be fulfilled, however, in part because two-thirds of the 681 soldiers Spain dispatched to Montevideo in 1812 drowned in a shipwreck. A long siege of Montevideo by *porteño* forces was finally crowned with success in June 1814 after a fleet set up in Buenos Aires—manned largely by British natives— forced the royalists to surrender.[81] Tumultuous years followed in Montevideo, during which Brazil and Buenos Aires asserted their respective rights to govern the east bank. Both finally ceded independence to Uruguay in 1828.

Without reinforcements from Spain, Peru was forced to take on Buenos Aires alone, which it did in Upper Peru. The first success was achieved when an army sent from Lima raided the encampments of the Buenos Aires troops, triggering massive desertion at the so-called Battle of Huaqui (20 June 1811). But that victory was followed by an anti-Spanish revolt in La Paz. Furious about the complicity of local whites with the Peruvian troops, Indigenous men and mestizos killed the governor and demanded the death of all Spaniards. Although smaller in scale, their uprising brought back memories of Túpac Amaru's revolt 30 years before. In other parts of Upper Peru, Indigenous men sympathetic to the regime in Buenos Aires also seized power, however temporarily, while at least six "little republics" were created that were longer-lived.[82] Many Indigenous people also joined the Cuzco revolt of 1814–15 as it spread to rural areas and encompassed Upper Peru. Its creole leaders rejected the Cádiz constitution and envisioned the creation of an independent country that included Lima, Buenos Aires, and Montevideo.[83]

Finally, in April 1814, a Spanish regiment arrived from Cádiz, which gave hope to Lima's resident Spaniards. However, as William Stevenson, a British native who was in town at the time noted, "they had soon cause to regret having solicited the assistance of an armed force from Spain, for all the expenses incurred in the equipment of the expedition at Cádiz were to be defrayed by the merchants of Lima. The officers and soldiers were also of the worst character, the former having been dispelled from different corps in the mother country for crimes which they had there committed, and the latter were taken from the common **gaols**, places of exile, and the galleys."[84]

These fresh Spanish troops, called Royal Regiment of Talavera de la Reina or simply the Talaveras, would be deployed in Chile, a section of his viceroyalty that Abascal had initially ignored. As elsewhere in the empire, a junta had assumed power there in 1810. Although no declaration of independence was issued, the junta organized a Congress that met in Santiago on 4 July 1811, the same date that Venezuelans gathered on the other side of the continent to declare their independence. Like their Venezuelan counterparts, the Chileans chose the date as homage to the North American rebels. The course of Chilean independence deviated from the United States example, however, when one enemy of Spanish rule, José Miguel Carrera, seized power in a coup d'état. Two years later, in 1813, his regime finally faced a royalist army sent from Lima but survived its incursion. Reinforced by numerous Chileans who favored the restoration of Spanish rule, another royalist force, led by Abascal's son-in-law Mariano Osorio, met the insurgents again, now at Rancagua, a town more than 50 kilometers south of Santiago.[85]

In the battle that followed (1–2 October 1814), the Talaveras led the charge. On the opposite side, the commander-in-chief Bernardo O'Higgins earned himself fame for the heroic defense that he led against the troops of Osorio, who had expected an easy victory. For 36 hours O'Higgins's men fought in the streets of Rancagua until their supplies of water ran out, leaving them dehydrated and causing their cannons to explode. They had also exhausted their munitions and provisions. In addition to this, a relief force sent from Santiago suddenly turned around, leaving too small a force to resist the royalists, who emerged as victors. Nine hundred men were killed on the urban battlefield, with the insurgents losing twice as many men as their opponents.[86] An outpouring of popular support accompanied the restoration of Spanish rule to Santiago a few days afterwards. Although Osorio alienated locally born soldiers by raising the salaries of the Spanish soldiers, royalist rule remained unchallenged until the arrival of San Martín's Army of the Andes in 1817.[87]

NEW GRANADA: SOUTH AMERICA'S NORTHERN THEATER

In spite of emerging discontent and various conspiracies in the 1790s—in some respects echoes of the American, French and Haitian revolutions of the time—the elite in Caracas, Venezuela, did not waver in its commitment to the Spanish empire. Napoleon's internment of Fernando in 1808 elicited a different response. Prominent residents, a majority of them creoles, took the initiative to form an autonomous junta, in part to preempt Venezuela's **captain general** from doing the same. They were prompted in their actions by the news that the Central Junta had given way to the Council of Regency, a body the Caracas elite considered illegal because it had not been established by the Spanish juntas or the Spanish people. The main promoters of the junta were jailed, condemned, and then acquitted by the royalist authorities, but two years later, in April 1810, these same disgruntled elite men overcame the royal authorities and formed another junta. Despite some regions' continued loyalty to the Council of Regency, the junta organized elections throughout the province of Venezuela in order to make itself representative of the entire province. The **convocation** differed significantly from that for the Cortes—illegitimate in the eyes of the junta—in that it granted free males of all backgrounds, even the illiterate, the right to cast a vote. On 2 March 1811, the congress of Venezuela began its sessions, proudly declaring itself the first "Cortes" to be held in America.[88]

A group of young property-owning men was behind the growing radicalism in Caracas. Among them was Simón Antonio José Bolívar (1783–1830), a wealthy owner of horse and cattle farms, copper mines, and large cacao and cotton planta-tions. Convinced at a young age of the need to free America from Spanish rule, Bolívar had left his native soil in 1804 for a long stay in Europe. His journey took him to Paris, where he witnessed Napoleon's coronation as emperor, and Rome, where he solemnly swore to break "the chains that oppress us by will of the Spanish power." Bolívar may have decided to return to Caracas in 1807 because of the news about an expedition that aimed to unleash a colonial revolt in Venezuela.[89] Its organizer was the well-traveled Francisco Miranda (1750–1816), who had fought in the American Revolution at the Battle of Pensacola and had served the French Revolution as an army gen-eral. In 1806, he had already tried to

New Granada, 1795.

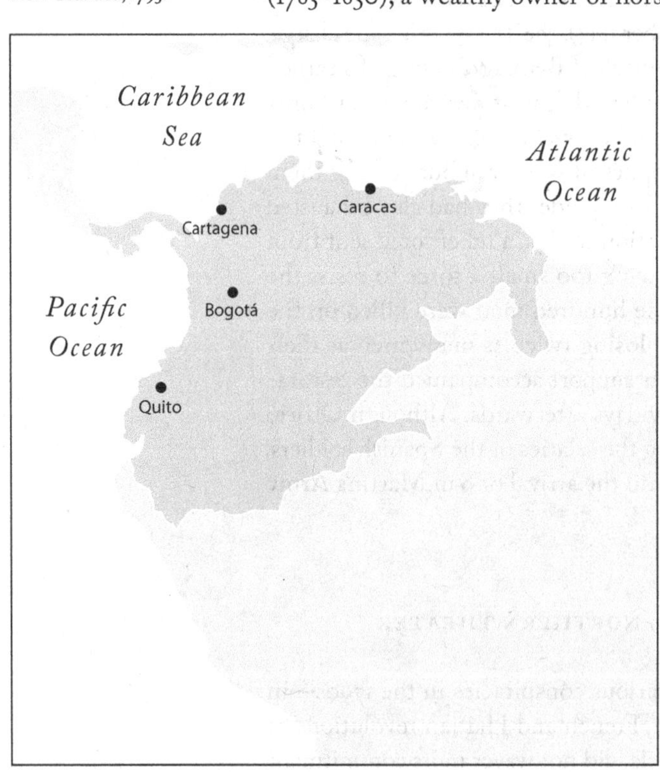

"liberate" Venezuela in an expedition launched from New York City with the help of John Adams's son-in-law William Stephens Smith. The attempt failed miserably; the residents who were supposedly under the yoke of the Spanish refused to join his cause.

Bolívar may have been jealous of Miranda's popularity, but along with his fellow radicals, he also admired him. A few years later, in 1810, he jumped at the opportunity of joining a small diplomatic mission that the Caracas junta sent to Great Britain, but ignored its orders and invited Miranda to return to Venezuela. Miranda accepted the invitation and campaigned with like-minded *caraqueños* for revolutionary measures, such as the introduction of equal rights for *pardos* and a declaration of independence. The congress decided on such a declaration on 5 July 1811, which inaugurated the first Venezuelan republic, "federal" only in name. Modeled to a large degree on its North American predecessor, the first republic would last less than a year and was later criticized by proponents of independence as a naive creation.[90]

From the start, the delegates from Caracas could barely conceal their contempt for most other parts of Venezuela, which they deemed unenlightened. The architects of the new regime realized they could not count on massive support as most inhabitants were so accustomed to Spanish rule that they did not see the benefits of independence. Royalists accused their enemies of chasing rainbows: they claimed that independence was a lie, a fiction that amounted to a rebellion against God, who had ordained the order of things. Those who had turned against Spain must therefore be in league with the Devil.[91]

Lack of support in the west of the country cost the new republic dearly. Although the new republic's forces won a battle with the town of Valencia, whose leaders remained faithful to Spain, it could not prevent the port of Coro from welcoming royalist troops that had set sail from Puerto Rico. Led by the Spaniard Domingo Monteverde, these men conquered western Venezuela. The first republic then unraveled quickly. An enormous earthquake killed 10,000 people in Caracas, but miraculously spared the royalist provinces of Coro, Maracaibo, and Guyana and suggested to the people that independence did not have God's blessing. But the state's leaders also helped bring about their own demise. The military governor José Félix Ribas put so many Spaniards in jail that there were not enough soldiers to guard them. Enslaved people ran away to the Spanish side in droves, as did free people fighting for the republic's army, with 2,000 arriving in the royalist camp within a few weeks.[92] Other enslaved people, east of Caracas, rose in revolt as they chose the king's side. To join the independence movement, in which many of their owners played prominent roles, was not the obvious choice for them.

In spite of his military experience, Miranda, who had been made *dictador*, could not stop Monteverde's threat. He capitulated after Simón Bolívar, the republic's commander of the port city of Puerto Cabello, abandoned that port as he faced another band of royalists. Accusing Miranda of neglect of duty, Bolívar and two others handed him over to the royalists, who wasted no time in sending him to Spain. Four years later, the **Precursor** died in an **insalubrious** prison cell in Cádiz.

The new royalist regime was not granted a long life. Almost immediately, new waves of unrest paved the way for the Second Republic. Defeated republicans were thrown in jail in violation of the treaty signed at the end of the first republic, and their property was confiscated. The regime also alienated *pardos* and the so-called *llaneros*—residents of the Llanos, the plains area of Venezuela, who sustained their frugal lifestyle by hunting cattle. Monteverde, too, committed military errors. Still, without what was soon called Bolívar's "Admirable Campaign" the royalists would have survived. The campaign started out in New Granada, where he received invaluable support from the republican government. From there, Bolívar took a great risk by invading Venezuela. Outnumbered by royalists, whose 10–12,000 men under arms dwarfed Bolívar's initial army of under 1,000, the insurgents avoided **pitched battles** and, in Napoleonic fashion, used speed and surprise to achieve victories. Helped by other republican advances in the east, Bolívar was able to enter Caracas, already vacated by Monteverde, in triumph on 6 August. He received the title "**the Liberator**."[93]

It is unclear if Bolívar's "war to the death" decree made a difference. On 15 June 1813, he declared: "Any Spaniard who does not work against tyranny in favor of the just cause, by the most active and effective means, shall be considered an enemy ... and in consequence shall inevitably be shot." Creoles, however, would be spared, even if they had supported Spain. This was no empty rhetoric. In February 1814, with Bolívar's consent or by his express orders, many Spaniards and natives of the Canary Islands were shot summarily. The most egregious case involved 800 people, most of them noncombatants, who had been arbitrarily arrested and kept as prisoners in **La Guaira**. Only about two dozen escaped. The others, even those staying in the hospital, were killed without mercy.[94] The carnage inflicted just days before by royalist troops in the town of **Ocumare**, who raped the women, killed 300 people, and cut up their corpses, may have led Bolívar to such ethnic cleansing. But he may also have feared a collusion between royalist prisoners and Spanish armies.[95]

Down but not out, the royalists staged yet another counterattack, due in large part to the troops commanded by José Tomás Boves, a native Spaniard who had managed to gain the support of the *llaneros* and shaped his cavalry around them. In peacetime, these horsemen herded cattle on Venezuela's plainlands, dreading the expansion of the aristocracy's ranches. Boves's promise of pillage and the redistribution of the aristocrats' lands was therefore attractive. By terrorizing the civilian population with arbitrary killings and atrocities, his men caused the residents of Caracas to flee by the thousands in panic.[96] The only town left to be conquered was Valencia. Although its inhabitants requested to discuss their surrender, according to a royalist eyewitness Boves rounded up all the men and took them outside the town where his troops speared them.[97] Boves completed his victory in August 1814, but would be killed in battle himself just four months later.

Meanwhile, the independence movement in New Granada had gone through various stages. Cartagena de Indias defied Spain first by introducing free trade in April 1809, thereby enabling the import of foodstuffs from United States ports. Although it had always been an important part of Spain's Atlantic trading system, Cartagena had also been a major center of smuggling with Dutch and British islands in the Caribbean. The unambiguous choice for free trade did not merely signal a rupture with the metropole; it also underlined the eagerness of the city's elite to break with Santafé de Bogotá, the seat of the viceroy. After Bogotá formed a junta on 20 July 1810, Cartagena established its own when elite creoles, under pressure from artisans and the urban poor, expelled the governor. The Cartagena junta soon introduced a new electoral system, which gave all males the votes, albeit indirectly. The only exceptions were made for vagabonds, enslaved people, and salaried bondsmen.[98]

The creation of juntas usually happened after distinctly anti-Spanish public demonstrations by the "people." In Bogotá, these people were small groups of agitators, apparently acting on orders from the town council, who recruited plebeians in exchange for financial rewards or drinks. Once the plebeians showed up at a major square, the agitators energized them with speeches in which they stretched the truth. One agitator, for example, spread the news that the viceroy and the members of the *audiencia* had sold the people to the French for three **cuartillos** apiece. A similar rumor, accusing a recently arrived Spanish military commander of having sold the local population to Napoleon, appeared in the town of Mompox.[99]

Following the rebellious examples of Cartagena and Bogotá, juntas were formed in four other New Granadan provinces (together forming the "united provinces"), while eight other provinces remained loyal to Spain. The united provinces recognized no decree adopted by the Cortes of Cádiz—which was largely ignored by the various parts of New Granada anyway—nor any other edict coming from Spain.[100] But even here, in an assembly dominated by men from Bogotá, **centrifugal** tendencies were present. One delegate from a small interior town voiced most clearly the logical implication of the return of sovereignty to the people(s). Just as Spain cannot impose its will on the viceregal capital, he argued, Bogotá cannot establish itself as the sovereign of the provinces, and neither can the provinces do so in the *pueblos.* Each, in other words, was sovereign.[101] These tensions persisted throughout the independence era. Politicians in the capital claimed to represent the provinces while the provinces themselves desired self-rule, and in turn villages challenged the continued **hegemony** of provincial capitals.[102] Bogotá became the capital of Cundinamarca, an area that did not declare itself independent until July 1813.

In Cartagena, armed plebeians and artisans, dissatisfied with their own junta's refusal to break completely with Spain, had forced the junta to sign the province's act of independence on 11 November 1811. A constitution was adopted seven months later which reflected the massive participation of *pardos* in the coup. Males who did not depend on others for their wage received the right to vote without any consideration of their ethnicity, while no more enslaved people were to be imported.[103] Some men of color even assumed politically active roles, such as the blacksmith Pedro Romero, one of three mulattoes elected to the convention that prepared the constitution of 1812.[104]

The royalist enemy took notice of this radical **bulwark** in New Granada. In May 1812, 300 Spanish regulars were sent from Cuba to Santa Marta, the closest port to Cartagena that was still loyal to Spain, in order to lead the modest local forces. Soon, the Cartagena insurgents responded by fitting out numerous locally owned ships as privateers. In 1813, an estimated 800 men served on Cartagena's **corsairing** schooners, capturing at least 41 Spanish vessels, many of them en route to and from Cuba, which remained a royalist stronghold. Many of these privateers at this time and in the years to come were foreigners: citizens of the United States, Haiti, France, as well as residents of the French Caribbean. Despite their efforts, two attempts by Cartagena's military commanders to capture Santa Marta failed. In the south of New Granada, the situation was not very different, as neither side could deal a decisive blow.[105] Internal strife distracted New Granada's independence movement. Despite the common goals of independence, an outright war broke out between Bogota and Cundinamarca on the one side, and the United Provinces of New Granada on the other, a federal **polity** of which Cartagena was a founding member, in 1812–13.

THE PERILS OF SELF-GOVERNANCE

Time and again American insurgents brought up the claim that they were being kept in a straitjacket by Spain. The constitution adopted in Tunja, another urban center in New Granada, argued that "the idea that a man is born as king, magistrate, legislator or judge is absurd and contrary to nature," given the equality of all men.[106] Economic disabilities were also criticized. One Chilean journalist argued: "Our good king didn't want us to cultivate vineyards so that we wouldn't get drunk; or to grow olives or almonds so that we wouldn't stuff ourselves with fruit ... or do business with each other...."[107] Such treatment was not worthy of Spain's supposedly maternal role. Whereas America behaved as a daughter, wrote the radical New Granada journalist Antonio Nariño in 1811, the mother country seemed actually more like a stepmother that treated some children (European Spaniards) better than others (American Spaniards).[108] Emancipation would end such discrimination in a natural way—after all, children grow up and become adults.

But were they prepared for independence? Wherever they toppled the old regime, Spanish American insurgents discovered how difficult it was to construct viable institutions to shape their new countries. Instead of harmony, it was discord that marked almost every level of the newly independent polities—within towns and cities, between provinces, and between capitals and provinces. In Chile, two kinship groups—the Larraíns and the Carreras—vied for supremacy in the independence movement, engaging in a family feud that compromised the overarching cause.[109] Under these conditions of disunion, some governments embarked on repressive policies to silence dissent, all the while presenting themselves as democratic.[110] Dissenting public opinion erupted across Spanish America and was increasingly expressed in print. During the colonial era prior to 1810, 45 newspapers had been published; in the 1810s, by contrast, 125 new ones appeared, with almost 400 in the 1820s. Of course, newspapers were largely an urban phenomenon. Outside of the cities, where literacy rates were low (in Mexico they were no higher than five percent), debates about politics continued to take place only orally.[111]

Since reliable information was scarce, rumors spread like wildfire, gaining currency as they traveled and reflecting real fears. In Quito in 1809, it was said that Spanish natives, including some royal officials, were planning to kill the local nobility in order to prevent them from forming a local junta.[112] Usually, however, Spaniards were accused of targeting the whole non-Spanish population. In Buenos Aires, for instance, anonymous wall posters appeared in 1812 that contained such conspiracy theories. Many believed in the existence of a Spanish plan that aimed at killing the governor and various other men, while expelling everybody who was not a European Spaniard. Likewise, Mexicans were afraid on several occasions that Spanish troops would kill everyone they could.[113] At times, the Spanish press portrayed the insurgents in similar terms. When Bolívar entered Caracas, he was said to have killed all the Europeans he could find, written letters in their blood, and ordered their eyes and hearts torn out while they were still alive.[114]

Despite this apparent dichotomy between Spaniards and Americans, a large number of people were not committed to one side or another. They simply wanted to be left alone to live their lives in peace, but often found themselves in the path of destruction. Insurgent and royalist armies frequently behaved like plagues of locusts, sacking houses and sometimes entire towns. Pillage was a common and accepted way to pay troops if no financial means were available; the alternative would be their desertion. Theft was also rampant, especially cattle for food and horses for the cavalry.[115]

Both sides used religion to rally people to their cause or to encourage soldiers on the battlefield. The insurgent army defending Bogotá in 1813 named Jesus Christ its *Generalísimo*, and its residents—civilian, military, and clerical—all appeared in public with cockades bearing his name. Some of the soldiers even claimed to have seen the Virgin Mary in the middle of a battle. In the enemy camp of royalist **Pasto**, the authorities invoked the Virgin of Mercy to defeat the heretics in Bogotá, going so far as to name her General.[116]

Apart from branding them as heretics, one could delegitimize enemies by labeling them bandits. After Hidalgo, **Allende**, and other insurgent leaders had been captured in 1811, brigadier **Félix Calleja** issued an official document announcing the end of the uprising in Mexico. Anybody who continued to fight the government was considered a bandit and thief and was deemed ineligible to receive a royal pardon.[117] Nonetheless, more than a handful of anti-government guerrilla bands sprang up in Mexico in the following years, none more than a few thousand men strong, and most varying in strength from a few dozen to several hundred. Some fought over grievances with authorities or merchants, others used the insurgency to justify their banditry.[118] Mexican bandits—ideologically motivated or not—made travel hazardous on the highway between Veracruz and Mexico City, and travelers in the mountain passes of Peru, New Granada, and Chile faced similar predicaments.[119] Chilean banditry was encouraged by the anarchy of the civil war between republicans and royalists, as many poor people were displaced or otherwise affected. Their persecution by the republican government drove scores of them into royalist hands.[120]

Meanwhile, the Constitution of Cádiz prompted different responses across Spanish America. The **Council of the Indies** in Madrid had hoped that the proponents of autonomy in Buenos Aires would stop their "rebellion" upon hearing the news about the opening of the Cortes. While that did not happen, the decrees adopted in Cádiz did affect the course of the political process in Buenos Aires. Its leaders, for example, copied into their own constitution the decree sanctioned by the Cortes that provided for press freedom and the end of censorship.[121] In Lima, the freedom of the press that had been introduced by the Cortes led to the emergence of public opinion and dissent, expressed in no fewer than 11 locally printed newspapers in the years 1811–15. They echoed concepts such as "liberty" and "citizenship" popularized by the Cortes of Cádiz. The newspapers' readership was not limited to educated men in the capital. Copies were also available in other towns, and sometimes the papers were read aloud, enabling illiterate people to inform themselves.[122] Press freedom was also briefly allowed in Mexico City until Calleja—who had been promoted to viceroy—did away with it, alleging that it had caused so much irritation and the flourishing of so many "seditious, incendiary, and insulting papers" that the city was on the brink of an uprising.[123]

In New Granada, the Cádiz constitution sparked a debate in 1813 about the admission of people of African backgrounds to administrative functions. Several black and mixed-race people in the town of Valledupar advocated this admission as they referred to the constitution's article that opened the door to deserving people of African descent. However, officials denied them citizenship, closing this avenue of social advancement.[124] In Cartagena, the effect of the Cortes's exclusion of people of African ancestry from citizenship was an enormous blow for people of color, who began to conceive of independence from Spain as the only way to advance their interests. As we have seen, they were soon instrumental in achieving that goal.[125]

FERNANDO'S RETURN

Four months after the Constitution of Cádiz was promulgated, Napoleon's hold on Spain was seriously weakened when French troops lost a major battle just south of the city of Salamanca against an Anglo-Spanish army. The battle proved to be the start of a campaign that would eventually lead to Spain's liberation. Over the course of 1813, numerous uprisings forced King José (Joseph Bonaparte) into exile, prompting his brother Napoleon to adopt a pragmatic solution to safeguard France's southern border. He freed Fernando VII and he signed an agreement with him that recognized *el Deseado* ("the Desired One," as he was known) as Spain's king in exchange for the guarantee that British forces would leave Spanish soil and that Spain would remain neutral for the remainder of the war.

After crossing the Spanish border, Fernando dropped hints that he did not intend to reach a compromise with the politicians who had come to the fore since his fateful internment at Bayonne. Liberal members of the Cortes anxiously followed Fernando's every move, still hoping he would obey the constitution. But on 2 May 1814—the anniversary of the anti-French uprising in 1808—officials in Madrid triumphantly installed a stone plaque reading "Royal Square of Fernando VII" on the side of a church. The old plaque, "Constitution Square," was destroyed.[126] The writing was now on the (church) wall. Two days later, all uncertainty ended when Fernando seized power, restoring **absolutist rule** and declaring all the decrees and laws generated by the Cortes null and void.

absolutist rule: Government based on the political doctrine of unlimited centralized authority, usually by a sole ruler.

One of Fernando's priorities upon his return to the throne was to handle the American rebellions. Metropolitan officials had been slow during his absence to understand why the revolts had occurred, and only in April 1812 did the Regency begin to obtain information from representatives from the colonies.[127] In 1814, it seemed likely that he would reconquer all of the American provinces, where only the Río de la Plata remained in insurgent hands—in Buenos Aires, Paraguay, and the Banda Oriental—although royalist control of the other colonies was not secure.[128] Most of the advice the king received, both from Spain and the colonies, suggested he opt for a military response instead of negotiations with the rebels. Full-fledged military action had been impossible while the **Peninsular War** (in Spain and Portugal) still raged, although a growing number of soldiers and officers had left for the Americas to bolster royalist ranks, totaling 16,092 in the years 1811–13. In 1814, however, virtually none were sent.[129] That would soon change. However, a major problem faced Fernando and his ministers. Sharply reduced trade with the colonies, a decline of American tax revenues, and the Peninsular War and the American revolts had emptied the treasury.[130]

Fernando decided on a large military expedition, although there was disagreement in royalist circles on the ideal destination. The man elected to lead the expedition, Field Marshal Pablo Morillo (1778–1837), had been a soldier since the age of 13. He had fought at the battle of Trafalgar (in which the British navy defeated the joint Franco-Spanish navy), where he was wounded and captured, and in the recent Peninsular War.[131] Once his fleet had crossed the Atlantic, disaster struck. Sailing off the Venezuelan coast, Morillo's flagship exploded, which made his mission exponentially more difficult. He lost one million pesos intended for wages, artillery, thousands of rifles, swords, and pistols, as well as gunpowder, bombs, grenades, and bullets.[132] Nonetheless, in April 1815 Morillo's men went ashore and began their march on Caracas. They entered the city welcomed by music, fireworks, and banquets.[133] The enthusiasm probably faded somewhat after the residents found out that Morillo was demanding 200,000 pesos from them to wage his campaign.[134]

Militarily, Morillo fulfilled all of his major tasks and restored royalist order in Venezuela and New Granada. However, he installed military governments in both regions and created a council that arrested hundreds and condemned and executed dozens, perhaps as many as 200 men. He also introduced conscription and arbitrarily confiscated monies from private persons to help finance the expedition. These actions did little to legitimize the new order.[135] In a speech to the inhabitants of New Granada he said: "Review in your memory the events of your insurrection and tell me if it is better for you to be the vassals of half a dozen lawyers or other adventurers who want to get rich at the cost of your blood, than the subjects of a powerful monarch, he who aspires only to be the idol of his people."[136] On the other hand, through a personal representative he sent to Madrid, Morillo did advocate sweeping changes in Venezuela to win the hearts and minds of plebeians. He proposed the abolition of the slave trade, gradual **manumission** of enslaved people, and the introduction of equal rights for blacks and mestizos. Somewhat at odds with these changes, he also proposed to counteract the growing black population by sending 500–600 families from the Canaries or Galicia to settle in Venezuela. His suggestions, however, were ignored.[137]

The Spanish government itself tried to persuade colonial inhabitants (not only those in Venezuela) by approaching Pope Pius VII to support its cause. The Pope complied with the request by issuing an **encyclical**, in which he called on the American bishops to do all they could to suppress revolts against Spain's legitimate rule and to stress "the illustrious and singular virtues of Fernando, your Catholic King."[138] Some residents of New Granada demonstrated a different view of the king. In four separate cases across class lines and regional borders, **iconoclasts** destroyed portraits and **effigies** of Fernando, for which a total of eight men were executed during Morillo's campaign.[139]

After Caracas, Morillo targeted the Caribbean port city of Cartagena, which was still in insurgent hands and ruled now by a governor who was unpopular with the local nonwhite majority. Morillo laid siege to the city in August 1815, blockading it for 116 days and eventually starving the people into submission. Famine and yellow fever killed 6,000 inhabitants, or one-third of the population. In his memoirs, Morillo described the city after its surrender as a vast cemetery in which one saw a few breathing skeletons wander around. Corpses, piled up inside houses and in the streets, spread a pestilential odor.[140]

Disease also began to wreak havoc on Morillo's expeditionary force, which had already been cut in half compared to its strength six months earlier in Caracas. High mortality due to dysentery, smallpox, and scurvy, but probably especially yellow fever and malaria, meant that Morillo was in a race against time.[141] Although he filled the vacated ranks with American-born soldiers, Morillo feared that tropical ailments would make it impossible to complete his mission. He was right. Morillo's army "faced a slow death," winning some battles, but losing men steadily to disease and desertion.[142] These factors allowed insurgents in New Granada a comeback. The chief beneficiary was Simón Bolívar.

After the loss of Venezuela's second republic, Bolívar briefly tried to revitalize the independence movement in New Granada, but news of Morillo's landing had made him rethink his course of action. He decided to go into exile again, leaving on a British brig for Jamaica. From there, he went to the republic of Haiti, ruled by Alexandre Pétion. Pétion, who provided aid to many supporters of Spanish American independence, proved to be immensely helpful to Bolívar's plan to invade Venezuela, offering him ammunition, arms, and above all soldiers. He insisted on only one condition: Bolívar had to abolish slavery in his native country.[143]

Although Bolívar and his men managed to go ashore in Caracas, their expedition was a spectacular failure. The Liberator did not accomplish much of anything and even abandoned his troops. It did teach him important lessons, though, which he would implement following his next arrival in Venezuela at the end of 1816. He gave up on the idea that he had to conquer Caracas first before extending his liberation campaign elsewhere. Likewise, he came to understand that he must quell the dissension and jealousy of each other's success among the independence fighters. Bolívar identified Manuel Piar, a *pardo* general in his armies, as a key threat to unity, and he accused of him inciting a race war. Piar was tried and convicted by a court martial, and executed by a firing squad. Whether the accusation was true is unclear. Bolívar may have simply used his accusation to get rid of a powerful rival.[144]

Bolívar did all he could to create a power base in Guyana, east of Venezuela. "This was a new and visionary strategy," one historian has written, "to base the revolution deep in the hinterland, among the great plains of the Orinoco, impenetrable in their vastness, wide rivers and malarial swamps, a great barrier against defeat, a springboard for attack, and a source of wealth in their rich reserves of livestock."[145] For soldiers, though, Bolívar had to look outside Guyana. Just as the end of the Peninsular War made it possible for Spanish officials to send more soldiers to the Americas, Napoleon's defeat and the return of peace to Europe enabled Bolívar to recruit European soldiers and officers who were now out of work. Similarly, the British government allowed recruitment efforts to take place, although it officially did not intervene in the wars between Spain and its colonies. A London-based agent working for the insurgents had no difficulty finding men who were willing to fight on the other side of the ocean. The prospects were alluring: they would be promoted, their wages would be equal to those of the British army, and they could count on financial compensation for any injuries they might sustain. Apart from genuine soldiers, these offers attracted adventurers who wanted to get rich quick and romantics longing to visit distant lands. Perhaps unsurprisingly, they were not always good fighters. On several occasions, British recruits jeopardized the insurgents' cause by their lack of discipline. One conquest, for instance, was followed by a bout of hard drinking after the soldiers discovered the town's rum supplies, and in the months that followed, the mercenaries deserted frequently, exasperated with the lack of food and clothes and worn down by royalist guerrilla fighters.[146]

Bolívar's successful attempt, his third, to make Venezuela independent in 1819 was therefore not due to British contributions. His own achievement did play a large role. Originally, each soldier in these small private armies was personally tied to the **caudillo** who headed the army; they specialized in guerrilla warfare. Bolivar transformed these private armies into a unified and formidable fighting force, whereupon republican prospects began to look brighter. In 1819, Bolívar made New Granada the theater of war. Morillo's troops had largely abandoned the region in order to focus on the fighting in Venezuela. Bolívar's implementations and strategies succeeded remarkably well, and were aided further by surprise tactics, which Bolivar employed at both the Battle of Boyacá (7 August 1819) and Carabobo (24 June 1821), defeating the royalist foe and heightening the rebels' spirits.[147]

As the tide turned, Bolívar started to shape a permanent union between the countries in which he defeated the royalists. He received support from the delegates gathered in the **Congress of Angostura**, who adopted the so-called Fundamental Law that united New Granada and Venezuela as a single new polity. Only vast countries, Bolívar asserted, would impress politicians in Europe and the United States, who he believed looked down on the tiny states in Spanish America that were the product of divisiveness. Although it was not represented at the congress and had not been conquered yet by insurgent forces, Quito was also added to the new nation. The new country, called Colombia, would only exist until 1830, when it collapsed into its constituent parts. Bolívar passed away in the same year, suffering from tuberculosis and troubled by the demise of the Colombian state over which he had presided.[148]

PERU AND SAN MARTÍN'S ACHIEVEMENT

If the war in northern South America is most associated with the name of Simón Bolívar, his counterpart in the southern regions was José de San Martín. Born in a former Jesuit mission town in the Río de la Plata, San Martín had spent most of his life in Europe and North Africa fighting against France for the Spanish Crown and distinguishing himself during the Peninsular War. In 1812, he offered his services to the rebel government in Buenos Aires, securing a position in the army due to his military experience and political connections. San Martín disagreed with Buenos Aires's

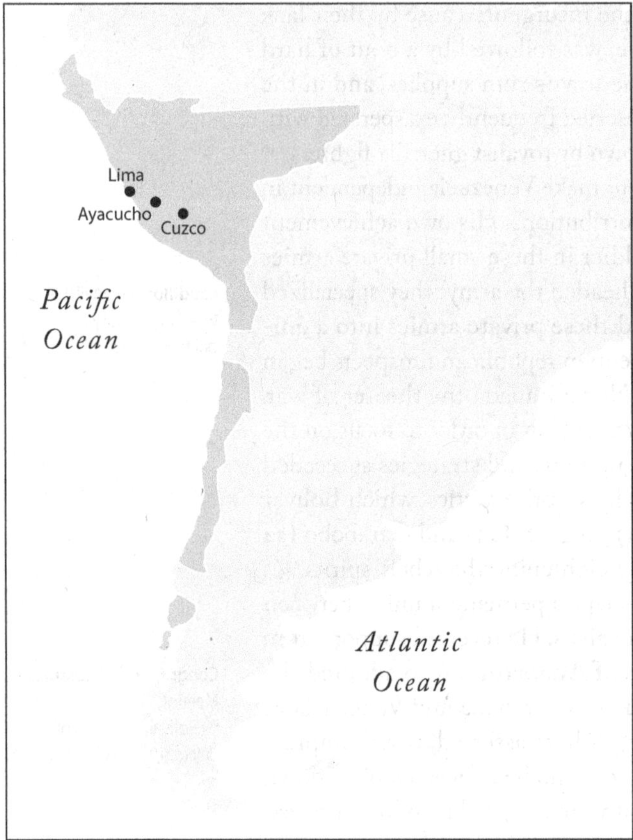

Peru, 1795.

existing strategy of focusing on Upper Peru before taking on Peru. Rather, he embraced a continental strategy. He established a base at Mendoza, the first step in a long journey that included crossing the Andes, conquering Chile, and then waging war with the Peruvians. Slowly his Army of the Andes grew, increasing from 400 soldiers in late 1814 to over 5,000 men two years later. In Mendoza, peasants were drilled relentlessly, provided with uniforms, and vast numbers of enslaved domestic servants and field hands were freed to join the army. Men with African backgrounds ended up forming 40 percent of all soldiers.[149] Without their involvement, San Martín would have been unable to execute his plans. Since the preparations took more time than anticipated, it was only in January 1817 that the army's trek across the Andes could begin. That was half a year after the delegates (half of them priests) at a congress convened by the government in Buenos Aires had declared "the independence of the United Provinces of South America." This declaration did not amount to a sudden break with the past, but rather an acknowledgment that compromise with Fernando's regime was no longer possible. Most delegates were not radicals. Instead of a republic, they supported a constitutional monarchy for the country that one day would be called Argentina.[150]

Although San Martín had made meticulous preparations, the crossing of the Andes was arduous and costly. San Martín himself wrote: "The army started with 10,600 mules, 1,600 horses, and 700 heads of cattle and arrived in Chile with 4,300 mules and 511 horses, in very bad conditions."[151] Furthermore, on the other side of the Andes, a Spanish army was waiting to confront the Army of the Andes, provoking the Battle of Chacabuco (12 February 1817). Due in part to the disciplined performance of the Chilean soldiers commanded by Bernardo O'Higgins, with whom San Martín had allied himself, the battle ended in a rebel victory. Just as there had been three years before when the royalists had won, there was again rejoicing in

Scene depicts market activity in downtown Buenos Aires.
Emeric Essex Vidal, "Market Place," from *Picturesque Illustrations of Buenos Ayres and Monte Video*, 1820. Image courtesy of Wikimedia Commons

Santiago de Chile; however, this time a republican regime was installed. Celebrations were also held in Buenos Aires, and theater plays were staged in the city to generate funds for the widows of the men who had perished on the battlefield.[152]

Continued royalist activity in Chile prevented San Martín from executing his plan to move his troops north to Peru. The Buenos Aires leadership had not provided their general with naval support, and it came back to haunt them. Royalists were able to maintain their control over the northern ports of Callao and Lima in Peru, and Valdivia in southern Chile.[153] Spanish warships and privateers used Callao as a base from which they harassed rebel shipping. In response, the Chilean government built a navy by buying ships from Great Britain and the United States, which it later supplemented with captured Spanish vessels. Most sailors of the new navy were also recruited in those two countries, including the commander-in-chief: the Scotsman Thomas, Lord Cochrane, who had earned a reputation in the British navy for his success against the French. Despite using state-of-the-art rockets and brand-new torpedoes, Cochrane failed to dislodge the Spanish from Callao, but in early 1820 he succeeded in capturing Valdivia in a risky and unauthorized expedition, facilitated by the hasty flight of the local garrison. Spanish naval power in the Pacific was thus significantly reduced, and the rebels suddenly found themselves in possession of a large amount of military equipment.[154]

Meanwhile, San Martín eliminated the royalist forces that had managed to escape after the battle of Chacabuco. In 1818 at Maipú near Santiago de Chile, his troops convincingly defeated the royalists, whose army of 4,500 was reduced to one-third of its size after 1,000 deaths in battle and the imprisonment of 2,000 men.[155] It was no easy victory, though. The losses suffered by the insurgents amounted to 1,000 dead or wounded, which led them to introduce forced recruitment among the population of Chile. The Chileans were also required to help the patriot cause with food and other resources. As a consequence, banditry spread around the region, desertion was rampant, and a week-long uprising occurred in the north among Indigenous people, who loudly proclaimed their support for the royalists.[156] Under these circumstances, the republican government introduced military-style rule. A diplomat from the United States remarked that all the towns resembled military barracks and that the country was more or less covered with soldiers.[157]

It would have made sense for the insurgents to push through and enter Peru. However, the government in Buenos Aires feared a Spanish invasion in their own city and blocked that design; they might need San Martín's troops to return by crossing the Andes again. Three times, San Martín himself traveled back to Buenos Aires to discourage such a scenario. Eventually, in 1820, the government in Buenos Aires was defeated at the hands of an army of interior provinces, and the defeat cleared the path for San Martín to carry out his own plans and invade Peru. An impressive **amphibious operation**, planned by Bernardo O'Higgins and financed by the Chilean government, left from the Chilean port of Valparaiso on 19 August 1820. On board the 16 **merchantmen**, escorted by 8 warships, were 4,400 soldiers and officers, 800 horses, 35 cannon, and 15,000 muskets.[158]

At the orders of San Martín, the fleet made landfall at the small port of Pisco, just south of Lima. The rebels set about distributing **broadsides** directed to various sectors of Peruvian society in a campaign to draw public opinion to their side.[159] This alarmed Peru's viceroy Joaquín de la Pezuela, who had succeeded Jose de Abascal in 1816 and was already dealing with public unrest. When he assumed his position, Pezuela found to his dismay that the treasury was more than 11 million pesos in debt. The recent loss of Chile in 1817/18 had effected profound financial consequences for the viceregal regime in Lima. Deprived of their main trading partners, Lima's merchants instantly

José de San Martín proclaims the independence of Peru.
Juan Lepiani, *Proclamation of the Independence of Perú*, oil painting, 1904. Image courtesy of Wikimedia
Commons

lost almost one million pesos, and their support of Pezuela began to falter
as a consequence.[160] In a desperate bid to reduce debt, Pezuela introduced
a forced loan of one million pesos from Lima's 150 wealthiest residents and
had the houses of two defaulters occupied. This increased his alienation from
the *limeño* elite, a gap that widened yet further when Pezuela embarked on a
policy targeting direct trade with foreigners.[161] Pezuela also alienated Peru's
military leaders by his response to the arrival of San Martín's army. Though
his army was many times stronger than that of the San Martín's, Pezuela
refused to field his troops in Pizco, preferring instead to defend Peru from
Lima. Blaming him for his handling of the war and for his treatment of the
city's merchants, conspiring army officers forced him to resign.

> *limeño:* Of or from Lima.

The Peruvian army now left Lima in an attempt to better defend the
viceroyalty, but this enabled San Martín to take possession of the capital
city. Twelve days later, on July 28, he proclaimed Peru's independence, but
in the months that followed he failed to complete the removal of royalist
troops. Nor did his policies draw Lima's elite to his side. San Martín ruled
in an authoritarian fashion—the *limeños* started to call him "emperor"—with
the help of many foreign ministers. As well, part of his army was defeated
by the remaining royalists, and it was not long before San Martín stepped
down, leaving a three-man junta to govern Peru.[162]

Prior to his resignation, though, San Martín had had a famous meeting
with Simón Bolívar, who had extended an offer of military help to his

counterpart. Although little is known about what the two men actually discussed in Guayaquil (in present-day Ecuador) in July 1822, it seems that San Martín considered Bolívar's military offer not good enough to complete the "liberation" of the viceroyalty. Conversely, Bolívar did not accept San Martín's proposal to make Peru a constitutional monarchy. Realizing that Bolívar's assets were superior, San Martín stepped down and departed for Europe, leaving the war against the royalists to the Liberator. The latter did not take on that task until September 1823, since he was still securing the complete independence of the areas that jointly formed the republic of Colombia.[163]

SOUTH AMERICA'S FINAL BATTLES

The window of opportunity for Spain to intervene in the wars of independence was now closed. In 1817, the ***Comisión de Reemplazos*** had sent a total of only 4,321 men on four different expeditions to Spanish American ports in order to regain political control. The one sizable expedition that departed in 1818 destined for Lima was captured by rebel privateers. In 1819, a massive fleet of 14,000 men was to set sail to the Río de la Plata to begin the reconquest of that viceroyalty.[164] The fleet, however, would never raise anchor. On 1 January 1820, Major Rafael Riego, commanding some of the troops stationed in Cádiz, issued a demand to restore the 1812 Cádiz constitution. Riego had been embraced by many in the army who supported the Cádiz constitution, as well as by agents of the American insurgents. His ***pronunciamiento*** echoed around the country, where town after town proclaimed the constitution. In the end, Fernando decided to give in and accept the constitution, and plans to reorganize an expedition to Buenos Aires did not find favor among the members of Spain's new government.[165]

During the period between San Martín's arrival in Lima in 1820 and Bolívar's arrival in 1823, the survival of royalist Peru was still a distinct possibility. The new viceroy, José de la Serna, had moved the government to the interior and based his rule on the reintroduced Constitution of Cádiz.[166] The only time an armed confrontation took place with troops from Lima, the royalists recorded a decisive victory. The independent regime centered in Lima, by contrast, fell prey to strife and even a civil war. As belief in its survival diminished, politicians and officers defected, significantly complicating Bolívar's mission. It meant that "liberation" had to come from Colombians, who would face royalist armies made up largely of Peruvian mestizos and Indigenous men. The first battle took place in the mountains of Junín (6 August 1824), where Bolívar's troops were victorious in just 45 minutes. The Venezuelan llanero cavalry distinguished itself; remarkably, only lances and sabers were used, and not a shot was fired during military action. The decisive battle happened three months later, on 9 December at Ayacucho while Bolívar was back in Lima tending to government business. Fellow Venezuelan Antonio José de Sucre assumed command in his absence and, although outnumbered, his men defeated the royalists and made their enemies sign an unconditional surrender.[167] The victory was followed by Sucre's capture of Upper Peru, which was renamed Bolivia in honor of the Liberator.

The last stand against South American independence was that of General José Ramón Rodil, the commander of Callao, Lima's walled port, who refused for over a year to accept the capitulation signed at Ayacucho. He hoped in vain to receive fresh troops from Spain. During the insurgents' siege, scurvy and other diseases spread in the town, and many of Rodil's 4,000 soldiers died from starvation while others simply gave up. When he finally surrendered to the Venezuelan general Bartolomé Salom in January 1826, Rodil himself observed that no living animals remained in Callao. The people who had remained loyal to him had exhausted the supply of dogs, cats, rats, birds, and sea lions in order to stay alive.[168]

The death toll of the independence wars had been uneven across Spanish South America. It was particularly high in areas such as Venezuela and Upper Peru. A census held in La Paz in 1824—at the tail end of the major conflicts—revealed "an excessively low number of men" between ages 15 and 25; women of marriageable age, however, were present in abundant numbers.[169] Many of the men serving in the armies on both sides must have died young, since youth was one of the soldiers' distinguishing characteristics. Mestizo, Indigenous, and white soldiers as young as 15 served in the royalist armies. Soldiers active in New Granada in 1815 averaged 17 years of age, while officers of the insurgent army in Santiago de Chile in 1814 were instructed to recruit enslaved people starting at the age of 13. In Buenos Aires, boys as young as 10 to 12 years of age were incorporated into the army, where they probably served as drummers.[170] Mortality did not affect every population group equally. Men from Buenos Aires' lower-class casual labor force died in much greater rates than those from other walks of life. By 1827, women outnumbered men almost two to one in the city's black and mulatto population groups.[171]

MEXICAN INDEPENDENCE

By the time the Battle of Ayacucho took place in Peru in 1824, Mexican independence had also been assured. Many inhabitants of the viceroyalty of New Spain received the news of the reintroduction of Spain's Cádiz constitution in 1820 with great enthusiasm. As two separate elections in New Spain were organized to elect the delegates of a new Cortes, political discussions took place in public, in pamphlets and in newspapers from June 1820 through March 1821, energizing more than one million Mexican men with voting rights. Once in session back in Spain, the Cortes adopted laws that met with the disapproval of the Mexican army and clergy, as it saw their traditional privileges reduced or abolished. For their part, the Mexican delegates, along with other American deputies in Madrid, were upset about their inadequate representation and the resulting inability to be heard. Indeed, the same issue that had earlier pitted peninsular Spaniards against American ones again divided the Spaniards on both sides of the ocean.[172]

Ultimately, these debates did not matter for Mexico, where instead an ambitious royalist officer with a cruel streak set the viceroyalty on the path to independence. One of the leading figures of the royalist counterinsurgency against rebel bands, Agustín de Iturbide (1783–1824) had initially eagerly eliminated insurgent commanders in public executions after bogus trials whose outcomes were a foregone conclusion. To the dismay of many, he also imprisoned numerous women and other noncombatants and treated them cruelly. Iturbide eventually overplayed his hand and was dismissed in 1816 after plundering estates, confiscating large amounts of silver, and robbing the treasury of Guanajuato.[173] The viceroy reinstated him four years later, when he was named general of southern New Spain, but Iturbide had come to resent the royal authorities in the interim and had embraced the cause of independence, or at least that of autonomy. Cultivating close ties with the local elites, he worked out the Plan of Iguala (24 February 1821), named for the village where it was first issued. The Plan left the social structure unaffected and declared "the absolute independence of this kingdom," although it extended an invitation to Fernando VII or one of his family members to govern New Spain.[174]

After authorities in the provinces and the capital accepted the plan, the newly arrived Spanish captain general Juan O'Donojú struck a deal with Iturbide and recognized New Spain's independence as a constitutional monarchy. When the ruling junta in Mexico City confirmed this agreement on 28 September, it was still possible for Fernando or a Spanish prince to take the reins. However, the Spanish government, at the time still bent on recovering control of Spanish America, declined. This left Iturbide as the obvious person to assume command and, supported by the Mexican elite, he was enthroned as Emperor Agustín I. Although he was supposed to respect Congress—which had been elected after suffrage was extended to all nonwhites and the voting age lowered from 25 to 18—Iturbide dissolved it, as long-simmering tensions between politicians favoring a strong legislative and those supporting a strong executive boiled over. He then abdicated in the mistaken belief that the provinces intended to oust him. When he later returned from his self-imposed exile in 1824, he was captured and killed.[175]

Three minor revolts occurred in central New Spain in the years 1811–14, during which some creoles, supported by mulattoes, aimed to declare independence, but no organized insurgent movement emerged.[176] Rather, the Plan of Iguala was the impetus. Should the provinces side with Mexico, remain in the Spanish empire or break with both? Different groups had different answers, of course. Chiapas's elite accepted the Plan and became part of Mexico, while Guatemala's authorities voted for complete independence. The remaining provinces could have chosen to be annexed to Guatemala, from which they had been ruled by a captain-general and an audiencia, but El Salvador, Nicaragua, and Costa Rica also chose full independence, while there was no consensus in Honduras. Appalled by the Central Americans' refusal to join his Mexican empire, Iturbide threatened to launch a military invasion, which allowed local conservatives to seize the momentum and propose to join the empire. For one year, Mexico included all of Central America, but the overthrow of Iturbide put an end to the ties that had bound them. On 1 July 1823 a congress declared Central America independent under the name "United Provinces of the Center of America."[177]

Spain's authorities did not recognize any of the new independent states, not even Mexico, despite the blessing that O'Donojú had given to Iturbide's empire. And Fernando did not waver in his belief that the American provinces would return one day to Spanish rule. His advisers told him that the new countries were in chaos and that most inhabitants wanted to be governed by Spain. The Council of the Indies did not waver either. Favoring a military solution, it proposed the reconquest of America by sending a military expedition to New Spain. A force of 4,000 soldiers finally left in 1829 that was intended to conquer all of the former viceroyalty of New Spain and use its resources to launch invasions throughout South America. A Mexican army quickly stopped the advance of the Spaniards, but new expeditions were launched immediately. Only the death of Fernando VII in 1833 led to Spain giving up its quest to regain its former colonies.[178]

POLITICAL RENEWAL

Iturbide's imperial experiment as Agustín I contrasted with the republican regimes that arose in other parts of Spanish America. Their choice for republics obviously constituted a deliberate break with the monarchical past. Simón Bolívar, for example, believed that only republics, ruled as they were by laws and not the royal will, could resist the tendency of men to pursue only their own personal interest.[179] By 1825, however, he was flirting with

North America, 1826.

monarchism—and thus implicitly with a society that was fundamentally hierarchical. A British diplomat quoted him as saying in a private conversation: "Of all Countries South America is perhaps the least fitted for Republican Governments. What does its population consist of but Indians and Negros who are more ignorant than the vile race of Spaniards we are just emancipated from. A country represented and governed by such people must go to ruin." It would take a while, though, for the inhabitants of the former Spanish colonies to embrace the notion of a new king, as the same diplomat observed: "The title of King would perhaps not be popular at first in South America and therefore it might be as well to meet the prejudice by assuming that of 'Inca' which the Indians are so much attached to. This enslaved and miserable Country has hitherto only heard the name of King coupled with its miseries and Spanish Cruelties, and a change of Vice-King had invariably proved a change of one rapacious oppression for another."[180] Bolívar was not alone during his presidency of Colombia to advocate a constitutional monarchy. A French agent wrote that the clergy, the army, and the common people all favored that option. Some wanted Bolívar himself to be crowned, while others worried that if he died he might be succeeded by a European prince. The *Libertador* stopped short of following this advice, although he did claim extraordinary authority when he made himself dictator of Colombia in 1828.[181]

Despite a commitment to republicanism, Bolívar was one of many postcolonial politicians to admire Great Britain's constitutional monarchy. He showed this unequivocally in the constitution he wrote for Bolivia in 1826, which contained key elements copied from England's **Magna Carta**, such as the **right of habeas corpus** and trial by jury.[182] The first constitution of his native Venezuela (that of 1811) had been indebted both to Britain's constitution and that of the United States as it incorporated a **bicameral system**, separation of powers, and an electoral college. Argentina's constitutions, starting with that of 1819, borrowed some of the same elements, while Mexico's 1824 constitution included various ingredients of the US example: a federal form of government, a supreme court, a bicameral legislature, and a native-born president of at least 35 years of age who was elected for a four-year term.[183] The French constitution of 1791 also echoed in the charters adopted in Spanish America, as did the **Rights of Man and Citizen**, which were incorporated into the 1811 constitutions of Cundinamarca and Venezuela.

Many of these same elements, such as the separation of powers, also arrived by way of the Constitution of Cádiz, which exercised a significant influence over the Spanish empire and its successor states. Former American members of the Cortes of Cádiz adopted the spirit of the Spanish constitution. Among them were two subsequent presidents of Ecuador as well as

Magna Carta: Charter of rights first adopted in England in 1215.

right of habeas corpus: The right to be brought before a judge or into court after arrest.

bicameral system: Political system of two chambers, a lower one (such as the House of Representatives) and a higher one (like the Senate).

Rights of Man and Citizen: The French Declaration of the Rights of Man and Citizen (1789) was a compilation of human rights.

Miguel Ramos Arizpe, chair of the committee that wrote Mexico's constitution of 1824 which, perhaps unsurprisingly, contained entire sections copied verbatim from the Spanish charter.[184] A notable legacy of absence in the Cádiz charter, however, was the lack of guaranteed religious freedom: the laws would protect the Roman Catholic religion and prohibit the exercise of any other.[185] When the Irish native William Burke made an exceptionally rare proposal for a measure of religious freedom in the *Gazeta de Caracas* in 1811, he unleashed a storm of protest in favor of religious intolerance.[186]

The numerous constitutions adopted in the new republics did nothing to alter the position of women. In the colonial era, women had not been completely powerless. They could own property and had more property rights than women in Britain or the United States, but during her marriage a woman's property was controlled by her husband and most of her other rights also belonged to him. Single women could initiate court cases, but once married, they usually needed the approval of their husbands. While they did make changes in public law, the leaders of the countries newly forged in the independence wars did not even consider reforming private law. Paternal power remained entrenched.[187]

SOCIAL CHANGES

Apart from legal continuity, colonial social structures tended to persist beyond independence. The men leading Costa Rica to independence, for instance, had all belonged to the colonial elite, were tied to each other through familial bonds, and had been prominent figures in the town councils.[188] Nonetheless, the independence movements made efforts to introduce social reforms. In the Río de la Plata, José Gervasio Artigas proposed in 1815 to confiscate lands that belonged to Spaniards who had emigrated in recent years, although his plan stipulated that the widows and children of these men could count on keeping enough of those lands to sustain themselves. The lands of these enemies of the revolution would be distributed for free to "the poorest among us [who] will benefit the most," including freed blacks, poor mulattoes, Indigenous people, and poor creoles.[189] Artigas's proposal came to naught.

Across Spanish America, enslaved black people availed themselves of the language of liberty that permeated the discourse of the insurgents, who were fond of referring to themselves as slaves of the Spanish. An actual enslaved man, Fernando Guzmán—an organist and violinist working in a convent—appeared before the audiencia in Mendoza in 1811 and told the judges: "I have always been convinced that the slave, in the midst of his servitude and dark gloom, has no other contentment than the hope to gain

South America, 1826.

his freedom."[190] Rumors of an emancipation decree signed by the king surfaced time and again during the age of revolutions, often causing enslaved men and women to revolt and thereby claim what they believed was their legitimate freedom. In the most common version of the rumor, the king had decreed the emancipation of all the enslaved, but the local authorities and the slaveholders refused to accept it.[191] It should be no surprise, therefore, that many enslaved men eagerly fought on the royalist side in the independence wars. In Venezuela and New Granada, they seized the opportunity to defend the king while fleeing from and possibly taking revenge on their masters.[192]

The unwillingness of insurgent leaders and republican politicians to extend freedom to the enslaved populations was not only obvious to the captives. Bolívar once wrote: "It seems to me madness that a revolution for freedom expects to maintain slavery."[193] Ultimately, the reluctance to abolish slavery betrayed the elites' fears of an uprising from below. In 1798, Francisco Miranda had written to a British friend that his desire to see liberty and independence emerge in the New World was as strong as his fear of anarchy. "May God," he wrote, "not wish that these beautiful countries are transformed, like **Santo Domingo**, into a theater of blood and crimes under the pretext of establishing freedom. They are better off remaining for another century under the idiotic and barbarous oppression of Spain."[194]

Fourteen years later, as the leader of Venezuela's embattled first republic, Miranda saw himself forced to promise freedom to enslaved men who would take up arms against the royalists. Insurgent leaders everywhere did the same. Bolívar may have done so to keep the promise he made to Haiti's president, Pétion, but at the same time he argued that enslaved people could not be granted their freedom without some form of compensation—which came by having to prove their worth to his cause on the battlefields.[195] Eager to escape from slavery in whatever way possible, numerous men offered their services in response. Those who managed to survive the wars to enjoy their freedom were few and far between. One exceptional case was that of Andrés Ibáñez. A native of Africa, he had been sold as a slave in Buenos Aires at the age of 16. Manumitted to serve in San Martín's army, he rose to the rank of captain and was awarded five medals for his military service. When the war ended, he returned to Buenos Aires and bought a *pulpería*, a store that sold clothing, tools, food, and other everyday objects.[196] The overwhelming majority of the men and women who languished in slavery would not live to be freed by the new republics. Instead of an outright abolition of slavery, the political class introduced a gradual abolition, adopting laws that decreed the "freedom of the womb," which allowed children of enslaved females to be free at birth.[197]

Sometimes, Indigenous people also invoked the notion of liberty in presenting their demands. During Pablo Morillo's restoration of New Granada

to the Spanish Crown, the Indigenous Tunebo of the Tunja region used
liberty—as well as poverty—in their opposition to the payment of royal
tribute.[198] Tribute, which Indigenous people had paid throughout the colonial
period in exchange for royal protection, played a role in almost all negotiations between Indigenous men and the belligerent parties, whether rebel
or royal. It featured, for example, in a document jointly penned around 1811
by various insurgent Indigenous leaders in Upper Peru. Stating their aims
and expressing their grievances, they stressed that they were not seeking
independence but wanted to renegotiate their ties with the colonial government. Invoking the anarchical situation that had been produced by the
imperial crisis, they insisted that they would refuse to pay tribute until they
knew whom they should pay.[199]

The objectives of the creoles who led the independence movements did
not square with those of most Indigenous communities, despite the veneration by some creoles of the indigenous nations that had opposed Spanish
invaders during the original conquest. Building on the creole patriotism
of the late colonial period, they presented the previous three centuries as
an era that had seen relentless Spanish oppression of Indigenous people.
The Chileans, for example, found similarities between themselves and the
sixteenth-century **Araucanians**, who had likewise resisted Spanish oppression, thereby preserving their autonomy.[200] Paradoxically, creole admiration
did not extend to contemporary Indigenous men and women, who were
seen as victims of Spanish tyranny and therefore incapable of emulating
the greatness of their ancestors.

Many Indigenous leaders preferred to honor their pact with the Crown,
consenting to be ruled by a just king who opted for laws rather than violence.[201] The loyalty displayed by different Indigenous groups in New Spain
to the King—and their jubilation when the news arrived of his return to
Spanish soil—is conspicuous, especially since these groups were not in
contact with each other.[202] The relationship between Indigenous people
and the royalists changed after the Cortes of Cádiz abolished tribute on
13 March 1811 and established civil equality for Indigenous men. Peru's
viceroy Abascal ignored the decree because tribute payments financed his
army and thereby underpinned his regime. His only option was to find
ways to convince Indigenous people to keep paying tribute. Indigenous
men used these occasions to renegotiate their colonial agreements. Some
communities in Lower and Upper Peru, however, rose in revolt and joined
the insurgent armies when King Fernando unilaterally reinstated tribute
payments in 1814.[203] Throughout the independence struggle, native communities in Upper Peru responded to favorable conditions by organizing
themselves autonomously or allying with the insurgents. Or, if they did not
see realistic chances of furthering their agenda, they could do only what

was strictly necessary during the war between insurgents and royalists in a wait-and-see strategy.[204]

In breaking up Spain's vast American empire, not only did the insurgents striving for independence pit themselves and their followers against those who wished to preserve the status quo—rather, like sorcerer's apprentices, they also unleashed forces far beyond their control. The rebellions gave new fuel to old feuds, such as the ones in which towns opposed capital cities that wielded power over them. In Venezuela, Chile, and Upper Peru, the conflicts morphed into genuine civil wars with high death tolls. Rebel leaders did not succeed in forging a postwar world marked by international harmony. Experiments with composite states like Colombia and Central America ultimately failed, and some newly independent countries even went to war with each other, such as Colombia and Peru in 1828–29. This was not the future the enemies of Spanish rule had imagined. The numerous divisions and knotted conflicts called into question the whole independence project.

Had all their efforts been in vain? José Miguel Carrera, the Chilean revolutionary, wrote just days before his execution that "we have succeeded in nothing but covering America in blood."[205] And one month before his own death, Simón Bolívar agreed with the debilitating futility of the insurgents' achievements, lamenting: "He who serves the revolution, ploughs the sea."[206]

NOTES

1   Carole Leal Curiel, *El discurso de la fidelidad: Construcción social del espacio como símbolo del poder regio (Venezuela, siglo XVIII)* (Caracas: Academia Nacional de la Historia, 1990), 107, 123–24, 126–29, 132, 142, 144.

2   Cited in Manuel Lucena Giraldo, *Naciones de rebeldes: Las revoluciones de independencia latinoamericanas* (Madrid: Taurus, 2010), 39.

3   The *peninsulares* tended to form less than one percent of the population in most urban areas, while their share of the population was even smaller in the countryside.

4   Ann Twinam, *Purchasing Whiteness: Pardos, Mulattos, and the Quest for Social Mobility in the Spanish Indies* (Stanford: Stanford UP, 2015), 63.

5   Marcela Echeverri, *Indian and Slave Royalists in the Age of Revolution: Reform, Revolution, and Royalism in the Northern Andes, 1780–1825* (Cambridge: Cambridge UP, 2016), 12, 14.

6   Gabriel di Meglio, "La participación popular en la revolución de independencia en el actual territorio argentino, 1810–1821," *Anuario de Estudios Americanos* 68:2 (2011), 429–54: 430–31.

7   Di Meglio, "Participación popular," 433.

8   François-Xavier Guerra, "The Spanish-American Tradition of Representation and Its European Roots," *Journal of Latin American Studies* 26:1 (1994), 1–35: 11.

9   Steve J. Stern, *Peru's Indian Peoples and the Challenge of Spanish Conquest: Huamanga to 1640* (Madison: U of Wisconsin P, 1982). Bianca Premo, *The Enlightenment on Trial: Ordinary Litigants and Colonialism in the Spanish Empire* (Oxford: Oxford UP, 2017). Sergio Serulnikov, "Disputed Images of Colonialism: Spanish Rule and Indian Subversion in Northern Potosí, 1777–1780," *Hispanic American Historical Review* 76:2 (1996), 189–226: 192.

10 Alberto Flores Galindo, *Buscando un Inca: Identidad y utopía en los Andes* (La Habana: Casa de las Américas, 1986), 97–99. Charles F. Walker, *The Tupac Amaru Rebellion* (Cambridge, MA: The Belknap Press of Harvard UP, 2014), 12, 15, 19–20, 25, 47, 119, 126–27.

11 Mario Aguilera Peña, *Los Comuneros: Guerra Social y lucha anticolonial* (Bogotá: Universidad Nacional de Colombia, 1985), 104. Anthony McFarlane, *Colombia before Independence: Economy, Society, and Politics under Bourbon Rule* (Cambridge: Cambridge UP, 1993), 262.

12 Brian H. Hamnett, *The End of Iberian Rule on the American Continent, 1770–1830* (Cambridge: Cambridge UP, 2017), 97–103.

13 Claudia Rosas Lauro, "El miedo en el Perú: Siglos XVI al XX: El miedo a la revolución: rumores y temores desatados por la revolución francesa en el Perú, 1790–1800," in Claudia Rosas Lauro, ed., *El miedo en el Perú, siglos XVI al XX* (Lima: Fondo Editorial PUCP, 2005), 139–66: 148–53.

14 Claudia Rosas Lauro, *Del trono a la guillotina: El impacto de la Revolución francesa en el Perú (1789–1808)* (Lima: Instituto Francés de Estudios Andinos, Fondo Editorial de la Pontifica Universidad Católica del Perú, Embajada de Francia en el Perú, 2006), 186–87.

15 McFarlane, *Colombia before Independence*, 285–89.

16 Lyman L. Johnson, *Workshop of Revolution: Plebeian Buenos Aires and the Atlantic World, 1776–1810* (Durham, NC: Duke UP, 2011), 149–78.

17 *Documentos de la insurrección de José Leonardo Chirinos* (Caracas: Fundación Historia y Comunicación, 1994), 46–47, 51.

18 Anne Pérotin-Dumon, "Les Jacobins des Antilles ou l'esprit de liberté dans les Îles-du-Vent," *Revue d'histoire moderne et contemporaine* 35:2 (1988), 275–304: 298.

19 Frédérique Langue, "Los extranjeros en el Caribe hispano en vísperas de la Independencia: Enemigos, revolucionarios, héroes errantes y hombres de buena fe," *Cuadernos de Historia Moderna* X (2011), 195–222: 212.

20 Aline Helg, *Liberty and Equality in Caribbean Colombia, 1770–1835* (Chapel Hill: U of North Carolina P, 2004), 109.

21 Michael Zeuske, "The French Revolution in Spanish America," in Alan Forrest and Matthias Middell, eds., *The Routledge Companion to the French Revolution in World History* (London: Routledge, 2016), 77–95.

22 Barbara H. Stein and Stanley J. Stein, *Crisis in an Atlantic Empire: Spain and New Spain, 1808–1810* (Baltimore: Johns Hopkins UP, 2014), 8–15, 33–36.

23 Carlos A. Villanueva, *Napoleón y la independencia de América* (Paris: Casa Editorial Garnier Hermanos, 1911), 238–41.

24 Marco Antonio Landavazo, "La fidelidad al rey. Donativos y préstamos novohispanos para la guerra contra Napoleón," *Historia Mexicana* 48:3 (1999), 493–521: 495.

25 Lucena Giraldo, *Naciones de rebeldes*, 93. Jaime E. Rodríguez O., *"We Are Now the True Spaniards": Sovereignty, Revolution, Independence, and the Emergence of the Federal Republic of Mexico, 1808–1824* (Stanford: Stanford UP, 2012), 89.

26 José David Cortés Guerrero, "La lealtad al monarca español en el discurso politico religioso en el Nuevo Reino de Granada," *Anuario Colombiano de Historia Social y de la Cultura* 37:1 (2010), 43–83: 48, 53.

27 Sandra L. Díaz de Zappia, "A visão de Fernando VII e o passado espanhol entre a emancipação e a independência (1810–1816)," *Jahrbuch für Geschichte Lateinamerikas* 53 (2016), 117–41: 125–26.

28 Landavazo, "Fidelidad al rey," 512.

29 Ada Ferrer, *Freedom's Mirror: Cuba and Haiti in the Age of Revolution* (New York: Cambridge UP, 2014), 243, 249–50.

30 Cited in Timothy E. Anna, "Spain and the Breakdown of the Imperial Ethos: The Problem of Equality," *The Hispanic American Historical Review* 62:2 (1982), 254–72: 255–56.

31 Jeremy Adelman, *Sovereignty and Revolution in the Iberian Atlantic* (Princeton, NJ: Princeton UP, 2006), 191. Rodríguez, *We Are Now the True Spaniards*, 103, 105, 109.

32 Valentín Paniagua Corazao, *Los orígenes del gobierno representativo en el Perú: Las elecciones (1809–1826)* (Lima: Fondo Editorial de la Pontificia Universidad Católica del Perú, 2003), 106–09.

33 Marie Laure Rieu-Millán, *Los diputados americanos en las Cortes de Cádiz (Igualdad o independencia)* (Madrid: Consejo Superior de Investigaciones Científicas, 1990), 36–37.

34 Rodríguez, *We Are Now the True Spaniards*, 150.

35 Mónica Quijada, "Una constitución singular: La Carta gaditana en perspectiva comparada," *Revista de Indias* 68 (2008), 15–38: 19. Jaime E. Rodríguez O., "La antigua provincia de Guayaquil durante la época de la independencia, 1809–1820," in Jaime E. Rodríguez O., ed., *Revolución, independencia y las nuevas naciones de América* (Madrid: Fundación MAPFRE TAVERA, 2005), 511–56: 538–39.

36 Samuel Alcides Villegas Páucar, "Las Cortes de Cádiz y la cuestión indígena, 1808–1814," *Revista de Antropología* 5 (2007), 199–220: 211–12.

37 Rieu-Millán, *Diputados americanos*, 146–68, 273–94. Roberto Breña, *El primer liberalismo español y los procesos de emancipación de América, 1808–1824: Una revisión historiográfica del liberalismo hispánico* (México, DF: El Colegio de México, Centro de Estudios Internacionales, 2006), 146.

38 Quijada, "Constitución singular,"19.

39 Juan Pablo Domínguez, "Intolerancia religiosa en las Cortes de Cádiz," *Hispania* 77:255 (2017), 155–83: 157–61, 163, 172, 178.

40 Breña, *Primer liberalismo español*, 146.

41 Stein and Stein, *Crisis in an Atlantic Empire*, 166.

42 Timothy E. Anna, "The Last Viceroys of New Spain and Peru: An Appraisal," *The American Historical Review* 81:1 (1976), 38–65: 43.

43 Rojas, "Las ciudades novohispanas," 294–302.

44 Stein and Stein, *Crisis in an Atlantic Empire*, 265, 276, 294–95, 302–07, 338, 343, 348.

45 Eric Van Young, *The Other Rebellion: Popular Violence, Ideology, and the Mexican Struggle for Independence, 1810–1821* (Stanford: Stanford UP, 2001), 75, 383. Rodríguez, *We Are Now the True Spaniards*, 11.

46 Hugh M. Hamill, Jr., *The Hidalgo Revolt* (Gainesville: U of Florida P, 1966), 68–76, 80–83, 87–88, 97–99, 104–05, 107–10.

47 Hamill, *Hidalgo Revolt*, 107–08, 114–15, 118–23.

48 Hamill, *Hidalgo Revolt*, 135–41. Rodríguez, *We Are Now the True Spaniards*, 140–41.

49 Rodríguez, *We Are Now the True Spaniards*, 131.

50 Christon I. Archer, "The Royalist Army in New Spain: Civil–Military Relationships, 1810–1821," *Journal of Latin American Studies* 13:1 (1981), 57–82: 64, 66.

51 Juan Ortiz Escamilla, *Calleja: Guerra, botín y fortuna* (Xalapa: Universidad Veracruzana; Zamora: El Colegio de Michoacán, 2017), 76–77.

52 Ortiz Escamilla, *Calleja*, 79. Van Young, *The Other Rebellion*, 347.

53 Anthony McFarlane, *War and Independence in Spanish America* (London: Routledge, 2014), 269.

54 Peter F. Guardino, *Peasants, Politics, and the Formation of Mexico's National State: Guerrero, 1800–1857* (Stanford: Stanford UP, 1996), 64–65. Jaime E. Rodríguez O., *The Independence of Spanish America* (Cambridge: Cambridge UP, 1998), 165–67. McFarlane, *War and Independence*, 253–69.

55 Van Young, *The Other Rebellion*, 166.

56 Theodore G. Vincent, *The Legacy of Vicente Guerrero, Mexico's First Black Indian President* (Gainesville: UP of Florida, 2001).

57 François-Xavier Guerra, "Identidades e Independencia: La excepción americana," in François-Xavier Guerra and Mónica Quijada, eds., *Imaginar la Nación* (Münster, Hamburg: Lit, 1994), 93–134: 119–20.

58 McFarlane, *War and Independence*, 48.

59 Halperín-Donghi, *Politics, Economics and Society*, 151–52.

60 Henry Ph. Vogel, "Elements of Nationbuilding in Argentina: Buenos Aires, 1810–1828" (PhD Dissertation, University of Florida, 1987), 131–32.

61 Gabriel di Meglio, "Un nuevo actor para un nuevo escenario: La participación política de la plebe urbana de Buenos Aires en la década de la Revolución (1810–1820)," *Boletín del Instituto de Historia Argentina y Americana "Dr. Emilio Ravignani"* 3rd series, 24 (2001), 7–43: 32–33.

62 Vogel, "Elements of Nationbuilding," 95. One historian has argued that the loyalty of the Buenos Aires leadership to Fernando VII in these years was tactical and not sincere: Carlos S.A. Segreti, *La mascara de la monarquía, 1808–1819* (Córdoba: Centro de Estudios Históricos, 1994).

63 Mariana Alicia Pérez, "Viva España y mueran los Patricios! La conspiración de Álzaga de 1812," *Americanía: Revista de Estudios Latinoamericanos de la Universidad Pablo Olavide* 3 (2015), 21-55.

64 John Lynch, *San Martín: Argentine Soldier, American Hero* (New Haven: Yale UP, 2009), 24, 42–47.

65 Di Meglio, "Participación popular," 436.

66 McFarlane, *War and Independence*, 147.

67 Tulio Halperín-Donghi, *Politics, Economics and Society in Argentina in the Revolutionary Period* (Cambridge: Cambridge UP, 1975), 241–45. Rodríguez, *Independence of Spanish America*, 129–32. John Lynch, *The Spanish American Revolutions 1808–1826*, 2nd ed. (New York and London: Norton, 1986), 50–52, 121–23.

68 Jacqueline Vassallo, "Algunas notas sobre las mujeres y los primeros años de la revolución en el Río de la Plata," in Sara Beatriz Guardia, ed., *La mujer en la Independencia de América Latina* (Lima: Centro de Estudios la Mujer en la Historia de América Latina, 2010), 352.

69 Alberto Baena Zapatero, "Las mujeres ante la independencia de México," in Izaskun Álvarez Cuartero and Julio Sánchez Gómez, eds., *Visiones e revisiones de la Independencia Americana: Subalternidad e Independencias* (Salamanca: Ediciones Universidad de Salamanca, 2012), 115–35: 122, 124–26. Marisa Davio, "Mujeres militarizadas: En torno a la búsqueda de fuentes para el análisis de la participación de las mujeres en Tucumán durante la primera mitad del siglo XIX," *Revista Electrónica de Fuentes y Archivos* 5:5 (2014), 81–96: 85–86.

70 Baena Zapatero, "Las mujeres ante la independencia," 121. F. Burdett O'Connor, *Independencia americana: Recuerdos de Francisco Burdett O'Connor*, ed. F. O'Connor d'Arlach (Madrid: Editorial América, 1915), 51.

71 Evelyn Cherpak, "The Participation of Women in the Independence Movement in Gran Colombia, 1780–1830," in Asunción Lavrin, ed., *Latin American Women: Historical Perspectives* (Westport, CT: Greenwood Press, 1978), 219–34: 221–22.

72 Catherine Davies, Claire Brewster, and Hilary Owen, *South American Independence: Gender, Politics, Text* (Liverpool: Liverpool UP, 2006), 137–40.

73 Nidia R. Areces, "La construcción de identidades políticas en Paraguay: De la invasión porteña a la dictadura de Francia," in Beatriz Bragoni and Sara E. Mata, eds., *Entre la Colonia y la República: Insurgencias, rebeliones y cultura política en América del Sur* (Buenos Aires: Prometeo Libros, 2008), 51–74: 52–60.

74 Jerry W. Cooney, "Paraguayan Independence and Doctor Francia," *The Americas* 28:4 (1972), 407–28.

75 Richard Alan White, *Paraguay's Autonomous Revolution, 1810–1840* (Albuquerque: U of New Mexico P, 1978), 62–63.

76 John Hoyt Williams, *The Rise and Fall of the Paraguayan Republic, 1800–1870* (Austin: Institute of Latin American Studies, The University of Texas at Austin, 1979), 43–99.

77 Ana Frega, *Pueblos y soberanía en la revolución artiguista: La región de Santo Domingo Soriano desde fines de la colonia a la ocupación portuguesa* (Montevideo: Banda Oriental, 2007), 85.

78 Di Meglio, "Participación popular," 438–39.

79 McFarlane, *War and Independence*, 167–73.

80 William H. Katra, *José Artigas and the Federal League in Uruguay's War of Independence (1810–1820)* (Madison: Fairleigh Dickinson UP, 2018), 18–19, 49–50.

81 McFarlane, *War and Independence*, 206–07.

82 McFarlane, *War and Independence*, 160–61, 184, 186, 197.

83 Hamnett, *End of Iberian Rule*, 168–74.

84 William Bennett Stevenson, *Historical and Descriptive Narrative of Twenty Years' Residence in South America* (London: Longman, Rees, Orme, Brown and Green, 1829), III: 123. Stevenson wrongly dates the arrival of the regiment in 1813.

85 Simon Collier, *Ideas and Politics of Chilean Independence, 1808–1833* (Cambridge: Cambridge UP, 1967), 92–102.

86 Juan Luis Ossa Santa Cruz, *Armies, Politics and Revolution: Chile, 1808–1826* (Liverpool: Liverpool UP, 2014), 51–55. Stephen Clissold, *Bernardo O'Higgins and the Independence of Chile* (New York: Frederick A. Praeger, Publishers, 1969), 127–30. Jay Kinsbruner, *Bernardo O'Higgins* (New York: Twayne Publishers, 1968), 79–84.

87 Ossa Santa Cruz, *Armies, Politics and Revolution*, 59.

88 Inés Quintero, "Soberanía, representación e independencia en Caracas, 1808–1811," *Procesos: Revista Ecuatoriana de Historia* 29:1 (2009), 5–20: 8–17.

89 Salvador de Madariaga, *Bolívar* (London: Hollis & Carter, 1952), 97.

90 Véronique Hébrard, "Opinion publique et représentation dans le Congrès Constituant Vénézuélien (1810–1812)," *Annales historiques de la Révolution française* 365 (2011), 153–75: 167–73. Hamnett, *End of Iberian Rule*, 143–44.

91 Tomás Straka, *La voz de los vencidos: Ideas del partido realista de Caracas, 1810–1821* (Caracas: Comisión de Estudios de Postgrado, Facultad de Humanidades y Educación-Universidad Central de Venezuela, 2000), 140–43.

92 C. Parra-Pérez, *Historia de la primera República de Venezuela* (Caracas: Academia Nacional de la Historia, 1959), 328, 372, 379. Clément Thibaud, *Repúblicas en armas: Los ejércitos bolivarianos en la Guerra de Independencia en Colombia y Venezuela* (Bogotá: Planeta, 2003), 91. Lynch, *Spanish American Revolutions*, 195–99.

93 McFarlane, *War and Independence*, 115–21.

94 Madariaga, *Bolívar*, 224–26. Juan Uslar Pietri, *Historia de la rebelión popular de 1814: Contribución al estudio de la historia de Venezuela* (Caracas: Edime, 1962), 112–14.

95   Uslar Pietri, *Rebelión popular*, 118–19. Simón Bolívar to Juan Jurado, Campo de Techo, December 8, 1814, in *Memorias del General O'Leary*, XXIX (Caracas: Imprenta y Litografía del Gobierno Nacional, 1887), 29.

96   Miguel Izard, *El miedo a la revolución: La lucha por la libertad en Venezuela (1777–1830)* (Madrid: Editorial Tecnos, 1979), 132.

97   José Francisco Heredia, *Memorias del Regente Heredia* (Caracas: Academia Nacional de la Historia, 1986), 177–78.

98   Hamnett, *End of Iberian Rule*, 131–33. Edgardo Pérez Morales, *Cartagena's Privateers and the Masterless Caribbean in the Age of Revolutions* (Nashville: Vanderbilt UP, 2018), 50.

99   Manuel Pareja Ortiz, "El «pueblo» bogotano en la revolución del 20 de julio de 1810," *Anuario de Estudios Americanos* 71:1 (2014), 281–311: 283–84, 287. Helg, *Liberty and Equality*, 123.

100 Isidro Vanegas, "La constitución de Cundinamarca: Primera del mundo hispánico," *Historia Constitucional* 12 (2011), 257–79: 265–66.

101 Clément Thibaud, "Des républiques en armes à la République armée: Guerre révolutionnaire, fédéralisme et centralisme au Venezuela et en Nouvelle-Grenade, 1808–1830," *Annales historiques de la Révolution française* 348 (2011), 57–86: 67.

102 Garrido, *Reclamos y representaciones*, 316–21.

103 Helg, *Liberty and Equality*, 128–31.

104 Alfonso Múnera, *El fracaso de la nación: Región, clase y raza en el Caribe colombiano (1717–1810)* (Bogotá: Banco de la República/El Áncora Editores, 1998), 200–02.

105 McFarlane, *War and Independence*, 104, 133–37. Edgardo Pérez Morales, *El gran diablo hecho barco: Corsarios, esclavos y revolución en Cartagena y el Gran Caribe, 1791–1817* (Bucaramanga: Universidad Industrial de Santander, 2012), 123–25. Pérez Morales, *Cartagena's Privateers*, 70–71, 95, 98.

106 Isidro Vanegas Useche, "El rey ante el tribunal de la revolución: Nueva Granada 1808–1819," *Historia y Sociedad* 31 (2016), 17–47: 26.

107 Mary Lowenthal Felstiner, "Family Metaphors: The Language of an Independence Revolution," *Comparative Studies in Society and History* 25:1 (1983), 154–80: 159.

108 Hans-Joachim König, *Auf dem Wege zur Nation: Nationalismus im Prozeß der Staats- und Nationbildung Neu-Granadas 1750 bis 1856* (Stuttgart: Steiner, 1988), 129.

109 Mary Lowenthal Felstiner, "Kinship Politics in the Chilean Independence Movement," *The Hispanic American Historical Review* 56:1 (1976), 58–80: 73–77.

110 Adelman, *Sovereignty and Revolution*, 212–18.

111 Rebecca Earle, "The Role of Print in the Spanish American Wars of Independence," in Ivan Jaksić, ed., *The Political Power of the Word: Press and Oratory in Nineteenth-Century Latin America* (London: Institute of Latin American Studies, 2002), 31. Van Young, *The Other Rebellion*, 311.

112 Jaime E. Rodríguez O., "Los orígenes de la revolución de Quito en 1809," *Procesos: Revista Ecuatoriana de Historia* 34:2 (2011), 91–123: 117.

113 Di Meglio, "Participación popular," 435. Van Young, *The Other Rebellion*, 329–30.

114 Michael P. Costeloe, *Response to Revolution: Imperial Spain and the Spanish American Revolutions, 1810–1840* (Cambridge: Cambridge UP, 1986), 26.

115 Van Young, *The Other Rebellion*, 89. Helg, *Liberty and Equality*, 159. McFarlane, *War and Independence*, 131.

116 Margarita Garrido, *Reclamos y representaciones: Variaciones sobre la política en el Nuevo Reino de Grabada, 1770–1815* (Santafé de Bogotá: Banco de la República, 1998), 353.

117 Archer, "Royalist Army," 69.

118 Rodriguez, *We Are Now the True Spaniards*, 195.

119 Karen Racine, "Death, Destiny, and the Daily Chores: Everyday Life in Spanish America during the Wars of Independence, 1808–1826," in Pedro Santoni, ed., *Civilians in Wartime Latin America: From the Wars of Independence to the Central American Civil Wars* (Westport, CT: Greenwood, Press, 2008), 31–53: 38.

120 Leonardo León, "Montoneras Populares durante la gestación de la República, Chile: 1810–1820," *Anuario de Estudios Americanos* 68:2 (2011), 483–510: 487–88, 492.

121 Costeloe, *Response to Revolution*, 31. Alberto Ricardo dalla Via, "La constitución de Cádiz de 1812: Su influencia en el movimiento emancipador y en el proceso constituyente argentino," *Revista de Derecho Político* 84 (2012), 165–93: 178.

122 David Velásquez Silva, "La guerra de opinión y el vocabulario político de los plebeyos durante las guerras de independencia del Perú," in Manuel Chust and Claudia Rosas Lauro, eds., *El Perú en Revolución: Independencia y Guerra: Un proceso, 1780–1826* (Castelló de la Plana: Publicacions de la Universitat Jaume I; Michoacán: El Colegio de Michoacán, 2017), 297–312: 298–300.

123 Ortiz Escamilla, *Calleja*, 112.

124 Suárez Araméndiz, "Conflictividad política," 153.

125 Múnera, *Fracaso de la nación*, 200–03.

126 María del Carmen Pintos Vieites, *La política de Fernando VII entre 1814 y 1820* (Pamplona: Editorial Gómez Gorriti, 1958), 78.

127 Rebecca A. Earle, *Spain and the Independence of America, 1810–1825* (Exeter: U of Exeter P, 2000), 27.

128 McFarlane, *War and Independence*, 285–86.

129 Edmundo A. Heredia, *Planes españoles para reconquistar Hispanoamérica (1810–1818)* (Buenos Aires: Editorial Universitaria de Buenos Aires, 1975), 79, 94, 105.

130 McFarlane, *War and Independence*, 291–94.

131 Stephen K. Stoan, *Pablo Morillo and Venezuela, 1815–1820* (Columbus: Ohio State UP, 1974), 64–65.

132 Stoan, *Morillo*, 74.

133 Lucena Giraldo, *Naciones de rebeldes*, 155.

134 Racine, "Death, Destiny, and the Daily Chores," 41.

135 Daniel Gutiérrez Ardila, *La Restauración en la Nueva Granada (1815–1819)* (Bogotá: Universidad Externado de Colombia, 2016), 56–57.

136 Speech of 23 September 1815, cited in Nubia Fernanda Espinosa Moreno, "La cultura política de los indígenas del norte de la provincia de Tunja durante la reconquista española," *Anuario Colombiano de Historia Social y de la Cultura* 37:1 (2010), 121–48: 126.

137 Anna, *Spain and the Loss of America*, 147.

138 Cited in Anna, *Spain and the Loss of America*, 149.

139 Gutiérrez Ardila, *La Restauración en la Nueva Granada*, 209–11.

140 Pablo Morillo, *Mémoires du général Morillo, comte de Carthagène, marquis de la Puerta, relatifs aux principaux événements de ses campagnes en Amérique de 1815 à 1821* (Paris: P. Dufart, 1826), 60–61.

141 Rebecca Earle, "'A Grave for Europeans'? Disease, Death, and the Spanish-American Revolutions," in Christon Archer, ed., *The Wars of Independence in Spanish America* (Wilmington, DE: Scholarly Resources, 2000), 283–97: 286–88.

142 J.R. McNeill, *Mosquito Empires: Ecology and War in the Greater Caribbean, 1620–1914* (New York: Cambridge UP, 2010), 280. Margaret L. Woodward, "The Spanish Army and the Loss of America, 1810-1824," *The Hispanic American Historical Review* 48:4 (1968), 586-607: 590-91.

143 Ernesto Bassi, *An Aqueous Territory: Sailor Geographies and New Granada's Transimperial Greater Caribbean World* (Durham, NC: Duke UP, 2016), 158–66.

144 McFarlane, *War and Independence*, 318–19. Clément Thibaud, "'Coupé têtes, brulé cazes.' Peurs et désirs d'Haïti dans l'Amérique de Bolívar," *Annales. Histoire, Sciences Sociales* 58:2 (2003), 305–31: 328.

145 Lynch, *Spanish American Revolutions*, 210.

146 Günter Kahle, *Simón Bolívar und die Deutschen* (Berlin: Dietrich Reimer Verlag, 1980), 53–55, 62. José M. Rivas, *Biografía del ilustre procer General Rafael Urdaneta* (Maracaibo: Imprenta Bolívar–Alvarado & Ca., 1888), 154–55. Madariaga, *Bolívar*, 309–12.

147 McFarlane, *War and Independence*, 315, 320, 324.

148 Lynch, *Spanish American Revolutions*, 245, 247, 253–54.

149 Lynch, *San Martín*, 74–75, 87.

150 David Bushnell, "The Independence of Spanish South America," in Leslie Bethell, ed., *The Independence of Latin America* (Cambridge: Cambridge UP, 1987), 93–154: 124.

151 Lucena Giraldo, *Naciones de rebeldes*, 171.

152 Vogel, "Elements of Nationbuilding," 167.

153 McFarlane, *War and Independence*, 355.

154 Brian Vale, *Cochrane in the Pacific: Fortune and Freedom in Spanish America* (London: I.B. Tauris, 2008), 13, 25, 46–56, 65–73. Gaspar Pérez Turrado, *Las marinas realista y patriota en la Independencia de Chile y Perú* (Madrid: Ministerio de Defensa, 1996), 146–47.

155 McFarlane, *War and Independence*, 355–56.

156 Igor Goicovic Donoso, "De la indiferencia a la resistencia: Los sectores populares y la Guerra de Independencia en el norte de Chile (1817–1823)," *Revista de Indias* LXXIV:260 (2014), 129–60: 141–45.

157 Juan Luis Ossa Santa Cruz, "El gobierno de Bernardo O'Higgins visto a través de cinco agentes estadounidenses, 1817–1823," *Co-herencia* 13:25 (2016), 139–66: 146.

158 McFarlane, *War and Independence*, 357–58, 360.

159 Patricia H. Marks, *Deconstructing Legitimacy: Viceroys, Merchants, and the Military in Late Colonial Peru* (University Park, PA: Pennsylvania State UP, 2007), 192.

160 Marks, *Deconstructing Legitimacy*, 173, 177, 211–12.

161 Marks, *Deconstructing Legitimacy*, 216–18, 258–59, 316.

162 McFarlane, *War and Independence*, 375–82. Mónica Ricketts, "Spanish American Napoleons: The Transformation of Military Officers into Political Leaders, Peru, 1790–1830," in Belaubre, Dym, and Christophe Belaubre, Jordana Dym, and John Savage, eds., *Napoleon's Atlantic: The Impact of Napoleonic Empire in the Atlantic World* (Leiden: Brill, 2010).

163 McFarlane, *War and Independence*, 393–97.

164 Costeloe, *Response to Revolution*, 80–81, 83–84, 110–11.

165 Anna, *Spain and the Loss of America*, 216–19.

166 Núria Sala i Vila, "El Trienio Liberal en el Virreinato peruano: Los ayuntamientos constitucionales de Arequipa, Cusco y Huamanga, 1820–1824," *Revista de Indias* LXXI:253 (2011), 693–728.

167 McFarlane, *War and Independence*, 400–04. John Miller, *Memoirs of General Miller, in the service of Peru*, 2nd ed., 2 vols. (London: Longman, Rees, Orme, Brown, and Green, 1829), II: 164.

168 M.-D. Demélas and Y. Saint-Geours, *La vie quotidienne en Amérique du Sud au temps de Bolívar 1809–1830* (Paris: Hachette, 1987), 109.

169 Racine, "Death, Destiny, and the Daily Chores," 36.

170 Alexandra Sevilla Naranjo, "'Al mejor servicio del rey': Indígenas realistas en la contrarrevolución quiteña, 1809–1814," *Procesos: Revista ecuatoriana de historia* 43 (2016), 93–118: 101. Thibaud, *Repúblicas en armas*, 225. Hugo Contreras Cruces, "Artesanos mulatos y soldados beneméritos: El Batallón de Infantes de la Patria en la Guerra de Independencia de Chile, 1795–1820," *Historia* 44:1 (2011), 51–89: 72. Gabriel di Meglio, "Soldados de la Revolución. Las tropas porteñas en la Guerra de Independencia (1810–1820)," *Anuario IEHS* 18 (2003), 39–65. Carmen Bernand, "La población negra de Buenos Aires (1777–1862)," in Mónica Quijada, Carmen Bernand, and Arnd Schneider, eds., *Homogeneidad y Nación con un estudio de caso: Argentina, siglos XIX y XX* (Madrid: Consejo Superior de Investigaciones Científicas, 2000), 93–140: 128.

171 Mark D. Szuchman, "Household Structure and Political Crisis: Buenos Aires, 1810–1860," *Latin American Research Review* 21:3 (1986), 55–93: 68–69. Bernand, "Población negra," 129.

172 Rodríguez, *We Are Now the True Spaniards*, 242–47.

173 Christon I. Archer, "Royalist Scourge or Liberator of the Patria? Agustín de Iturbide and Mexico's War of Independence, 1810–1821," *Mexican Studies/Estudios Mexicanos* 24:2 (2008), 325–61: 333. Brian R. Hamnett, "Royalist Counterinsurgency and the Continuity of Rebellion: Guanajuato and Michoacán, 1813–20," *Hispanic American Historical Review* 62:1 (1982), 19–48: 42.

174 Rodríguez, *We Are Now the True Spaniards*, 253–63.

175 Rodríguez, *We Are Now the True Spaniards*, 278–79, 289, 298, 301–04.

176 Timothy Hawkins, "Napoleonic Subversion and Imperial Defense in Central America, 1808–1812," in Belaubre, Dym, and Savage, *Napoleon's Atlantic*, 97–117: 99.

177 Timothy Anna, "The Independence of Mexico and Central America," in Leslie Bethell, ed., *The Independence of Latin America* (Cambridge: Cambridge UP, 1987), 49–92: 77, 88–91.

178 Costeloe, *Response to Revolution*, 96–100.

179 Anthony Pagden, *Spanish Imperialism and the Political Imagination: Studies in European and Spanish-American Social and Political Theory 1513–1830* (New Haven and London: Yale UP, 1990), 136.

180 The diplomat was Captain Thomas Maling. Harold Temperley, *The Foreign Policy of Canning 1822–1827: England, the Neo-Holy Alliance, and the New World*, 2nd ed. (London: Frank Cass & Co., 1966), 557–58.

181 C. Parra-Pérez, *La monarquía en la Gran Colombia* (Madrid: Ediciones Cultura Hispánica, 1957), 95, 105, 129, 323.

182 Karen Racine, "Proxy Pasts: The Use of British Historical References in Spanish American Independence Rhetoric, 1808–1828," *English Historical Review* CXXXII:557 (2017), 863–84: 871.

183 George Athan Billias, *American Constitutionalism Heard round the World, 1776–1989: A Global Perspective* (New York: New York UP, 2009), 125, 130, 133.

184 M.C. Mirow, "The Age of Constitutions in the Americas," *Law and History Review* 32:2 (2014), 229–35: 234–35. Rodríguez, *We Are Now the True Spaniards*, 343.

185 José Barragán, "Sobre la vigencia en México de la constitución española de Cádiz de 1812," *Revista de Derecho Político* 84 (2012), 385–433: 411–12.

186 Pedro Grases, ed., *Pensamiento político de la emancipación venezolana* (Caracas: Biblioteca Ayacucho, 1988), 91.

187 Reuben Zahler, *Ambitious Rebels: Remaking Honor, Law, and Liberalism in Venezuela, 1780–1850* (Tucson: U of Arizona P, 2013), 158–59.

188 Eduardo Madrigal, "Poder económico y lazos sociales de una elite local en los últimos años del régimen colonial y en la Independencia: Costa Rica, 1821–1824," *Caravelle* 101 (2013), 87–108: 92–93.

189 Katra, *Artigas and the Federal League*, 33–34.

190 Silvia C. Mallo, "La libertad en el discurso del Estado, de amos y esclavos, 1780–1830," *Revista de Historia de América* 112 (1991), 121–46: 136.

191 Wim Klooster, "Slave Revolts, Royal Justice, and a Ubiquitous Rumor in the Age of Revolutions," *The William and Mary Quarterly* 3rd series, 71:3 (2014), 401–24.

192 Marcela Echeverri, "Popular Royalists, Empire, and Politics in Southwestern New Granada, 1809–1819," *Hispanic American Historical Review* 91:2 (2011), 237–69: 250.

193 Peter Blanchard, "The Language of Liberation: Slave Voices in the Wars of Independence," *Hispanic American Historical Review* 82:3 (2002), 499–523: 514.

194 Francisco Miranda to John Turnbull, 12 January 1798. Cited in C. Parra-Pérez, *Historia de la primera República de Venezuela* (Caracas: Academia Nacional de la Historia, 1959), 416.

195 Simón Bolívar, *Obras completas*, ed. Vicente Lecuna, 2nd ed., 3 vols. (Habana: Editorial Lex, 1950), 1:717.

196 Bernand, "Población negra," 129.

197 Magdalena Candioti, "Regulando el fin de la esclavitud: Diálogos, innovaciones y disputas jurídicas en las nuevas repúblicas sudamericanas 1810–1830," *Jahrbuch für Geschichte Lateinamerikas* 52 (2015), 149–71. Daniel Gutiérrez Ardila, "La politique abolitionniste dans l'État d'Antioquia, Colombie (1812–1816)," *Le Mouvement Social* 252 (2015), 55–70.

198 Nubia Fernanda Espinosa Moreno, "La cultura política de los indígenas del norte de la provincia de Tunja durante la reconquista española," *Anuario Colombiano de Historia Social y de la Cultura* 37:1 (2010), 121–48: 132–33.

199 María Luisa Soux, "Tributo, Constitución y renegociación del pacto colonial: El caso altoperuano durante el proceso de independencia (1808–1826)," *Relaciones. Estudios de historia y sociedad* XXIX:115 (2008), 19–48: 25–26.

200 Rebecca Earle, "Creole Patriotism and the Myth of the 'Loyal Indian,'" *Past & Present* 172 (2001), 125–45: 129. Collier, *Ideas and Politics*, 213–14.

201 Brian P. Owensby, "Pacto entre rey lejano y súbditos indígenas: Justicia, legalidad y política en Nueva España, siglo XVII," *Historia Mexicana* 61:1 (2011), 59–106.

202 Manuel Ferrer Muñoz, "Las comunidades indígenas de la Nueva España y el movimiento insurgente (1810–1817)," *Anuario de Estudios Americanos* 56:2 (1999), 513–38: 522.

203 Soux, "Tributo, Constitución y renegociación," 29, 31. Echeverri, *Indian and Slave Royalists*, 153.

204 María Luisa Soux, "Insurgencia y alianza: Estrategias de la participación indígena en el proceso de independencia, 1809–1812," *Studia Histórica: Historia Contemporánea* 27 (2009), 53–73: 56.

205 Manuel Reyno Gutiérrez, *El pensamiento del Gral. José M. Carrera* (Santiago de Chile: s.n., 1975), 102.

206 Simón Bolívar to Juan José Flores, 9 November 1830, in Bolívar, *Obras completas*, III: 501.

CHRONOLOGY

March 1780–January 1782	Túpac Amaru rebellion in Peru.
March–June 1781	Comuneros revolt in New Granada.
June–August 1806	First British invasion of Buenos Aires, which is eventually repelled.
July–August 1807	Second British invasion of Buenos Aires, after the invaders had first taken Montevideo. On this occasion, local forces again defeat the British expedition.
May 1808	Napoleon Bonaparte forces Spanish King Fernando VII and former Spanish King Carlos IV to resign, naming his brother Joseph as their successor. A massive uprising across Spain against the French occupiers follows.
September 1808	The merchant guild of Mexico City organizes a coup d'état in which members of the audiencia, the archbishop, and the Inquisitor General also take part. Viceroy Iturrigaray and his supporters are arrested.
May 1809	A decree by Spain's Central Junta calls for a meeting of delegates from Spain and Spanish America to meet in a Cortes, which will serve as the Spanish empire's legislative body and prepare a constitution.
July 1809	A junta is formed in La Paz that seeks to remain independent of both Spain and Buenos Aires. Forces sent from Lima and Buenos Aires crush the movement.
April 1810	Members of Caracas's elite form a junta that organizes elections in all of Venezuela.
May 1810	The Buenos Aires elite establishes a junta, which deposes and exiles the viceroy, thereby achieving autonomy.
July 1810	Paraguay's "notables" gather to declare their loyalty to Spain's Council of Regency.
September 1810	Miguel Hidalgo issues his Cry of Dolores, calling for a revolt against Napoleon's France, and promising Indigenous people an end to their tribute payments. His small army soon grows into a formidable force, at least in size.
January 1811	A decisive victory in battle by the royalists outside Guadalajara is the beginning of the end for Hidalgo's movement.
January–March 1811	Paraguayan militias twice defeat an army from Buenos Aires, after that city's leadership is angered by Paraguay's independent course.

July 1811	First declarations of independence in Venezuela.
November 1811	Armed plebeians and artisans force the junta of Cartagena de Indias to sign the province's act of independence.
November 1811	A coup d'état by the Carrera clan in Chile enables José Miguel Carrera to become the sole ruler.
March 1812	The constitution of Cádiz is promulgated. It abolishes Indigenous tribute and forced labor, eliminates most privileges acquired by birth, and created a unicameral legislature.
July 1812	Royalist victories put an end to the first Venezuelan republic.
October 1812	José de San Martín joins a successful army coup against the triumvirate in charge of Buenos Aires.
June 1813	Simón Bolívar issues his "war to the death" decree.
July 1813	Cundinamarca (capital city: Bogotá) declares itself independent.
August 1813	Bolívar enters Caracas in triumph and is granted the title "The Liberator." He then establishes a military dictatorship.
October 1813	De facto declaration of independence of Paraguay.
December 1813	Napoleon releases Fernando VII, allowing him to return to Spain, where he will soon declare the Constitution of Cádiz null and void.
June 1814	A long siege by naval forces from Buenos Aires finally defeats the royalist bulwark of Montevideo.
July 1814	The second Venezuelan republic comes to an end as Bolívar and his army leave Caracas prior to the landing of a huge Spanish army.
October 1814	A royalist victory at the Battle of Rancagua ends the Chilean regime of José Miguel Carrera.
April 1815	Arrival in Venezuela of Fernando VII's restorative army, led by Pablo Morillo.
November 1815	Defeat and execution of José María Morelos in Mexico.
June 1816	Paraguay's Congress declares Dr. Francia dictator for life.
July 1816	Congress of Tucumán, convened by the government in Buenos Aires, announces "the independence of the United Provinces of South America."

September 1816	At the Battle of La Laguna in Upper Peru, Manuel Padilla's army is defeated by royalist forces. Padilla is killed, but his wife, the famous army commander Juana Azurduy, escapes. She cannot prevent the collapse of Padilla's republic.
February 1817	Following the 25-day crossing of the Andes by San Martín's army, the Battle of Chacabuco takes place, ending in a rebel victory. A republican regime is subsequently installed in Santiago de Chile.
August 1819	The battle of Boyacá, in which Bolívar's men are victorious, lays the foundation for New Granada's independence.
December 1819	Delegates at the Congress of Angostura approve the union of New Granada and Venezuela.
January 1820	The long-awaited departure from Cádiz of a royalist fleet of 14,000 men that is to restore order in the Río de la Plata is thwarted by the *pronunciamiento* of Major Rafael Riego, who demands the reintroduction of the Cádiz constitution.
February 1821	Agustín de Iturbide issues his Plan of Iguala, which declares "the absolute independence of this kingdom," although it extends an invitation to Fernando VII or one of his family members to govern New Spain.
June 1821	At the Battle of Carabobo (24 June), Bolívar's army defeats its royalist foe once again.
July 1822	Meeting in Guayaquil between San Martín and Bolívar, which leads to San Martín's decision to leave the conduct of the war to the Liberator.
July 1823	The brief inclusion of Central America in Mexico ends, and a congress declares Central America independent under the name "United Provinces of the Center of America."
August 1824	In the Battle of Junín, royalists lose against Bolívar's troops.
December 1824	The decisive Battle of Ayacucho is won by the army commanded by Antonio José de Sucre. His enemies sign an unconditional surrender.
July 1824	Death of Mexican emperor Iturbide, to be followed three months later by the adoption of a constitution.
August 1825	After Sucre's troops conquer Upper Peru, delegates for a constitutional Congress gather to create the new country of Bolivia, named in honor of Bolívar.
January 1826	The last stand against the independence of South America takes place in Lima's port of Callao. Starved to death, the royalists surrender.

QUESTIONS TO CONSIDER

1. What do the rumors in Documents 2 and 3 tell us about the societies that produced them?
2. How do the authors of Documents 4, 9, 12, and 28 think about the "fatherland" (*patria*)?
3. Which similarity does the cabildo of Bogotá notice between the situation in the Spanish empire and that in the British empire a few decades earlier (Document 7)?
4. How do Manuel Abad y Queipo and Juan Bautista Díaz Calvillo try to halt Hidalgo's insurgency (Documents 11 and 12)?
5. Analyze the differences in tone and content between the issue of *El Diario Politico de Santafé de Bogotá* and the declaration of independence of Cartagena de Indias (Documents 10 and 17).
6. According to Robert Semple, what constitutes the main difference between the North American war of independence and the independence struggles in Spanish America (Document 19)?
7. Compare the assessments of Dr. Francia's rule in Paraguay in Documents 26 and 42.
8. What does Simón Bolívar write about the future of Spanish America (Document 30)?
9. What is the difference between the economic ideas of Mexico City's *consulado* and Javier Mina (Documents 14 and 34)?
10. Why did Spanish army leader Pablo Morillo decide against enlisting enslaved black people (Document 39)?
11. What do the letters of Manuel Belgrano and Pablo Morillo (Documents 27 and 40) have in common?
12. How do Sucre's views of the future compare to those expressed in the *Gaceta del Gobierno de Lima* (Documents 50 and 52)?
13. How inclusive are the citizenship rights granted by the Constitution of Cádiz and that of Bolivia (Documents 20 and 54)?

PART 1

Prelude

DOCUMENT 1:

Doña Micaela Bastidas to Messrs. Governors Don Baltasar Cárdenas, Don Tomás Enríquez, and Don Mariano Flores, Tungasuca, 15 December 1780[1]

Micaela Bastidas (1744–81) was essentially the co-leader of the Peruvian revolt against Spanish rule instigated by her husband, Túpac Amaru, as this letter shows, written at the height of the revolt in which perhaps as many as 100,000 people died.

My dear sirs, you will have heard already how my husband is presently taking the necessary steps in order to free this Kingdom from the many taxes and burdens by which the thievish **corregidores** submerged us. This will be a common benefit for the whole Kingdom, and we will be free from such abuses.

So far, all is going well, and we have on our side the provinces of Urubamba, eight parishes of **Cuzco**—Paucartambo, Quispicanchi, Paruro, Tinta, Lampa, Azángaro, Carabaya, and Paucarcolla—the city of Chucuito, and others.

We are in the midst of the greatest victory; and in order to emerge with laurels and enter the city of Cuzco and root out the vexations and the bad government, it is necessary that all come [our way] with the people of their respective towns.

Therefore, having seen this, you will get your people ready and send them here to Tungasuca, for which purpose I give you ample power and authority to send Indians as well as Spaniards, and to carry out the death penalty vis-à-vis those who are disobedient …; I advise you to come with a cross on your cap or hat as the insignia of good Christians.

I hope you will comply without giving rise to any other measures. May God be with you for many years. From your dependable servant.

corregidores: District officers with local administrative and judicial powers.

Cuzco: City in the Peruvian Andes; capital of the Inca Empire until the Spanish conquest in the sixteenth century.

---

1   In Francisco A. Loayza, ed., *Mártires y heroínas (Documentos inéditos del año de 1780 a 1782)* (Lima: Librería e Imprenta D. Miranda, 1945), 13–14. Unless otherwise noted, all documents in this volume have been translated by Wim Klooster.

DOCUMENT 2:

Interrogation of José Ortiz, Medellín (New Granada), 21 December 1781[2]

In August 1781, in the shadow of the Comuneros revolt (see page 5),
the authorities in the town of Antioquia in New Granada (present-day
Colombia) were alarmed by what they perceived as a slave conspiracy
involving more than 5,000 blacks, although it had not led to a full-blown
uprising. Many of those who had been ready to join the revolt believed in the
existence of a royal decree that emancipated the enslaved people, a recurrent
belief during this age of revolutions.

Asked what his name is, where he resides, which marital status, age, social
rank, and job he has, he says his name is José Ortiz, slave of Don Vicente
Tamayo, resident of Hato Viejo, to whom he has been passed as part of the
inheritance of the goods of the late Don Francisco Díaz, who was the priest
of San Jerónimo, to whom he was passed around twenty-four days ago, that
his marital status is that of a married man, his social rank is that of mulatto,
that he is around forty-six years of age, and his job is that of field hand.

Asked if it is true that the defendant was involved in the crime of a
planned uprising by slaves in order to ask for freedom for good or ill, and
if he was likewise one of those named captains of the revolt, he said that
coming from Urrao and arriving at the **salados de Noarque**, he met a slave
of Juan Ignacio Ruiz named Prudente, who told him that he was looking for
him to convey the message from a slave of Don Antonio de Lora called Lino
that the defendant should come to Antioquia, and although he asked what
he was sent for, he [the slave] did not give a reason other than saying that
he did not know, and having come to this city, he met the aforementioned
Lino next to the main gate of Don Bernardo Martínez' house, and when he
asked him to what end he had sent for him, he answered that a royal decree
had appeared, which a mulatto scribe in this city had mentioned, that he
did not mention his name, and the **cédula** said that the slaves were free
and that they would be granted their freedom by each giving two *tomines*
of gold to that scribe; the same Lino said that that scribe had read it [the
royal decree] and if it would happen that members of the **cabildo** knew that
he had it and had taken it out, he would have to be put among the slaves so
that they could defend him; the abovementioned Lino … asked if he would

salados de Noarque: An unidentified spot.

cédula: Royal decree.

tomines: Coins.

cabildo: Town council.

---

2   In *Documentos para la historia de la insurrección comunera en la Provincia de Antioquia, 1765–1798*
(Medellín: Universidad de Antioquia, Facultad de Ciencias Humanas, Departamento de Historia,
1982), 460–62.

give his two *tomines*, to which he responded that he would not only give the two *tomines* but ten pesos if it were true, after which, without discussing the matter any further, the defendant walked to San Jerónimo and he does not know if he was named captain of the insurgent slaves.

Asked if after the event that he mentioned, he sought out other slaves to gather in order to ask for the said cédula, he stated with clarity whom he summoned for that purpose and the masters that they serve, he said that it is true that Pelayo, slave of the aforementioned master Don Antonio de Lora, ordered him to convene the slaves of San Jerónimo and the San Jacinto mines, and that he had already gathered those from Medellín, Guarne, el Páramo, and the valley of San Andrés, but that in San Jerónimo he did not invite any of his comrades, and in San Jacinto he talked to the slave who is the captain of the gang of Doctor Don Sancho Londoño, called Faustino, who asked him what news there was in Antioquia, [and] he answered that the mulatto scribe had shown the blacks a decree that said that they would be free by each giving two *tomines*, at which that black captain answered that it had already been said for a long time that the decree was there, and that they did not speak more about the topic, and that in the parish of San Pedro de Osos he met a black man and asked him if he was a slave, since he did not know him, and when he said yes, he also told him that the decree had appeared and that by giving two *tomines* that scribe would deliver it [freedom], to which the man replied that he would give it at any time, after which each went their way....

Asked on which day they had determined to assemble and ask for the mentioned decree, he said that the abovementioned Pelayo had told him that they had to gather on New Year's Day to ask for the cédula, and that in order for all those the defendant had invited to be ready, he would dispatch a laborer [*peon*] to summon them and after that, he [Pelayo] said that he did not know if it would be that day, because he had to go with his master to kill a tiger at the hacienda, but that he would arrange in time which day it had to be.

Silvestre García, royal councilor, to [Governor Luis de Las Casas], Havana, 9 February 1795[3]

The year 1795 saw more slave revolts and conspiracies than ever before or afterwards in the Americas. The Haitian Revolution in full swing, the French Convention had decided the previous year to abolish slavery in France's colonies, and the agent of the French government in the Caribbean, Victor Hugues was trying to destabilize the non-French Caribbean by promising freedom for enslaved people, equality for free people of color, and autonomy for the white elites. The notion of possible collusion between blacks and Frenchmen struck fear into the hearts of many whites.

e

Your Excellency, ever since it was reported that an uprising was being plotted in this city, I have, in order to fulfill the task you have given me, done everything to make inquiries about the rumors going around and their background. The goal was to monitor and investigate with the most deliberate secrecy and without intervention of a scribe so as to operate with the greatest caution the source of the rumors, the apparent or real proofs of the plot, and the persons who had joined hands for it....

By law, it was established that the cruel act committed by the black man Joseph Maria, slave of Doña Maria Candelaria Aldana on 20 October in the boys' and girls' school run by Doña Maria Montero, killing one boy, two girls, and one man, and wounding six boys and a young woman, was the indeliberate consequence of a fit of madness from which the black man suffered. But despite the careful endeavor to make this known to the public, the events made people talk publicly and rashly about their distrust of people of color, particularly in the present circumstances in which those of **Guarico** and other French possessions have risen cruelly and ferociously against the whites. When the blacks themselves heard these rumors, some of them started saying that they could castigate the whites, and that the latter had made much noise about a trifle, namely the killing by a black man of a few whites, and other propositions of the same kind. It could not be discovered who these men were since they uttered these phrases as they walked through the streets. In this situation, the repeated conversations heard among them about the said event coincided with the presence of many French prisoners distributed among the forts, some of whom were seen coming with

Guarico: Saint-Domingue; a reference to the Haitian Revolution.

---

3   Archivo General de Simancas [Spain], Secretaria de Estado y del Despacho de Guerra [SGU], LEG 6854, 57.

a guard to the Plaza Vieja to stop for food and conversing with one or the other black or mulatto man, perhaps because they were French artisans or peddlers working in the Plaza or because of any other reason, but none of any significance. This made the public suspect collusion between them, and accordingly the rumors began to take shape, while others which I will mention below were added, making them so potent that people assumed the plot was real and the outbreak of the uprising inevitable.

… When the people were in a state of agitation because of the value they attached to the stories that were told, the passage (which I related to you) took place of the navy brigadier **Don Carlos de la Ribiere**, a French émigré. On that occasion, the Spanish black man Blas Joseph Melgarejo said to the mulatto slave of another naval official, also an émigré: "Don't you think we have to do the same as the blacks of Guarico? While that mulatto opted out of appearing in court, and you acquiesced in it, apprehensive that forcing him to do so would lead to a misstep and also, for good reasons, to appease the brigadier, I was able to ascertain … that the black man Melgarejo lived in a room below **Licenciado** Don Ventura Perez, whom I asked about his character, conduct, and occupation. After informing me that he was levelheaded and of good behavior, and that both he and his wife occupied themselves in buying eggs, chickens, and hens in the countryside, which his wife sold in the Plaza, the Licenciado interviewed him personally without telling him for what purpose, and … learned that he had had a conversation about the current hearsay but that he had not had dealings or discussions with others of his class that merits even the smallest consideration, and that he was just trying to make a living.…"

Don Carlos de la Ribiere: Charles François de Riffardeau, Marquis de Rivière (1763–1828).

Licenciado: Recipient of a university degree, equivalent to a BA.

PART 2

Imperial Crisis

DOCUMENT 4:

Juan Pablo Viscardo y Guzmán, *Letter to the American Spaniards*, Philadelphia, 1799[1]

Born in Peru, Juan Pablo Viscardo y Guzmán (1748–98) joined the Jesuit order at a young age. In 1767, he was forcibly shipped to Italy after Spain's King Carlos III expelled all Jesuits from his American colonies. Residing near Genoa, Viscardo heard the news about Túpac Amaru's rebellion, of which he became a distant supporter. When he presented himself to British diplomats as a native Peruvian with inside knowledge of the rebellion, the British government gave him a secret identity and paid him to write commentaries on Spanish American affairs. Under these conditions, Viscardo wrote this document around 1791, calling passionately on the Spanish Americans to break off ties with Spain. After his death, his fellow "precursor" of the Spanish American independence movements, Francisco Miranda, obtained Viscardo's papers and had the Letter published in London (although Philadelphia is listed on the book's cover). Copies of it were read by numerous insurgent leaders around the start of the independence movements.

These legitimate hopes [of the conquerors of America] having been frustrated, we, their descendants and those of other Spaniards who successively transported themselves to America, have respected, preserved and cordially cherished the attachment of our fathers to their first *patria*, although we knew only this one for our country …; it is to her [the *patria*] that we have sacrificed infinite riches of every kind; it is for her alone that we have until now worked ourselves into a sweat, and it is for her that in every encounter we have gladly shed our blood. Guided by a blind enthusiasm, we have not taken heed that so much enthusiasm for a country which is foreign to us, to which we owe nothing, on which we don't depend and from which we don't expect anything, turns into a cruel betrayal towards the one in which we are born, and which provides food for us and our children; our veneration of the feelings of our fathers' affection toward their first *patria* is the most decisive

---

1   Original title: *Lettre aux Espagnols Américains.*

proof of the preference we owe to ours; all that we lavished on Spain has been, against all reason, taken away from ourselves and our children; while our stupidity has left us in irons; and if we do not break them in time, all we can do is to patiently endure this ignominious slavery. If our present condition were as irremediable as it is distressing, it would be an act of pity to conceal it from your eyes; but having in our power the surest remedy, let us unveil this dreadful picture and consider it in the light of truth. It teaches us that every law which opposes the universal good of those for whom it is made, is an act of tyranny, and that to demand its observance is to impose slavery; that a law which would tend to directly destroy the basis of the prosperity of a people, would be a monstrosity beyond belief.... Since men began to unite in society for their greater benefit, we are the only ones whom the government has forced to supply its needs at the highest possible price, and to buy its products at the lowest price. In order that this violence should have the most complete success, they have silenced, as in a besieged city, all the voices by which we could have obtained from other nations, at moderate prices, and by equitable exchanges, the commodities which were needed. The government's taxes, the ministry's gratuities, the avarice of merchants authorized to exercise the most unrestrained monopoly ... didn't allow the consumer any choice; and since this mercenary tyranny might force us to resort to our industry to supply our needs, the government took care to chain it.

... Small wonder, then, that with so much gold and silver, of which we have nearly filled the universe, we have scarcely enough to cover our nakedness. What good is so much fertile land? If the tools necessary to plow it are lacking, it is useless to cultivate it beyond our consumption....

Let us consent on our side to be a different people; let us renounce the ridiculous system of union and equality with our masters and tyrants; let us renounce a government, the remoteness of which, so enormous, cannot procure for us, even in part, the advantages which every man ought to expect from the society to which he is attached; this government, which, instead of fulfilling its indispensable duty to protect the liberty and safety of our persons and our property, has been very eager to destroy them; and which, instead of striving to make us happy, piles on us all kinds of calamities. Since the rights and duties of government and subjects are reciprocal, Spain has become derelict towards us; she also broke the weak links that could bind us and hold us back.

Nature has separated us from Spain by immense seas; a son who would be at such a distance from his father would doubtless be a fool, if, in the conduct of his smallest interests, he was still waiting for his father's decision. The son is emancipated by natural right; and similarly, a numerous people, which does not depend on another people, which it doesn't need, should it be subjected to him as the lowliest slave?

… Finally, under whatever aspect our dependence on Spain is envisaged, we will see that all our duties oblige us to end it. We owe it by gratitude to our ancestors, who did not lavish their blood and their sweat for the theater of their glory and their work to become one of our miserable servitude. We owe it to ourselves, by the indisputable obligation to preserve the natural rights received from our creator, precious rights that we are not entitled to alienate, and of which they cannot rob us without committing a crime, whichever pretext they use.

Napoleon to Joachim Murat, lieutenant general of the Kingdom of Spain, Bayonne, 11, 21, and 26 May 1808[2]

Just over a week after he had forced Fernando VII and Carlos IV to renounce their rights to the Spanish throne, Napoleon started organizing expeditions to Spanish America, trying to preempt rumored British invasions or help the inhabitants fight off the British. No detail escaped this micromanager. His main activity was focused on Buenos Aires and Veracruz, as he tells Joachim Murat, one of his most prominent marshals, in these letters. Murat, who was married to Caroline, Napoleon's youngest sister, was named lieutenant-general of Spain before Napoleon appointed him as the King of Naples, succeeding Napoleon's brother Joseph, the new King of Spain.

11 May:

I have already told you that it was necessary that on all the ships which should be sent to America, rifles and pistols are to be embarked, which are badly needed in that country. It will be good to also transport a number of recruits on each ship. When we only put thirty or forty men on each ship, it would have a very good effect on America, because those colonies will see that we think of them. Have the Minister of the Navy survey the vessels sent to America and let him arrange to have rifles and recruits on board.

… What is the number of small ships, advice-boats, **avisos**, etc. we ship to America? There should be at least twelve. These small ships should carry letters from the junta, with the supporting documents and letters from the Minister of the Navy, of which twelve copies should be made. I think that the places where it is important to send these expeditions are Mexico and the Río de la Plata. For each of these places, it would be necessary to designate six frigates that sail well.

avisos: Light, fast vessels used for communication, usually within a naval squadron.

21 May:

I have read with great interest the reports of the ministers of war and the navy on the means of rescuing the Río de la Plata. There is no time to lose. It is necessary to arm the *Concepción* and the *San Fernando*, which, with the *Vengeance*, the *Magdalena*, the *Diana* and the corvette *Indagadora*, will

---

2   In *Correspondance de Napoléon Ier, publiée par ordre de l'Empereur Napoléon III*, 32 vols. (Paris: Imprimerie Impériale, 1858–70), XVII: 110–12, 205–06, 246–48.

easily carry 3,000 men. You must immediately appoint the rear-admiral who is to command this squadron, send the necessary funds to Ferrol, and choose the force of 3,000 men to be embarked on this expedition. I think it would take a light infantry battalion, a line infantry regiment, which comes to 2,200 infantrymen, a cavalry regiment on foot of 500 men, and 400 artillery men. The minister of war has to appoint these forces, as well as a brigadier, a sergeant-major, an artillery colonel, several artillery officers, and three officers of the engineers. 10,000 rifles will be loaded on the expedition's ships, 12 pieces of field cannon, with 300 rounds to be fired per round, 500,000 gun cartridges for the infantry, and 4,000 pioneer tools. This operation seems to me extremely important. By sending the required 5 or 600,000 francs, all this may be ready during the month of June, before the English can be informed of extraordinary activity in this matter and strengthen their squadron. They have only one ship, and when they have two of these they would make a quick pursuit ahead of the Spanish squadron. All this must be done secretly and unostentatiously. As for the landing, it would be necessary to order that the squadron should approach more toward the south, so that, if it finds the English to be superior near Montevideo, it could disembark lower.

26 May:

I have just written to Don Gregorio de la Cuesta, captain-general of Old Castile, to inform him that I have appointed him Viceroy of Mexico. Have him ship his certificates and commissions in good standing and order the frigate *La Flora* to be ready in Cádiz to take him to Mexico.

You will order the viceroy to bring with him four or five brigadiers general, corporals or colonels, to entrust them with the government of Veracruz and other important places. You must also prepare avisos in the small ports that are located between Cádiz and Portugal, from where one can, better than from everywhere else, leave for America, so that, if the frigate would be too much delayed to set sail, the viceroy could embark on one of the avisos. You will place on the *Flora* 3,000 rifles and other materials deemed necessary. Of the two **vessels of 64** which are at Cádiz, the *San Fulgencio* is a very fine fast ship. Have him commanded well, have his crew completed and prepared for a mission; my intention is to destine him for Buenos Aires. It is necessary to embark on this ship 4,000 men and 4,000 rifles. But it is necessary that its **copper** be inspected, in order to be certain about its journey. You need to fill it with supplies for six months.

You have appointed the brigadier general for the **intendanc**y of Veracruz. I have been assured that he is an officer who has no merit and who has bought his rank. My intention is to appoint as commander of the province of

vessels of 64: Sixty-four-gun ships.

copper: Copper plates protected the ship's hull from corrosion and biofouling (the accumulation of organisms such as algae).

intendancy: An administrative unit in which an intendant was responsible for administration, finance, and the military.

Caracas the brigadier Don **Vicente di Imbaran**, who is now in Madrid and who has been governor of Cumaná. It is necessary that this officer proceeds without delay to Ferrol, where he will embark on the brig the *Descobridor* and sail as soon as possible. You will embark on this brig 1,500 to 2,000 rifles.

… You will not fail to send my proclamation to the Council of the Indies, so that it may be sent to America in every possible way. Order that no moment be wasted at Ferrol to make provisions, for it is urgent that we send help to South America. *La Concepción* is ready, it is only a matter of hurrying its crew; the *Saint-Elme* and *Saint-Firmin* are in the roadstead as well as two frigates; the *San Fernando* is also ready. We can therefore, with a little activity, have four vessels and two frigates at Ferrol, which can carry 3,000 men, which, combined with the 400 men of the *San Fulgencio* of Cádiz, will secure the possession of **this part of America**.

If the weather is good, a brig will leave from here tomorrow with packages and rifles for Buenos Aires. These rifles are all good French rifles.

Salvador José de Muro y Salazar, Marquis of Someruelos, *Proclamation to the Inhabitants of Cuba*, Havana, 17 July 1808[3]

Immediately after receiving news of the events in Bayonne, where Napoleon had forced Spain's King and his predecessor to relinquish the Spanish throne, Cuba's Governor, the Marquis of Someruelos (1755–1813) sharply condemned French actions in this proclamation. At the same time, he urged his residents to treat the French nationals among them well. Many of the 20,000 natives of France and its colonies living in Cuba had first arrived as refugees from neighboring Saint-Domingue during the Haitian Revolution. As the popular mood turned against the French residents in 1809, Someruelos ordered them to leave.

Inhabitants of the Island of Cuba, Worthy Children of the Generous Spanish Nation

I inform you that I have just received today some manifestoes, proclamations, and edicts published and printed by order of the Supreme Junta that has been established in Seville, as a result of an act of perfidy more infamous than what has been seen or heard for centuries.… It appears from them … that the French government, falsely assuming the guise of friend and good ally, has seduced Fernando VII, the best and most virtuous of kings, abusing his generosity and good faith, to lure him into its territory with deceitful and insidious tricks, ensuring with the same cunning deviousness that his august parents followed him, as well as the whole royal family, treating them with the most shameful contempt, and finally consummating its horrible project by forcing them to renounce the Spanish Crown in favor of an odious foreigner with no more right than his insatiable ambition, at the same time that his executioners and murderers shed the precious blood of the inhabitants of Madrid in exchange for the hospitality and fraternity with which they had welcomed and entertained them.… Our language does not have the right phrase to characterize such a horrific conduct that has covered France in shame and Spain in grief and shaken even the most insensitive and barbarous nations. But don't imagine that for that reason the pride, great character, and majestic dignity of Spain have faded because of so much disorder and grievous calamity. Far from it, the virtuous and magnanimous children of the fatherland of heroism are determined to fight

---

3 John Carter Brown Library, Providence, RI.

until the last of the twelve million which their inhabitants total, gloriously dies, to avenge such a humiliating affront, as well as their offended religion, their raped women, and their murdered children, and to rescue their beloved Fernando from captivity. Yes: do not doubt it. They will make the perpetrators of so much wickedness tremble and exterminate them. They are animated by a holy fury capable of breaking and shattering the chains that oppress all European nations.

Persuade yourselves with confidence that united with Spain and England, the nations in whose homes and fields the innocent blood of its most florid youth that has been shed by an incomprehensible chain of events initiated by the **Genius of Desolation** is still dripping, will recover from their dejection. They will find courage to shake off the yoke, and they will come together to work on the greatest and worthiest enterprise that humans have ever carried out, with the same fury with which the lion rushes to recover her cubs. The French themselves, that illustrious nation, generous and worthy of better fortune, will rush to wash away the black stain with which it has smudged its luster by its own hands: have compassion for them and don't regard them with hatred and anger, because they are our brothers and will soon be our good friends. The Divine Author of men, the Arbiter of the fate of the nations is interested in this holy and august work, and we must not doubt His protection....

Genius of Desolation: Napoleon.

Memorandum of grievances (Memorial de Agravios), cabildo of Bogotá, 20 November 1809[4]

Bogotá's city council begins its message to Spain's Central Junta—which had assumed sovereignty in the King's absence—by expressing its joy about the decree issued by that body on 22 January 1809, in which "the vast and precious domains of America" are not called "colonies or factories, like those of other nations, but an essential and integral part of the Spanish monarchy." The councilors are highly critical, however, of the arrangements pertaining to American representation. The council, led by the document's author Camilo Torres (who would be executed by royalists in 1816), never sent it, because they thought it too radical. Note that this memorandum, like so many other independence documents, does not mention nonwhites.

It is impossible to express the joy that this sovereign resolution has caused in the hearts of all the members of this city council and of those who desire a true union and fraternity between the European and American Spaniards, which who can only endure on the foundations of justice and equality. America and Spain are two integral and constituent parts of the Spanish monarchy, and on the basis of this principle and that of their mutual and common interests, a sincere and fraternal love can only be founded on reciprocity and equal rights.

The city council, then, sees in this determination … a pledge of the true spirit that today animates the **two Spains**, and a sincere desire to walk in lockstep with the common good. If England's government had taken this important step, perhaps it would not lament the separation of its colonies now. But a tone of pride and a spirit of conceit and superiority made it lose those rich possessions, which did not understand how they could be vassals of the same sovereign nation, and integral parts of the same monarchy, while all other provinces of England sent their representatives to the nation's legislative body and wanted to dictate and impose taxes that they had not sanctioned with their approval.

But amidst the jubilation that this order has caused, the city council of the capital of New Granada has witnessed with great pain that even the less important provinces of Spain have sent two representatives to the supreme junta, while only one deputy is required for each of the kingdoms and

two Spains: European Spain and American Spain.

---

4 In *Representacion del cabildo de Bogotá capital del Nuevo Reino de Granada a la Suprema Junta Central de España, en el año de 1809* (Bogotá: Imprenta de N. Lora, 1832), 1–36.

captaincies of the vast, rich and populous domains of America, resulting in the remarkable difference between nine [American] and thirty-six [Spanish representatives].

… The Americas … are not made up of foreigners to the Spanish nation. We are children, we are descendants of those who have spilled their blood to acquire these new domains for the Crown of Spain; of those who have extended their limits and have given it in Europe's political balance a standing that Spain alone couldn't have. The natives that were conquered and subjected to Spain are no longer there today or are very few compared to the children of Europeans that populate these rich possessions. The continuous emigration from Spain during the three centuries that have passed since the discovery of America; the crafts and positions in the hands of European Spaniards, who came to settle successively and who have left their children and posterity here; and the benefits of trade and the rich gifts that nature offers have been the perpetual source and wellspring of our population.

… As for learning, America is not so vain to believe that it is superior or even equal to the provinces of Spain. Thanks to a despotic government, enemy of the Enlightenment, it could not expect to make rapid advances in human knowledge, since its intellect was hindered by obstacles placed in its way. The printing press, vehicle of the Enlightenment and the most reliable conduit for its spread, has been more strictly prohibited in America than anywhere else. Our study of philosophy amounts to no more than the use of a metaphysical jargon by the most obscure and worthless authors that are known. Hence our shameful ignorance of the rich treasures that surround us and their most common application in daily life. Not long ago, the chairs in natural and international law were abolished, to the amazement of all who are reasonable, because their study was considered harmful. Harmful, therefore, is the study of the first principles of morality that God has impressed in the heart of man! Harmful is the study that teaches him his obligations toward the **first cause** as his creator, himself, his country, and his fellow men! That is despotism's barbarous cruelty, enemy of God and of men, which only aspires to use people as a pack of vile servants, destined to satisfy its pride, whims, ambition, and passions!

first cause: God.

… What **this body** wants today, what it is asking for, is that the American deputies not be excluded from equal representation because of their limited learning. It is true that they will not be able to compete with their European colleagues in the deep mysteries of politics; but at least they will have practical knowledge of their country, which their counterparts cannot have. Every day the most monstrous and damaging errors are committed in the Americas for lack of such knowledge. Without it, a government two and three thousand leagues away, separated by a wide sea, must waver, and, guided by principles that cannot be adapted to vastly different circumstances,

this body: The city council of Bogotá.

must bring about wrongs more disastrous than those it seeks to remedy. Like a doctor who cures without knowledge and without the patient being present, it administers poison instead of an antidote and brings death instead of health....

Are you afraid of America's influence on the government? And why do you fear that? If the government is fair, just, and liberal, our hands will help sustain it. Man is not an enemy of his own happiness. If you want to tip the balance to the other side, understand that ten or twelve million souls with equal rights, weigh the same. The seven million people that form Great Britain undeniably outweighed the barely three million of English America; and yet, when justice increased the latter's weight, the scales were tipped.

Don't be afraid that the Americas will separate from you.... The Americas know your situation and your resources, and they know their own. One brother speaks to another in order to remain at peace with, and united to him. Both only have the right to give laws to the other when they agree to a mutual and reciprocal alliance.

... The law is the expression of the general will, and it is necessary that the people state it. That is the purpose of the Cortes; it is the medium for a general expression. If you do not listen, then, to the Americas, if they do not manifest their will through a competent and properly authorized representation, the law is not made for them, because it does not have their sanction. Twelve million men with different needs, in different circumstances, under different climates, and with different interests, need different laws.... If the sovereign were to move here, leaving you as dependent provinces, would you accept the number of deputies we would like to determine, three times fewer than that we'll assign for the Americas? If by some misfortune, which we are horrified to consider, the natural or violent death of all the offspring of the royal family in Europe would make it necessary to call on a member of the royal family who found himself in America to rule us, and he fixed his abode here, would you be satisfied at the convocation of the Cortes or the formation of a national representative body to be so much in the minority as nine vs. thirty-six, irrespective of the great advantages that the Americas offer you in the way of extension, riches, and perhaps population? No, we would be unfair if we did not allow you equal participation. Then apply this principle yourselves and don't wish for your brothers what in the other case you wouldn't wish for yourselves....

The fear that this number [of deputies] would consume many public funds would be shameful to bring up for such a great nation. Set at ten or twelve thousand pesos [per deputy], [the total] would barely amount to the sum of four hundred thousand. And how does that compare to the enormous sum spent by the members of the royal house, which must now be diminished for the benefit of the state? How would it compare to what the **despicable**

Godoy has devoured in the twenty disastrous years when he was the royal favorite and the cruelest despot? How, finally, would it compare to what the treasury has spent on that army of captain-generals and lieutenant-generals, field marshals, and squadron commanders who have so fruitlessly bled the country? [There are] so many luxury embassies like those in Constantinople, Russia, Sweden, Denmark, etc., with which we neither have nor need to have permanent and stable relations; and so many other savings that a prudent administration would make. These will create a large and safe fund with which we will be able to face the expenses....

Equality! Holy right of equality. Justice, may you … give each one what is his, inspiring in European Spain these feelings of American Spain. It strengthens the bonds of this union. May it last forever, and may our children, giving each other their hands from one continent to another, bless the happy days that brought them so much good. Oh! May heaven hear the sincere vows of the town council and may their sentiments not be misinterpreted! Heaven forbid that other principles and other less liberal ideas produce the fatal effects of an eternal separation!

The Superior Junta of Cádiz to Spanish America, 28 February 1810[5]

By early 1810, there was little hope left that Spain would remain independent. When French troops moved into Seville, the city's junta ordered the local authorities to accept French rule and recognize the government of Napoleon's brother Joseph. The Central Junta, which was based in Seville, now dissolved itself and was replaced by the Council of Regency. Because of the fear that Americans might not stand behind the new government, there was a need to communicate with them. One body that did this was the junta of Cádiz, the city where the Council of Regency would reside. Its message was not just meant for American settlers, however, but also for that Council. Almost entirely made up of merchants, the Cádiz junta put pressure on the Council to take its commercial interests into account through this message of self-congratulation.

Peoples of America:

During the dangerous crisis that the monarchy has just suffered, it was not only assaulted by a cloud of misfortunes in its external defense, but internally undermined by factions and frenzy, causing it to collapse to the ground; when the confusion and disorder did not seem to leave any path to take in the labyrinth of events and the tumultuous stirring of passions, the town of Cádiz, which nature and chance had put inside the whirlwind, had the good fortune to form one of the main pillars to sustain the unity and hope of the state. It speaks to you now through its superior junta, to inform you of the events that have actually occurred, to state its various operations, and to show you the course that you must loyally follow for the salvation of the country.

You will hear the news that the French have penetrated Andalusia, that they have occupied Seville, that they have expanded to the sea, that the sovereign authority deposited in the Central Junta now rests with a Council of Regency, and that we must start again to organize the resistance against the enemy.

After the French occupation of Seville, uncertainty spread across Spain. Each province, each city, each village had to take sides, and attend to its preservation, and defense on its own. Cádiz is different from all other cities

---

5   Original title: *La Junta Superior de Cádiz a la América Española*, John Carter Brown Library, Providence, RI.

in Spain because of its population, its opulence, and the immense reach of its commerce. It is a bulwark of strength. It is there that the Council of Regency resides, to which sovereign authority has been transferred.

Cádiz speaks to you, peoples of America, and trusts that the voices from your countries will be heard to adhere and fraternize due to the close ties that unites it with you. In what city, in what port, in what corner [of America], however remote and hidden, does Cádiz not have a correspondent, a relative or a friend?

The Governing Junta of Caracas to the Constituted Authorities of All Towns of Venezuela, 1810[6]

As in other parts of Spain and Spanish America, a junta was formed in Caracas to claim power while the King was in exile. Caracas's junta differed from most others, though, by failing to recognize the Council of Regency. Made up of men with radical ideas, the junta's initial intention was not to break off relations with Spain. Instead, it ruminates in this proclamation to the towns of Venezuela about the meaning of "fatherland" (*patria*). The radicalism comes through in the news about military organization, which was perhaps officially to ward off a potential French invasion, but may have been intended for a confrontation with Spanish forces.

… Caracas was the first to solemnly pronounce its resolution and has sworn to uphold it without dissolving the bonds of fraternity that so closely unite us with our European brothers; determined not to recognize another sovereign than Fernando the Seventh, Caracas has separated from the Council of Regency, and has sworn by the hands of the victims sacrificed by French barbarism, to defend its freedom in spite of those who conspire against her.

The eyes of Europe and the rest of America are fixed on the Department of Venezuela…. Let us be a worthy model of its conduct; let us sustain with nobility the brilliant role of being the first to have embraced the crown of freedom in the vast American continent. The undertaking is immense, and therefore needs great efforts; it is necessary that the citizen devotes himself entirely to the Fatherland, and that he proves to him that expressions of his love … are sincere and correspond to the feelings of his heart; it is necessary that the holy freedom of which we have made ourselves worthy is sustained at the expense of our possessions, our persons, and our blood itself. But it is necessary to know this Fatherland, it is necessary to know what this freedom consists of in order to love the Fatherland and sustain it with sacrifices….

The Fatherland is not the King, the government or the constitution; these are only the forms in which it exists. The Fatherland is the congregation of men who live under the same government, are subject to the same laws and follow the same usages and customs. The land in which we are born and the riches that we possess in it, are not exactly the Fatherland, but the means of subsisting comfortably and peacefully in the congregation that constitutes

---

6   Original title: *La Junta gubernativa de Caracas a las autoridades constituidas de todos los pueblos de Venezuela*, John Carter Brown Library, Providence, RI.

it. The Fatherland, then, is a whole, of which each citizen is an integral part, and he therefore commits a crime to consider himself separate from it. An honest man must not fear any other harm or desire any other advantage than that which harms or favors the country to which he owes everything he owns. When he lavishes his sweat, when he sheds his blood for it, he gives nothing of himself, he does nothing but return what it has lent him; he has been begotten, educated, and fed in the bosom of this Fatherland; it defends him with its laws against domestic insults and with weapons in external wars; … these benefits need sacrifices to maintain the Fatherland that provides them, and whoever refuses is an evil man, a bad patriot. If there is among us someone so infamous and so selfish, he must move out, he must absent himself from a society whose benefits he does not repay, he must become a desert dweller; there he will find no society, no country or reciprocal duties; may he live alone and as he pleases, covering himself with leaves of trees and feeding himself with the bread of solitude.

… [The governors, judges, and mayors] will see to it that all the individuals of their jurisdiction up to the age of sixty years form squads, divided into companies of 50 or 60 men, and organized by … judges according to the circumstances of the country. Each company will choose its officers, and all those that form a squad will do the same with respect to their commander. Men in the same squad will make sure that the companies meet once or twice a week for two or three hours, and that during this time they are instructed as much as the officers' ability allows in the simplest and most necessary military exercises such as marching in two files, turning half to the left, and rotating a quarter of a circle. The individuals that compose these squads will bring to these exercises whatever weapons they have, even if it is just a stick.

El Diario Político de Santafé de Bogotá, 18 September 1810

Non-existent prior to the independence era, newspapers proliferated in Spanish America in the years after 1808. Like most others, *El Diario Político de Santafé de Bogotá* was only granted a short life, appearing from 27 August 1810 until 1 February 1811. With funds obtained from Bogotá's governing junta, the editors took it upon themselves to "enlighten the people" and provide information about what they saw as a struggle for freedom. The newspaper also served as a mouthpiece of the city's junta, which here advocates the elimination of the rivalry of Spanish Americans and Spaniards. Independence is not yet expressed as a goal.

The Supreme Governing Junta of the capital city … feels obliged to interrupt its business for a few moments to wipe away the tears of a large number of mothers and sons of honorable Europeans, whose banishment an unknown author has called for, using the deplorable and irreligious medium of **pasquinades**. Instead of taking up a sword to cover his Fatherland in honor, it seems that the author only seeks to stain it with disgrace, making it the derision of other nations, which to this day must look at our happy revolution as the most peaceful and well-ordered of all in history.…

Therefore, it orders and commands:

Firstly: Since it is a crime against public security and tranquility to insult any citizen, of whatever class, or his wife, children, and family, he who does so himself or through an intermediary, orally or in writing, will be severely punished, whether he is a European Spaniard or an American Spaniard.

Secondly: Condemning the odious distinction between creoles and Europeans, the current government will reward and consider both groups based on their merit and patriotism. It will compensate the Americans for having been wrongfully neglected in the past when ecclesiastical, political, and military positions were filled.

Thirdly: The same government is following the cases of bad Europeans. To prevent them from being confused with the good ones in the capital city and to cover them with the hatred they deserve, the government will expel those who through their behavior have shown to be unworthy of staying in the capital and its provinces.

Fourthly: The same measure will be taken against those Americans who, forgetful of the obligations of love and loyalty towards the Fatherland, have become suspicious in the eyes of the government.

pasquinades: Also pasquins; publicly displayed satires or lampoons.

Lastly: To prevent the use of the scandalous and irreligious medium of pasquinades, the Justice section of the Supreme Junta will listen to any accusation justly made against European or American Spaniards whose behavior is contrary to the good cause and the current system of government in order to restrain and punish such delinquents according to their crimes....

PART 3

Independence Movements Take Off

DOCUMENT 11:

Edict of Manuel Abad y Queipo, bishop of Michoacán, Valladolid (Mexico), 24 September 1810[1]

The bishop-elect of Michoacán, Spanish-born Manuel Abad y Queipo (1751–1824), had advocated Indigenous equality in the years before the imperial crisis. But Abad y Queipo was no revolutionary, and he was quick to condemn Hidalgo's revolt. Eight days after its start, he wrote this text to the inhabitants of his bishopric. According to him, the revolt bore a close resemblance to the Haitian Revolution, in which all whites and 80 per cent of nonwhites had perished—a wild exaggeration.

Don Manuel Abad y Queipo, confessor canon of this Holy Church, bishop-elect and governor of this bishopric of Michoacán, to all its inhabitants, hail and peace in our Lord Jesus Christ: *Omne regnum in se divisum desolabitur.* Every kingdom divided against itself is brought to desolation, says Jesus Christ, Luke 11:17. Yes, my beloved faithful, the history of all centuries, of all peoples and nations, which has passed before our eyes, [including] the French Revolution and the one that is currently happening in the [Iberian] Peninsula, in our beloved and unfortunate fatherland, confirm the infallible truth of that divine oracle. But the example more analogous to our situation we find immediately in the French part of the Island of Santo Domingo, whose owners were the richest, wealthiest, and happiest men known on earth. The population was composed, almost like ours, of European Frenchmen, creole Frenchmen, Indians native to the land, blacks and mulattoes, and castas resulting from the first groups. Divisions were introduced because of the aforementioned French revolution, and everything was ruined and destroyed. Anarchy in France caused the death of two million Frenchmen, that is, about two-twentieths, the finest part of both sexes; it ruined its

---

1   In Genaro García, ed., *El clero de México y la guerra de independencia: Documentos del arzobispado de México* (México: Librería de la Vda. de Ch. Bouret, 1906), 20–27.

commerce and navigation, and set back industry and agriculture. But the anarchy in Saint-Domingue slaughtered all the French and creole whites, without even one remaining, and massacred four-fifths of all the other inhabitants, leaving the remaining one-fifth of blacks and mulattoes in eternal hatred and in a mortal war, in which they are bound to entirely destroy each other. It devastated the whole country, burning and destroying all the possessions, all the cities, towns, villages, so that the best-populated and cultivated country that existed in all the Americas is today a desert, a shelter of tigers and lions. That is the horrendous, but honest, picture of the ravages of anarchy in Saint-Domingue. New Spain, which Europe had admired for its most brilliant testimonies of loyalty and patriotism in favor of the mother country, having supported and sustained it with its treasures, with its opinion and its writings, having maintained peace and harmony despite the snares and intrigues of the tyrant of the world, today is threatened with discord and anarchy and with all the misfortunes that pursue it and that the aforementioned island of Santo Domingo has suffered. A minister of the God of peace, a priest of Jesus Christ, a shepherd of souls (and I don't want to say it), the priest of Dolores, Miguel Hidalgo (who had earned my trust and my friendship), associate of the captains of the Queen's regiment, **Ignacio Allende, Juan de Aldama, and José Mariano Abasolo**, raised the banner of rebellion, ignited the torch of discord and anarchy, and by seducing a portion of the innocent peasants made them take up arms, and arriving with them at the town of Dolores, on the 16th of the current month, at dawn, surprised and arrested the European residents, and plundered and stole their goods; and afterwards, at seven o'clock at night, at the town of San Miguel el Grande, he carried out the same [sort of] attack and took possession of the government. On Friday the 21st, he occupied Celaya in the same way, and according to our information, it seems that they have spread to Salamanca and Irapuato. He is taking the arrested Europeans with him, including the sacristan of Dolores, the priest of Chamacuero, and several Carmelites from Celaya, threatening the people of the towns that he will behead them if they put up any resistance; and insulting the religion and our sovereign Fernando VII, he painted on his banner the image of our august patroness, Our Lady of Guadalupe, and wrote the following inscription: Long Live the Religion, Long Live Our Blessed Mother of Guadalupe, Long Live Fernando VII, Long Live America, and Down with Bad Government.

Ignacio Allende, Juan de Aldama, and José Mariano Abasolo: Ignacio Allende (1769–1811) and Juan Aldama González (1764–1811) were the original leaders of the insurrection before Hidalgo took over. They were both executed. Although he was also an insurgent leader, José Mariano Abasolo (1783–1816) was not executed, but was sent to Cádiz, where he died in jail.

Juan Bautista Díaz Calvillo, *Discourse about the Ills that Disunity between Overseas and American Spaniards Can Cause*[2]

In late 1810, Juan Bautista Díaz Calvillo, a creole priest in Mexico City who was well-known for his eloquent sermons, presented this text for publication in response to Hidalgo's insurrection. Once it received the official stamp of approval, it joined a large number of pamphlets supporting either party. Calvillo unambiguously sided with the authorities and claimed that they had God on their side. Even if the insurgents had more fighting men in their ranks, God would allow those whose cause was just to emerge victorious.

Who would believe, noble and generous Americans, that after three centuries in which our fertile and beautiful soil had enjoyed the inestimable goods of peace, enriching with its products Old Spain as a just reward for the benefits that it had received; who, I say, would believe that the spirit of discord, the son of a restless heart, envious and ungrateful, intended to surprise the minds of the most faithful of this kingdom, until they conceived the most unjust and bloodthirsty project that perhaps exists in the annals of the world? By which faithful, grateful, religious America, having sheltered for so long the children of her mother, Catholic Hesperia, now wants to eject them from her coasts or make them suffer the ultimate desolation and a fatal extermination? By which those through whom they have acquired the best education, the assets of society, the knowledge of every scientific discipline, the comforts of life, and the company of men that we enjoy, must be mistreated, persecuted, and slandered, and must perish harshly at the hands of the French oppressors or some ungrateful Americans? By which our beloved parents, those who brought us the beautiful light of the Gospel, who announced to us a God of peace, who brought us back to spiritual life, who nourished us with the bread of sound doctrine, and prevented at the expense of their sweat and labor corruption and contagion to take root, will be precipitately expelled from a country that they have bought with their hardships, benefited with their instruction, and raised to the degree of brilliance in which it finds itself today, with their writings, preaching, and example? What a monstrous ingratitude! What an event worthy of drawing the execration and hatred of all nations! What a fertile ground for the most

---

2   Original title: *Discurso sobre los males que puede causar la desunión entre españoles ultramarinos y americanos* (México: Arizpe, 1810).

terrible evils to visit us, when it seems that we are looking for nothing but prosperity and goods!

There is no doubt: this unjust, cruel, atrocious project, was born of the rivalry and disunity that reigns in some petty and envious hearts, at the same time that it tarnishes the general reputation of America, without her own involvement, because neither the authorities that represent her, nor the different classes that compose it, nor the greater and better share of its natives have mixed with the rebels, rather they detest and persecute them; it must lead us to anarchy, to destruction, to death, and to the unbearable yoke of a tyrant who will put an end to our beloved homeland and will banish from it forever the holy religion of our elders. Do you deny that, restless spirits? ...

[They say that] *Europeans are placed in the most honorable jobs!* But isn't there also an equal or larger number of Americans who already occupy those positions in the cathedral churches, parochial churches, royal offices, and the military of New Spain? Don't we see that both in New and Old Spain, much kindness has been offered to natives of this land who have distinguished themselves in their services to the king and the oppressed fatherland? Don't we hear at the same time the bitter complaints of many children of the Peninsula, who say that they have not been treated as expected, as they think they deserve? ...

[They say that] *The Europeans take all the appreciation and esteem!* And don't they deserve it because of their prudent way of thinking and their orderly way of proceeding? And aren't there, on the contrary, many of them, whom their own countrymen have abandoned for being dissolute, and who find themselves in the unhappy condition of begging from door to door to spend the day? ... Why are the overseas Spaniards being persecuted and hated? Have they destroyed any house? Have they dishonored families? Have they been oppressors of the fatherland? Have they tyrannized the people? Have they ravaged cities, deranged provinces, and cut and burned the fields?

Who are the ones who stir up the fire of discord? Who are the inventors of such an inhuman project? Not the Americans of good conduct and those who are well-off, but a depraved person with the disposition of a wild beast like Allende, or one short of talents like Abasolo, or a perjurer like Hidalgo. These men are the heroes who will procure with their enterprise the happiness of our countries, these are the great benefactors of the country, who seek to break their imaginary chains, these are the liberators of the oppression and tyranny that they say we experience; or to state it properly: these men are a plague of the republic, traitors to the fatherland, disloyal to the king, enemies of God. Yes, only in the minds of this kind of men would such a cruel plan be possible.

Hence, if they have some supporters, who either follow them or wait anxiously for them, those are not exactly the children of this soil, but men loaded with debts, men of licentious living, the envious and restless, men with cruel intentions and inclined to form groups, men dedicated to gambling and idleness, those who because of their bad demeanor have not been able or even tried to settle down, confused young men who reject subjection to their parents or guardians so they can indulge in freedom, men deluded by vain hopes of better luck, and men seduced by the agents of the tyrant of Europe.

Miguel Hidalgo, *Proclamation to the American Nation*, Guadalajara, 21 November 1810[3]

A few weeks after Díaz Calvillo's publication came out, Miguel Hidalgo himself issued this proclamation. Like Simón Bolívar three years later, he presented the political conflict as one pitting Americans against Spaniards ("Europeans").

Is it possible, Americans, that you must take up arms against your brothers who are engaged at the risk of their lives in freeing us from the tyranny of the Europeans, and in ceasing to be their slaves? Do you not know that this war is only against them, and that therefore it would be a war without enemies, that it would be concluded in a day if you did not help them fight? Do not let yourselves be hallucinated, Americans, nor let yourselves be mocked any longer, and don't let them abuse your beautiful nature and gentleness, making you believe that we are enemies of God, and we want to upset your holy religion, trying with slurs and slander to make us look hateful to your eyes. No: the Americans will never move an inch away from the Christian maxims, inherited from their honorable elders.

We do not know any other faith than the Catholic, Apostolic, Roman religion, and to keep it pure and untouched in all its parts, we will not allow foreigners who deface it meddle in this continent. We are ready to happily sacrifice our lives in its defense, protesting before the whole world, that we would not have drawn the sword against these men, whose arrogance and despotism we have suffered with the greatest patience for three hundred years, in which we have witnessed the violation of the rights of hospitality, and seen the rupture of the purest bonds that should have united us, after having been the toy of their cruel ambition and unhappy victims of their greed, insulted and provoked by an uninterrupted chain of contempt and outrage, and degraded to the miserable rank of reptilian insects, if we did not know that the nation was going to perish irremediably, and that we would be vile slaves of our mortal enemies, losing forever our religion, our laws, our freedom, our customs, whatever we need to guard that is the most sacred and precious.

Consult the invaded provinces, all the cities, towns and places, and you will see that our constant concern is to maintain our religion, our law, the

---

3   Original title: *Proclama a la nación Americana*, in *Colección de documentos relativos a la época de la independencia de México* (Guanajuato: A. Chagoyan, 1870), 14ff.

fatherland, and the purity of our customs, and that we have done nothing else than seize the Europeans, and give them a treaty that they would not give us, nor have they given it to us. For the happiness of the kingdom it is necessary to take control and power away from the Europeans; that is the whole point of our endeavor, for which we are authorized by the common opinion of the nation and by the feelings that are nursed by all creoles, although they cannot express them in those places where they are still suffering from the harsh servitude imposed by an arbitrary and tyrannical government, anxious for our troops to come near and remove the chains that oppress them. This legitimate freedom has nothing in common with the disrespectful act committed by the Europeans when they captured His Excellency **Mr. Iturrigaray**, and overthrew the government at their will, without our knowledge, looking at us as stupid men and as a herd of four-legged animals, with no right to know our political situation. In view, then, of the sacred fire that inflames us and of the justice of our cause, encourage yourselves, children of the fatherland, that the day of glory and public happiness of this America has arrived. Rise up, noble Americans, from the state of deep dejection in which you have been buried, and deploy all the springs of your energy and your courage, making all nations see the admirable qualities that adorn you.… If you desire public calm, if you want your people, families and haciendas to be safe, and this kingdom to be prosperous.… In short, if you want to be happy, desert the armies of the Europeans, and come join us: let the overseas men defend themselves, and you will see that it is finished in a day, without harm to them or you, and without the death of a single individual, because our intention is only to strip them of their command without affecting themselves or their farms. Open your eyes: bear in mind that the Europeans intend to make creoles fight creoles, retiring themselves to watch from afar; and if battle ends to their advantage, they will assume all the glory of the victory, before scoffing and jeering at all the creoles, even the ones who had defended them; be aware, that even if they triumph with your help, the award that you should expect from your thoughtlessness is the doubling of your chains and your immersion in a slavery crueler than the previous one. We appreciate the safety and survival of our brothers much more; we only wish that we do not have to take up arms with them: a single drop of American blood weighs in our estimation more than the success of some battle, which we will try to avoid as much as possible … but with extreme pain in our hearts we declare, that we will fight against all those who oppose our just claims, whoever they may be, and to avoid disorder and bloodshed, from now on we will infallibly observe the laws of warfare and nations.

Statement by the Royal Trade Guild of Mexico against American free trade, Mexico City, 16 July 1811[4]

One of the demands of creole revolutionaries across Spanish America was free trade. At the start of Spanish dominion in the Americas, the Spanish state had established a monopoly over colonial imports and exports. Despite a wide array of laws prohibiting trade with foreigners, contraband trade thrived in every century. The beneficiaries of the monopoly system, such as the *consulado* (merchant guild) of Mexico, strongly opposed a reversal of time-honored commercial policies. Here, the guild explains why free trade was a bad idea.

Since the **peace negotiations at Utrecht**, Europe's public law assumes that each metropole enjoys the privilege of exclusive trade and navigation with its colonies; that every challenge from foreigners is a criminal violation, punishable by a country's statutes; that one cannot legally sail on the seas near a foreign settlement if such traffic is forbidden to foreigners; that reciprocal commercial treaties between nations have no implications for the colonies; that this national monopoly is a just compensation owed by the overseas dominions for the kind protection from the motherland; that remote provinces, which are so expensive and ruinous for the metropole, purchase their defense, peace, and preservation at a very low price. The Spanish government proclaimed these prudent maxims, anchored them in a constitution, backed them up in devastating wars, consolidated them with power and honor, made them prevail with humility and firmness, and introduced them in public law with tact and wisdom. Does the Spanish government, then, have to destroy those same principles maintained by courage, funds, and the shedding of blood? Whereas the other powers of coastal Europe scorch the whole world for a single **factory** or a precarious and sterile possession, should Spain not use the most beautiful empire on the globe? After having suffered for centuries hardships, losses, interruptions, and obstacles in its commerce and navigation in fighting foreigners' free trade, how could it authorize [precisely] that in the midst of maritime peace, abundance, mercantile activity, and easy communication?

peace negotiations at Utrecht: The negotiations that led to the Treaty of Utrecht (1713), which concluded the War of the Spanish Succession.

factory: Trading station.

---

4   Original title: *Informe del Real Consulado de México contra el comercio libre de América*, in J.E. Hernández y Davalos, ed., *Colección de documentos para la historia de la Guerra de Independencia de México de 1808 a 1821* (México, 1878), 2: 501–11.

It is not possible to guess what ideas those have who are devoted to the New World when they bring up the free interaction with the entire world. It suffices to realize that Asian manufactures will render our cotton and silk useless, that all merchandise will come from outside, robbing our workmen of their living, that New Spain alone will lose six million pesos each year, and that this advanced empire will return to the paralysis and inertia of earlier times…. Besides, the attachment of foreigners to contraband trade will drain our precious metals and disparage our indigenous products whose volume is not big enough for furtive extraction.

Universal trade would therefore be without any doubt the most terrible enemy of navigation, agriculture, textile mills, and handicrafts, in Spanish America, because it would make disappear in one moment the hard work of many years, the resources of all life, the hopes of future generations, and even the harmonious customs which form the cement of the social order.

DOCUMENT 15:

Manifesto for the World by the Federation of Venezuela, Caracas, 30 July 1811[5]

The lawyer and politician Juan Germán Roscio (1763–1821) was one of the authors of Venezuela's declaration of independence of 5 July 1811. In the spring of 1812, he was elected member of the triumvirate that ruled Venezuela's first republic. After its defeat, he was jailed in Cádiz and Ceuta, where he wrote the text of *Triumph of Liberty over Despotism*, which would appear in print in 1817. In this document, written a few weeks after Venezuela first gained independence, Roscio points to successful historical examples of peoples who broke their oaths of allegiance to chart their own course.

If the independence of the Hebrew people was not a sin against the written law, that of the Christian people against the law of grace cannot be either. The **Apostolic Chair** has never excommunicated any nation that rose up against the tyranny of kings or governments that violated the social pact. The Swiss, the Dutch, the French, and the North Americans proclaimed their independence, interfered with their constitution, and changed their form of government…. The Swiss were linked with an oath to Germany, as were the Dutch to Spain, the French to Louis XVI, and the Americans to George III. Neither they nor the other princes who favored their independence were excommunicated by the Pope. The grandfather of Fernando VII, one of the most pious and Catholic Kings who have occupied the throne of Spain, **protected** with his nephew Louis XVI the independence of North America without fearing ecclesiastical rebuke or heavenly anger; and now that the circumstances present independence even more rightfully to South America, those who call themselves the representatives of his grandson want to abuse the religion that Carlos III respected so much, to continue the most atrocious and unprecedented usurpation…. Just God! Almighty God. Merciful God! How long will fanaticism and empire argue about the sacred religion, which you sent to America in its early state for your glory and happiness?

Apostolic Chair: The Pope.

protected: A reference to Spain's involvement in the American Revolution on the side of the rebels.

---

5 Original title: *Manifiesto que hace al mundo la confederación de Venezuela*, in *Juan Germán Roscio: Escritos representativos* (Caracas: República de Venezuela, Ediciones de la Presidencia, 1971), 83.

DOCUMENT 16:

Speech by José Miguel Guridi y Alcocer, deputy of Tlaxcala (Mexico), in the Cortes of Cádiz, 4 September 1811[6]

The parish priest José Miguel Guridi y Alcocer (1763–1828) was elected deputy for Tlaxcala at the Cortes of Cádiz in 1810. During the next two years, he was one of the most prominent politicians in Cádiz, where he helped write the famous constitution. In September 1811, a few months after he had advocated the abolition of slavery, Guridi intervened in the debate on the respective numbers of deputies for Spain and America in the Cortes. Delegates discussed the question of whether the *castas*—free people with varying degrees of African admixture—were to be counted as Americans. In the eyes of the Spaniards, who wanted to keep the American delegation small, only "natives" of Spain and America (including Indigenous people) could be considered citizens, whereas the African roots of *castas* were more important than their birth in America. Guridi argues here that this line of reasoning does not make sense.

Justice requires and politics demands that the natives of Africa are citizens.... Rome, where the rank of citizen was better known and appreciated, became what the other Italian towns aspired to be. It established that being born free in Rome was enough to be a Roman citizen, which counted for more than privilege, adoption, and honorable employment, that also gave that right. The same practice was adopted by the Greeks, Germans, Swiss, and other nations.

Among us the term citizen's right has been unknown. We use the words citizen and **vecino** interchangeably. Native and foreign are the words found in our laws; and naturalization is what the privilege known to strangers has been called, which is the equivalent of citizenship in other countries.... Reason confirms this, because birth must be preferential even to origin.... If we were to go by this article and go about investigating the English, we would call them Saxons, while we could Spaniards Goths, **Alans**, **Callos**, etc., and we would see all men as natives of Noah's fatherland, if not go back all the way to Adam. And this being the case, on what ground would we deny the rank of citizens to those who were born in Spanish territory because of their African origin? But I want to allow for the requirement of remote origins in Spain. Who said that castas lack that? Many of them

vecino: Property-owning free man.

Alans: An Iranian nomadic people in Antiquity.

Callos: Probably the Calé, or Iberian Romani.

---

6   In *Diario de sesiones de las Cortes Generales y Extraordinarias,* 9 vols. (Madrid: Imprenta de J.A. García, 1870–74), III: 1762–66.

are of Spanish origin in not just one line, but three, and going back to their great-grandparents, they descend from Africa in only one line, and in the other seven from our territory....

On what basis would their origins hurt them? Could it be precisely because of Africa? No, because that part of the world does not compare unfavorably with others, and we have territory there, whose natives are Spanish. Is it the hatred of the Carthaginians who dominated us in another era or of the Moors who occupied the Peninsula for eight centuries? No, because the peoples from which our castas descend, have never been hostile to us; instead, we have been their enemies and have enslaved their inhabitants. Is it because of their dark skin color? No, because the castas have a brown color like the Indians, who are not denied the citizen's right on this ground; some have a lighter skin than the Indians, and others are as white as the Spaniards. Besides, in an age as enlightened as the nineteenth century and a country as cultured as that of Spain, we should address the subjects' physical and moral qualities and not their skin color ... The only conclusion left is that slavery infects the African origin.

I do know that among the Greeks it [slavery] was the greatest obstacle to obtain the citizen's right, which was never granted to the freedmen or their children, nor could Demosthenes persuade the Athenians to do so, despite his long speeches in favor of them; but it was different among the Romans, who laid down the law in this matter. Some add that ideas about slavery were very different then.... Back then, it derived from a law that came about because of war. It was like a mark reserved for the enemies of the state, whereas now it bears on innocent people who have not been hostile to the nation. It has its origin in a kind of rape, in violence, and in the most disgusting trade, which, far from arousing contempt for the people involved should provoke compassion. After having done the injustice to the castas to enslave their elders, why should we do the other injustice of denying them the citizen's right? One injustice cannot support or be the reason for another.

And I say that is such an injustice, if only because of the castas' commitments to the state. Like others, they contribute their dues and fees; they defend the country, making up the bulk of veteran regiments and militias, and they almost monopolize the arts and crafts in America, propping up a branch of industry that is both profitable for the treasury and indispensable to society. Justice demands that those who contribute in these ways enjoy the common right to everything, which implies that they have the rank of citizens. At the same time, whatever the aim of their unjust treatment, no goal will be achieved by it, nor will any evil be avoided. The collection of personal tribute is tangible proof. Not half or even a quarter of what had to be collected from the castas was actually brought in, because they have always tried to be mistaken for Indians or Spaniards, which is how they called themselves depending on the darkness of their skin. As a result, most did not pay anything, for lack of any scrupulous investigation, letting everyone enjoy a favorable reputation.... Although people deny it, the same will happen, and for the same reason, with the rank of citizen, which will be assigned to those who did not pay tribute, who are in the majority. The only ones who will be called castas are those who have been born in Africa or all of whose ancestors hail from there, i.e. the blacks, whose faces don't allow them to hide their rank; as well as the freed mulattoes, because the slavery which they have left behind is evidence....

Politics dictates the need to take advantage of this urgency by openly granting what would be useless to deny. In this way a large number of subjects will be created who will be more useful than they have been thus far. They are skillful, courageous, strong, and robust workers, and suitable for everything; but they have had no political existence; they have been dejected, which is the greatest obstacle to virtue and the most powerful inducement for vice. Grant them a right, which without removing them from their class or their condition as commoners, will make them realize that they are something, that they have a place in the state, and then their spirits will be raised, their powers activated, they will be fulfilled with ideas of honor and self-esteem, and they will acquire strength to better serve the country.

Act of Independence, Cartagena de Indias, 11 November 1811[7]

The reaction in New Granada to the formation of the Council of Regency in Cádiz was a mixed one. Some towns recognized the new Council, whereas others rejected its authority. In Cartagena de Indias, a pro-Spanish faction vied for supremacy with one resisting Spanish rule. When Bogotá established a junta in 1810, creole elite men formed a junta of their own after expelling the Spanish governor. A strong democratizing drive followed that resulted in an electoral system which provided for participation of male citizens in elections irrespective of their ethnicity. In November 1811, radicals organized a crowd invasion of the palace where the junta gathered, forcing that body to sign a declaration of independence. Immediately, the following document was compiled to justify the revolution.

ev

… We put aside with horror those three hundred years of humiliations, miseries, and sufferings of all kinds, which the Spanish conquerors and leaders ferociously heaped on our country, whose history cannot be read by posterity without admiring such long suffering: passing in silence, although without forgetting, over the unfortunate consequences of that time for the Americas, we want to concentrate only on the facts peculiar to this province, from the time of the Spanish revolution; in that light even the most determined devotee to the cause of Spain could not but confess that while our conduct with respect to the governments of the Peninsula has been the most liberal and selfless, that of our adversaries has been the most unjust, tyrannical, and oppressive.

We had to submit to such degrading inequality. We claim, we represent our rights with energy and with vigor, we support them with the reasons emanating from the same declarations of the National Congress; we ask for our internal administration, basing it on reason, on justice, on the example given by other wise nations.…

Those called deputies of America held up in the Cortes with much dignity the cause of the Americans; but obstinacy did not yield; reason cried out in vain to the souls that are blinded by prejudices and the ambition to dominate; always deaf to the clamor of our justice, they gave the last judgment to our hopes, denying us the equality of representatives and it was a truly singular and unbelievable spectacle to see that while European Spain with

---

7   In Manuel Ezequiel Corráles, ed., *Documentos para la historia de la provincial de Cartagena de Indias, hoy estado soberano de Bolívar* (Bogotá: Imprenta de Medido Rivas, 1883), 351–56.

one hand was demolishing the throne of despotism, and spilling its blood to defend its freedom, with the other it cast new chains to American Spain, and threatens with a raised whip those who would not put up with them.

Facing such a painful alternative, we have suffered all kinds of insults from the agents of the Spanish government ...; we are harassed, we are discredited, all communication with us is cut off, and because we submissively claim the rights that nature, before Spain, had granted us, they call us rebels, insurgents and traitors, the nation's government not deigning to answer our requests. Since all expedients to bring about a proper reconciliation have been exhausted, and because we expect nothing from the Spanish nation, now that the most enlightened government that it can have does not recognize our rights and does not match the goal for which governments have been instituted, which is the common good and happiness of the members of civil society, the desire for our own preservation and to provide for our political existence, forces us to use the imprescriptible rights that we reclaim after the resignations of Bayonne, and the power that each people has to separate from a government that makes it miserable.

Driven by these reasons of justice that only faintly sketch our sufferings, and by natural and political reasons that so urgently convince us of the necessity to separate as indicated by nature itself, we, the representatives of the good people of Cartagena de Indias, with its express and public consent, appointing the supreme being as witness of the righteousness of our course of action, and the impartial world as arbiter of the justice of our cause, we solemnly declare to the whole world that the Province of Cartagena de Indias is from now de facto and de jure a free, sovereign and independent state that is absolved of all submission, vassalage, obedience, and any other bond of any kind and nature whatsoever that previously linked her with the crown and governments of Spain, and that as such a free and absolutely independent state, it can do everything that free and independent nations do and can do. And to emphasize the resolution and validity of this declaration we solemnly pledge our lives and haciendas, swearing to shed every ounce of our blood rather than failing to succeed in such a sacred commitment.

Governmental Palace of Cartagena de Indias, the 11th day of November 1811, the first of our independence. Benito Carmona, President; Juan de Dios Amador; José María García de Toledo; Ramón Ripoll; José de Casamayor; Domingo Granados; José María del Real; Germán Gutiérrez de Piñeres; Eusebio María Cañamal; José María del Castillo; Basilio del Toro de Mendoza; Manuel José Canabal; Ignacio de Narváez y la Torre; Santiago de Lecuna; José María de la Terga; Manuel Rodríguez Tortees; Juan de Arias; Anselmo José de Urreta; José Fernández de Madrid; José María Benito Rerollo, Secretary.

Manuel Ignacio González del Campillo, bishop of Puebla, to José Maria Morelos, Puebla, 14 November 1811[8]

At the request of the secretary of New Spain's Viceroy Francisco Javier Venegas, Bishop Manuel Ignacio González del Campillo (1740–1813) of Puebla started a correspondence in September 1811 with José María Morelos, the rebel leader who had followed in Hidalgo's footsteps. The goal was to persuade him to give up arms in exchange for a pardon. Morelos refused. In this letter, Campillo takes Morelos to task for acting contrary to his calling as a priest. Morelos would answer the letter by calling on Campillo to join the insurgency, assuring him that he would find better reasons for this revolt than the American Revolution and the Jewish revolts against the Roman Empire. In 1812, Campillo would excommunicate all priests who sympathized with the independence movement.

$\mathcal{C}$

Dear Sir: Although my priest, **Licenciado** José María de la Llave, has received your letter of October 20, in which you grant him a passport and safe conduct to go to Chilapa to hand over the manifesto that I have written, which aims to make you desist from an undertaking that is so disastrous for religion and country, I have found it convenient to direct myself to you immediately through this person, both because said priest is still sick and in order not to expose him to the fate of other priests.

Licenciado: Recipient of a university degree, equivalent to a BA.

You say in your letter that to guarantee Llave's freedom and the preservation of his rights, his priesthood was enough to leave him unharmed. There is the priest of Ayutla, whom you separated from his flock ten months ago and confined in I don't know which town, full of misery. Another priest is that of Temaslaca, who was violently and sacrilegiously surprised by your soldiers in a village of his parish (restored at my order) through which he passed, and you have him imprisoned in Chilapa.

The priest of Tlapa is very venerable, and you keep him as a prisoner under the surveillance of a sentinel, without allowing him to exercise the duties of his sacred ministry. Is it conceivable that a priest treats the ministers of the sanctuary that way? Well, it is.…

You cannot ignore the privilege of immunity that the clerics enjoy, nor the very serious censures meted out by the church against those who offend against it, whom it will apprehend or imprison. We cannot hide from you the

---

8 In *Colección de documentos relativos a la época de la independencia de México* (Guanajuato: A. Chagoyan, 1870), 104–12.

very serious spiritual damage that this behavior causes among my beloved flock. It is inappropriate not only for a priest like yourself but for any Christian. Children are dying without baptism, and adults without the sacraments of penance, the Eucharist, and extreme unction.

I cry about the injustice of my diocesans' irreparable misfortunes; and amidst the bitterness caused by the consideration that so many souls are rushing to the abyss of hell, the only thing that consoles me is that I am not at all to blame for so many Christians missing out on Jesus' redeeming blood. Can you sleep peacefully, having caused damages that you can never compensate for? Go inside yourself for a moment, and think about it that as a minister of peace for your sacred ministry, you have ignited in the south the most disastrous war; that while you should by nature be the person to reconcile men with God and with himself, you have sowed the seeds of discord among them and between them and the Supreme Lord; and whereas you ought to be the person to perform the sacraments in order to lead the Christians to heaven … you render Christ's redemption useless by your example, by exhortations that are contrary to the gospel, and by your behavior that is certainly not that of a priest of the New Testament: You do not lead souls to heaven but you send thousands to hell.

It wouldn't surprise me that when you read this letter you will mock me, just like you mock the respectable discipline of the church, the work of the Councils, the Popes, and the venerable bishops, all the while marrying my parishioners, saying Mass in this diocese without my approval, residing in it against my will and that of the prelate, sending priests to the parishes, and committing other excesses, which to Catholics seem unbelievable…. On what grounds can you do what you are doing? As a priest? You must know the limits of a priest's authority…. Perhaps as the general of the south, as you call yourself? What delirium!

… Oh, Mr. Morelos! Surrounded by your cannons and your soldiers, you mock everything that is worthy of the greatest respect! To you, justice, laws, humanity, the fatherland, and religion are not worthy of your consideration; but God is making fun of you. The day of your justice will come, as it came for that other **unfortunate priest** whose general you became, as you announced in your first proclamations, and then you will know your impotence and the injustice of the projects that you have proposed, and of the means to carry them out.

When you are locked up in a prison and about to ascend a shameful scaffold like Hidalgo, when you lie in a bed having been captured, a few moments before exhaling your last breath, you will see all the horrors of the actions you are committing, of which you are not aware now because of the blindness caused by being carried away by your prejudices. You will see go up in smoke your projects that now amuse and delight you, and you will be bewildered and embarrassed for having been able to make so many sacrifices to the fabulous deity that you are worshipping. Then at last you will realize that neither revenge, no matter how fair it seems, nor the greatest affairs, nor the greatest happiness may come before the precepts of Jesus Christ.

The correct obedience to this divine Lawgiver is the only thing that makes us genuinely and unfailingly happy. I do not want you to concentrate on the countless and enormous evils that you bring to your fatherland, about which I speak extensively in the manifesto, or on the flaws and political and practical shortcomings of your project; I just want you to use your reason from the following vantage point. I allow you to succeed in all your endeavors: to establish independence of the America, to finish off the Europeans, and make this kingdom the most flourishing empire in the world. These feats, this glory, what good will it be for you in the afterlife? There is no political reasoning or worldly expediency there; they [souls in the afterlife] do not take revenge or engage in deeds that may be glorious in the eyes of contemptible mortals. To God's purest eyes, those are no more than crimes and abominations.

You will appear in God's tribunal with your hands stained by the blood of your neighbors and with a conscience overwhelmed by the enormous weight of the crimes that have been committed to carry forward the insurrection. When I start calculating them, my imagination stops, and I only see an ocean of offences and sins, and you submerged in it. Who could count the thefts, deaths, hatreds, revenges, profanations, and all the innumerable other transgressions that are the result of the disorder that the insurrection has produced?

And that a priest, a parish priest, that is, a teacher of the law, a light used by God to illuminate, was the first transgressor, he who pours out the darkness as the source of so many evils? How painful! What a dishonor for the priesthood! What opprobrium for the ministry! Since **Zwingli** changed from priest to heretic, I don't know if there has been a case so pernicious for the faithful and so sensitive to the church like that of you and your partner Hidalgo in the nineteenth century: a miserable century for America, one that our descendants will not be able to remember without tears.

Zwingli: Huldrych Zwingli (1484–1531), leader of the Swiss Reformation.

Robert Semple, *Sketch of the Present State of Caracas; Including a Journey from Caracas through La Victoria to Puerto Cabello*, 1812[9]

Boston-born Robert Semple (1766–1816) moved to Britain after the American War of Independence, dedicating his life to commerce and travel. He lived in the Cape Colony, visited the Ottoman Empire, traveled to the Caribbean and Brazil, and found himself in Venezuela during the days of that country's first republic. Here he notes the stunning transformation that had taken place in Venezuela, where the spirit of independence infected everyone.

It appears, then, that the Patriots of Spanish America have no just grounds for making a comparison of their conduct with that of the founders of the United States. The circumstances throughout are totally and essentially different. Their cause, however, is not, on that account, the less just; or rather, it may fairly be asserted, to be more so, in proportion as the wrongs and oppressions, which the Spanish colonies have suffered, are infinitely greater than were ever attempted, or even imagined towards the English. But even this will hardly account for the different conduct of the contending parties, for which we must have recourse to the marked difference of the English and Spanish characters, as exemplified both in the mother countries and their colonies. During the fierce civil war, of seven years' continuance, which ended in the establishment of the United States, scarcely a single individual perished on either side, except in battle. An honourable and decisive testimony of the general humanity of the English character. In Spanish America, on the contrary, in the short space of three years, we have seen murders, under the name of legal executions, precede and follow the slaughter of battle. Streets and private houses have been stained with blood; human heads suspended in cages, at the entrance of great towns; unwholesome prisons crammed with victims; and the charge of perfidy and cruelty urged by both parties, and with equal justice.

Within these few years, a new spirit has arisen in America, which is spreading with the rapidity of a religious fanaticism. I mean an affectation of total independence, as Americans, in every respect, not merely politically, but even to a fastidiousness of acknowledging any obligations to Europe. We revisit with delight the shores of Greece and Italy, and think it no disgrace to acknowledge all the benefits derived by our **rude** forefathers, and even by ourselves, from these great sources of taste and science. Not so with this

rude: Used here in the sense of "vigorous."

---

9 London: R. Baldwin, 1812, 145–51.

modern and numerous sect of Americans, who in spite of common sense, would fain persuade themselves and others, that arts and sciences, liberty and laws, are indigenous to the new world. Hence the proposal seriously made in the United States of adopting a new language, or changing the name of the present [citizen] to that of the Freedonian, that they might not any more be under the sad necessity of speaking English. Hence the pity with which the Spanish Americans affect to deplore the fate of the Aborigines of their country, and in all their new constitutions invite the Indians, hitherto treated with so much contempt, to a nominal participation of their privileges. In numerous and increasing instances, this spirit rises to a species of fanatical hatred against Europeans, who are termed ferocious, cruel, and perfidious, whilst the Americans are magnanimous, mild, and just. In others, this bitterness is vented against the subjects of the parent state solely. Thus the English are denominated freebooters, tyrants, and ruffians, by their descendants; and the Spaniards by theirs are contemptuously called **Godos, or Goths**; and all the cruelties committed since the days of the first conquerors are heaped upon the heads of the present generation, while the term of Madre Patria, or Mother Country, is used sneeringly, and by way of reproach.

From a consideration of this spirit, so prevalent, and so powerful, we are irresistibly led to conclude that America can never again be permanently brought under the dominion of European powers. That period has passed, or is fast passing away; and although much blood yet remains to be shed, the divisions established by nature must at length prevail. They are deceived, however, who thence conclude that the era of American happiness shall immediately commence, and that henceforward liberty and peace shall form a recompense for what they affect to term the Iron Sceptre of three Ages. But these ages were ages of peace, and rapid improvement in population and agriculture. The greater part of the vast continent of America acknowledged one Sovereign, spoke one principal language, and enjoyed internal quiets. Now the scene is to be changed. Feuds have arisen between provinces, and towns, and villages; and have been followed by bloodshed. Revenge rankles between Monte Video and Buenos Ayres; Caracas and Valencia and Coro; Mexico and numerous interior towns. The Creoles have supplanted the European Spaniards; for a short time every inferior rank feels elevated in the scale, but how long will they remain contented with a single step? and what will be the consequences of restraining them in their desire of advancing farther? These are not difficult to foresee. Discontent and civil war. America will become divided into a vast variety of petty States and Governments. A boundless field will be opened for talents and exertion, and European Warriors will repair to a country where rewards almost equal to those of the first conquerors await them. As individuals, they will arise to eminence and power, but Europe, as a whole, is about to lose her despotic sway for ever. The immediate descendants of Europeans in America hear without emotion of the land of their forefathers. They acquire mountains and streams, and forests of their own, which are endeared to them by early recollection; and every soldier transported to effect conquests in America becomes a source of increase to the country which he is sent to subdue. It is evident therefore that the various revolutions in the European colonies in America have originated in principles and are affected by causes which are common to all. It has been, and is every where, the native population, struggling for the possession of power against foreigners, who, by appealing to arms, have irreparably weakened the ties which so long gave them a powerful influence over the minds of the colonists. In Spanish America, it may be said, that the slave has dared to lift his hand against his master, and in most instances has not merely escaped unpunished, but has met with high rewards. The examples have been too numerous and too tempting, not, in time, to be universally followed; and then what power can retain in subjection this immense continent, which includes so many climates, and will ere long be peopled by numerous and powerful nations?

Political Constitution of the Spanish Monarchy, Promulgated in Cádiz on 19 March 1812[10]

> The Constitution of Cádiz, adopted in 1812 by a legislature that included representatives from Spain and Spanish America, would have immediate consequences in various parts of the Spanish empire. It also echoed in numerous constitutions adopted by the new republics that were founded in Spanish America as an outcome of the independence movements.

CHAPTER IV. On the Spanish citizens.

Art. 18. Citizens are those Spaniards who, **in both lines**, trace their origin from the Spanish domains of both hemispheres and are living in any town in the same domains.

in both lines: In the male and female lines.

Art. 19. Foreigners who already enjoy the rights of Spanish citizens are also citizens and obtain a special citizen's card from the Cortes.

Art. 20. In order for a foreigner to obtain such a card from the Cortes, he must be married to a Spaniard and must have brought with him or established in Spain a noteworthy practice or industry, or have acquired real estate for which he pays a direct contribution, or have established himself in business with a substantial amount of capital of his own according to the Cortes, or have performed services for the good and defense of the Nation.

Art. 21. Citizens are also the legitimate children of foreigners domiciled in Spain, who, having been born in the Spanish domains, have never left without a license from the Government, and having reached the age of twenty-one, have come to live in a town in the same domains, practicing a profession, trade or useful industry there.

Art. 22. The door to virtue and merit to become citizens is open to Spaniards who are known and reputed to be of African origin. Consequently, the Cortes will grant a citizen's card to those who perform marked services for the country, or to those who distinguish themselves by their talent, industry, and conduct, on the condition that they are the children of a legitimate

---

10   Original title: *Constitución política de la Monarquía española, promulgada en Cádiz a 19 de marzo de 1812* (Madrid: Imprenta Real, 1812).

marriage of freeborn parents, that they are married to a freeborn woman, and that they live in the domains of Spain, and that they practice some profession, trade or useful industry with their own capital.

Art. 23. Only those who are citizens may obtain municipal jobs….

Art. 24. The status of citizen is lost: First: by acquiring citizenship in a foreign country. Second: by admitting to being employed by another government. Third: By a sentence for felonies or infamous crimes, unless rehabilitation is obtained. Fourth: For having resided five consecutive years outside Spanish territory, without assignment or license from the government.

Art. 25. The exercise of the same rights is suspended. First: By virtue of judicial prohibition because of physical or moral incapacity. Second: By virtue of the status of bankrupt debtor or debtor to public funds. Third: By virtue of the status of domestic servant. Fourth: For not having a job, trade, or known way of making a living. Fifth: For being criminally prosecuted. Sixth: From the year one thousand eight hundred and thirty, those who for the first time enter into the exercise of the rights of citizenship must know how to read and write.

Art. 26. Only for the reasons indicated in the two preceding articles may the rights of citizens be lost or suspended, and not for any other reasons.

Interrogation and punishment of Francisco Cudina, April–August 1812[11]

For most individuals, it is impossible to establish why they offered their services to one of the two warring parties. Some changed their allegiance. One Spanish native who fought for the insurgents of Buenos Aires in the Battle of Huaqui (20 June 1811) was subsequently hired by the royalists to carry papers from General Juan Manuel de Goyeneche (1776–1846), who had won at Huaqui, to Viceroy Elío in Montevideo. From there, he carried a letter from the Governor of Montevideo, General Gaspar de Vigodet, to Goyeneche when he was arrested. After initially denying all charges, he ultimately confessed, and explained why he switched sides.

… [A] man who is imprisoned in this royal fortress was brought in for the purpose of receiving his confession, and having sworn the oath, which he did in the ordinary way, promising to tell the truth, he was asked for his name, age, religion, birthplace, social class, and profession, and if he knows the cause of his imprisonment or presumes what it is, and he said that his name is Francisco de Paula Cudina y Cermeño, that his age is twenty-five years, his religion is the Catholic, Apostolic, Roman; his birthplace the [Catalan] capital of Barcelona, his civil status is that of man married to María Felipa Peñalva, and his current job none, and that the cause of his imprisonment is that of having brought a letter from General Goyeneche to Viceroy Elío and another from General Vigodet to Goyeneche. Question: If it is not true that he carried the sealed documents from General Goyeneche for Mr. Elío, and those from General Vigodet in response to Goyeneche himself, these two generals being enemies of the sacred cause that this capital so rightly supports, on which the charge is based. He said: That it is true that he carried the documents that the question mentions; and that he does not doubt the justice of the cause that the **capital** supports, and in that same belief he took up arms in its defense, and served with honor in the auxiliary expedition that left for Peru, until the unfortunate **event on the Desaguadero** [River].

    Counterclaim: How he could serve the enemies of a cause that he knew as just, and for which he confesses to have risked his life; if he does not know the seriousness of this crime, and that it is more serious for a soldier who has solemnly sworn his allegiance and vowed to die under the banners

capital: Buenos Aires.

event on the Desaguadero: The lost battle of Huaqui.

---

11 In Adolfo P. Carranza, ed., *Archivo General de la República Argentina: Período de la Independencia, Segunda Série, Tomo IX* (Buenos Aires: G. Kraft, 1897), 74–78, 84–86.

for which he is enlisted, as the penitent has done, for which he is charged. He said that he knows the seriousness of his crime with regard to the sacred tasks he had born to defend, the just cause of this capital: but that the abandonment and misery in which the penitent ended up after the engagement at the Desaguadero [River], can and do explain his conduct, because all of that was the result of the want and scarcity that surrounded him … and he considers it his greatest misfortune having found no other means to subsist.…

Asked if it is not true that before carrying the documents to Mr. Elío, he brought others to Santa Cruz, on the road to **Mato Grosso**, knowing that these were addressed to the court of Brazil in order to coordinate operations with the Portuguese army, and put pressure on the capital, subjugate it along with the other provinces that are united to it, which is what the charge is based on, he said: That it is true that he brought the papers to which the question refers and that he suspected that they were going to combine their forces with the Portuguese and perhaps later attack the capital, but that he has already made known the considerations that drove him to this conduct.

Asked if it is not true as well that as a reward for bringing the documents to Santa Cruz, General Goyeneche gave him the position of Grenadier Lieutenant in one of his companies, remaining thereby the declared enemy of our cause and in a position to act actively against those who support it, on which a new charge is based, he said that the content of the question is true.

Asked if it is also not true that the penitent opened the two documents or letters of General Goyeneche and General Vigodet, which would involve a new kind of crime for which charges can be made, he said that is true that he opened the two documents, but he was driven by the suspicion or distrust that General Goyeneche was trying to surrender these domains to Portuguese domination, and as the penitent detested this, he wanted to find it out from the documents themselves, and not deliver them, but decide on other measures and make them known to the Superior Government.

Asked if it is not true that the confessor in his first two statements before the Superior Government lied about the facts that were asked, thus betraying the religion by the oath under which he promised to tell the truth; and if he does not know the punishment which he has deserved for such perjury, for which he is charged, he said that the fear and shock made him forget the duties in which he was constituted, but that he was calmer [now] and free of fear because of the **guarantee** of this Superior Government, and has constantly told the truth in all his subsequent statements, without omitting circumstances that he knows should harm him.…

In which state these proceedings were suspended to continue as long as is deemed convenient, and the penitent declared and confirmed all that had

been set forth, and after having read it he signed it with the Commissioner
to which I bear witness.

Tagle—Francisco de Paula Cudina—José Ramón de Basabilvaso.

Having seen these indictments against the aforementioned Francisco de
Paula Cudina, courier of documents from General Goyeneche to Viceroy
Elío, who was apprehended on his return from Montevideo when he carried
the documents which Governor Vigodet sent to the same General …, and
against those involved in this case: Manuel Ramón de Basabe, José Garcia
and José Maure; the first, Cudina, is condemned to death by hanging.…

Feliciano Antonio Chichina—Bernardino Rivadavia—Juan Martin de
Pueyrredon.

On the eighteenth day of said month and year [August 1812], at about
eleven o'clock in the morning, in the Plaza de la Victoria, the death sentence
was carried out on the person of Francisco Cudina, whose corpse was left
hanging.…

Tagle: Gregorio García de Tagle (1772–1845), general counsel of the Buenos Aires government.

El Grito del Sud [Buenos Aires], 21 July 1812

1812 was a year of growing radicalization in Buenos Aires. Monarchical symbols were taken down and discriminatory measures taken against Spanish natives. Politicians stopped short, however, of declaring independence. This newspaper article in *El Grito del Sud* ("The Cry of the South"), dismissed the notion that Spain was America's mother country, arguing that Spain and America are actually orphan brothers. *El Grito del Sud,* one of many short-lived newspapers (1812–13) was written by Bernardo de Monteagudo (1789–1825), a lawyer who became a leading politician during the independence wars in Buenos Aires, Chile, and Peru. He was probably the author of Chile's proclamation of independence in 1818.

Spain and America are no more than two brothers. It is true that it has been commonly said that one is the mother country, but I don't know how true that is, and perhaps that is why the error thus remains. Let's see if we can dispel it. A king has always been considered the father of his kingdom; if other kingdoms are added to this kingdom, they are all sons of that father, who is the king; therefore, they are all brothers, with no other difference than some being older than others. Well that is how Spain's relationship to America should be considered. When the king only had Spain, we can say that he had only one son. Then he came into possession of the Americas, and had two. This father absented himself and died without leaving a guardian for these children. They now take for themselves the share of the inheritance to which they are entitled. Spain has taken its own share by resuming his rights; America did the same, and I have not pretended otherwise. But what is happening? Spain is not content with his share, and as a big brother wants to swallow the little one; and after he lost or let himself be robbed by Napoleon of its inheritance, due to carelessness or lack of skills, he tries to see if he can nibble at some part of America or keep all of it. To be sure, Spain cannot come here in person, because they have left him no more than a trifle, but he has sent his agents and representatives like Venegas, Abascal, Elío, and Vigodet to see if they can steal something. What a scandal! After Spain said that we would no longer have a viceroy! To come with a viceroy when there is no king! Who can bear it! European Spaniards, don't you deceive yourselves with so much villainy?

That we have sworn obedience to the king we can concede to the Spaniards; but since he is captive and all hope of rescuing him is lost, the only obligation required by the oath is to behold Fernando's shadow with respect while not depriving us of the necessary clarity to understand each other. Meanwhile, these two orphan brothers Spain and America will look after each other, since they are old enough for that; each one will be responsible on behalf of the king (if he ever returns) for his relevant part of the inheritance, and if the king doesn't return, each one will enjoy it as his own. America, for one, doesn't want to place himself in the care of his brother, Spain, because he fears that he will take care of him the way he took care of himself. But what about the obedience that America owes to Spain? America owing obedience to Spain! What nonsense! But shouldn't America be faithful to the Spanish nation? That is also nonsensical talk. What confusing ideas! Little surprise that the Europeans are on bad terms with us, that they treat us as rebels, and believe that they are rebels themselves, if they follow our method. It is necessary to disabuse them of that notion and show them that the Americans don't think that way.

No, the Americans are not rebels; because they have not denied obedience and loyalty to the one who owes it, the king, to whom alone they have sworn … the oath of loyalty and obedience is not sworn by one kingdom to another, which would be required for one of them to rightly demand obedience…. However, they say (and this, I think, is their strongest argument) that America, like Spain, as being two equal parts of a whole, must obey the king, and in his absence, who legitimately represents him; and that since it is beyond doubt that the Cortes meeting in Spain legitimately represents the king, Spain as well as America must swear allegiance and render obedience to it.

To this argument, the *Gazeta Extraordinaria de Buenos Ayres* of Monday, 25 February 1811, gave the perfect answer in an article about the nullity of the Cortes, an article that all patriots must read again, and even Europeans who want to be disillusioned. In the meantime, I will only say that this Cortes is not inclusive, and therefore that it does not legitimately represent the king in all his domains. It is not inclusive because compared to Spain, it does not have the appropriate number of American deputies, according to the population. All of America has only 27 deputies and Spain 75, whereas our population, without counting the slaves, is much larger than Spain's, even if we assume that all the French have been evacuated. That is a substantial issue, which alone is enough to annul the Cortes, and I don't know how the Regency and the European deputies that compose the Cortes have deluded themselves to such a degree.

George Dawson Flinter, *A History of the Revolution of Caracas: Comprising an Impartial Narrative of the Atrocities Committed by the Contending Parties, Illustrating the Real State of the Contest, Both in a Commercial and Political Point of View, 1813–14*[12]

> In contrast to Robert Semple's enthusiastic account of independent Venezuela (document 19), George Dawson Flinter left a sobering description of the same independence movement by focusing on atrocities committed by the insurgents. Flinter (ca. 1792–1838), an Irishman who served in the British and Spanish armies, lived in Caracas for a number of years working for the royalists.

The City of Caracas, under the new government, exhibited a picture of the most shocking depravity; all the outrages, inseparable from military despotism, were now arrayed in their greatest horrors, before a people, who had long been accustomed to the sweets of uninterrupted tranquillity. The shrill clarion of war had never echoed through their vallies, and their peaceful habitations had never been before disturbed by the clamor of contending legions. The tale of distant wars, related by some wounded soldier, used to draw from the tears of sensibility: little did they expect to have been so soon the melancholy spectators of scenes, much more dreadful than their warmest imaginations could have pictured.

Under the plausible pretence of retaliation, the patriot general, Bolivar, ordered many hundreds of innocent unsuspecting victims to be dragged from the bosoms of their families, and to be consigned to breathe the foetid air of subterraneous dungeons, where many died from actual suffocation. All the Spaniards, who had not been able to leave the country, previous to the arrival of the patriots, were treated in this inhuman manner, without any imputed crime, but the casual circumstance of having been born in Spain.

… What a heart-rending spectacle, to behold decrepid old men, whose grey locks and venerable appearance would have excited compassion in hearts of the most obdurate villany, brought in from the country, and marched through the public streets, tied on the backs of asses, amidst the sighs and tears of their children, their grandchildren, and domestics, exposed to the insulting sneers of an unprincipled mob, and destined to languish their few remaining days, in misery and chains. These arbitrary transactions were rendered still more abominable, by money being extorted from these

---

12   London: T. and J. Allman, 1819, 57–63.

unfortunate captives, on pretence of the public service, and by holding out to them promises of setting them at liberty; but in a few days, they would, on the most frivolous pretences, be again remanded to their prisons, and when their exhausted finances could no longer contribute to feed the avarice of these monsters, they would be brought out to the market place, and shot.… These unfortunate victims of cruel persecution would be first shot through the legs and arms; whilst the anguish of pain, which they endured, and their supplications for mercy, afforded a great fund of mirth to the assembled spectators; nor would the executioners dispatch them, till the multitude expressed their wishes to have a fresh object brought on the theatre, by crying out, "kill him, kill him!" their sufferings would then be put an end to, by shooting them through the head; bands of music striking up at the same time the most lively airs, formed a shocking contrast, and shows, more forcibly, the cruel levity of these people, than could all the reasoning of philosophy. At the same moment were to be seen the gay frolic of the midnight revel, and the tears and supplications of the wretched wife and children of some unfortunate Spaniard, who was next morning to be launched into eternity. The airy music of the dance was continually blended with the death peal of the cathedral bell, which announced the approaching execution. Many wretched females, in the hopes of averting the impending fates of their fathers, their brothers, or their husbands, have delivered themselves to prostitution to gratify the impure desires of these monsters; but after passing a night of bitter infamy, the dawn of morn came but to renew, with tenfold violence, the agony of their sufferings, the first object that presented itself to their view, would be the murdered bodies of their relatives, for the preservation of whose lives they had sacrificed their honour, hanging on some neighbouring tree, or nailed to the door of their apartment. Many of these injured females have I heard recount the tale of their sufferings, and, with showers of tears and uplifted hands, invoke the vengeance of heaven on the murderers of their family and despoilers of their honour.

José de Bustamante, governor and captain-general of Guatemala, to the Council of Regency, Guatemala, 3 March 1813[13]

The highest political rank in Central America was occupied in the years 1811–17 by José de Bustamante (1759–1825), former naval officer and governor of Paraguay. Responding to some small revolts, he created what one historian has called a "counterinsurgency state," which successfully sought to nip in the bud any opposition to Spanish rule.[14] Bustamante feared the creole elites, which he suspected of hiding their dream of independence behind their stated goal of more autonomy and their support of the Cádiz constitution. In this document, he lays the blame for all unrest squarely on the creoles and their "spirit of oligarchy."

The spirit of oligarchy is what has dominated these provinces. Those who make up the commoners are unhappy people who blindly follow the impulse that is imprinted on them. They proclaim our desired monarch; celebrate excellent news from the Peninsula; respect the authorities or turn against their legitimate judges; insult their leaders and overthrow the laws, according to who has influence over them.

Distracted by their bad habits or busy with their jobs; without funds, without education to lift them up, they don't yearn for jobs, think of trade or wish that vacancies are filled by their class rather than another one.

Job-hunting and commercial greed have in previous times and will in the future be the only source of upheaval in America. People will exaggerate how harsh the laws are, they will emphasize the rights of towns, talk with horror about despotism, pretend to have tender feelings for the wretched, etc., but the only motives are those mentioned, and wretched people do not seek jobs or engage in commerce.

From the first news of the disastrous events in the Peninsula, ideas and feelings that had not manifested themselves previously began to be expressed.

… It was not nothing what was observed in this kingdom before I took command. Restless men, who ignored their true interests, judged them mistakenly. They believed to find in disorder and upheaval what makes them really happy; they spread false news; they imagined other falsehoods; exaggerated bad news; spread doubt about the most plausible messages;

---

13   In León Fernández, ed., *Documentos relativos a los movimientos de Independencia en el Reino de Guatemala* (San Salvador: Talleres tip. del Ministerio de Instrucción Pública, 1929), 53–65.

14   Timothy Hawkins, *José de Bustamante and Central American Independence: Colonial Administration in an Age of Imperial Crisis* (Tuscaloosa: U of Alabama P, 2004), Chapter 5.

multiplied the pasquinades; praised the government's shortcomings and undermined the foundations of legitimate authority....

In March of ... 1811 I took command. I received confirmation of the news that I had been given of a secret spirit of restlessness in this kingdom; I feared its effects in the province of San Salvador, of which my predecessor was less afraid; and in order to remove from that environment whatever factors might become the stimulus of insurrection, I ordered the arms and funds in San Salvador to be transferred to this capital; and in fulfillment of that were transferred in August of the same year 11,700 rifles, 95,201 pesos and 3¼ **reales** from the public treasury, 20,621 pesos from the consulate and 12,177 pesos of private individuals.

Later, after the election of the deputy for the Cortes, the municipal council of this capital agreed to draw up instructions for him and they presented me a handwritten version of them.

It was necessary to twist my feelings and sacrifice my opinion to allow the instructions to be created. I did that to obey the sovereign decree of press freedom to avoid complaints and to prevent people from saying that corporations or individuals were deprived of the powers that the National Congress had given them to publish their political thoughts and ideas. In that document ... the spirit of the oligarchy was openly on display.

[It stipulates that] the members of the municipal councils should be elected by the same town councils; that two-thirds of them should be elected for life and the remaining one-third biennially ...; that in each capital a board is established, composed of individuals appointed by the town councils; that half of its constituents should be members of town councils and the other half either members from the same councils or neighbors.... [The document] circulated in printed form in all the provinces; the ideas of the capital penetrated everywhere....

A few months later, on the 5th and 6th of November of the same year of 1811, the fire that secretly burned manifested itself in the public. Stirred into action, the people of San Salvador deposed Mayor Mr. Antonio Gutiérrez Ulloa, without having verified any of his responsibilities; they established a governmental junta; they closed the tobacco shops;[15] abolished royal claims; persecuted honorable Europeans well-known for their patriotism, including Mr. Gregorio Castrisiones, who had performed distinguished public service and donated 11,000 pesos for the expenses of the present war; and they invited the other towns to follow their detestable example, and join in the project they had begun to carry out.

... Once the peace in the province of San Salvador was restored, disturbances began in the province of Nicaragua. The following 13 December, the

---

15 The colonial state monopolized production and sale of tobacco.

same kind of commotion as in San Salvador occurred in the capital León; the same cry was raised against European clerical workers and merchants; the Intendant, Mr. José Salvador, was deposed; and a governing junta was established that tried to abolish the tobacco monopoly and [royal] claims.

… The fire was expanding throughout the province, but for the same reason as in San Salvador, it was extinguished in Nicaragua.

… From the start of the unrest in this kingdom, I realized that it was necessary to maintain a regular armed body to facilitate the policy of prudent conciliation that I had decided to follow, and I would use it if necessary. The obstacles were not trifling in a kingdom …: the character of the inhabitants, the scarcity of funds, the misery of the people, the absolute lack of militias in some districts, the lack of discipline of the few militias that did exist in other districts, the seduction of bad people and the same spirit of restlessness, which was penetrating everywhere.

However, by overcoming obstacles, arousing the zeal of honest residents, stimulating that of the officers, appealing to that of worthy parish priests and influential residents, and making considerable savings in the public treasury, I finally managed to arm four thousand men without taxing the towns, and place them in the appropriate districts to quickly move into to the provinces in upheaval in order to impose respect for the law and arrive with strength where necessary.

It was necessary in Granada, that unhappy city that resisted the peaceful method of conciliation that was offered to it, and that wanted to follow the method of restlessness when it had already ceased in the other districts of the province. It was necessary to bring in the troops, despite my peaceful sentiments.…

Tegucigalpa did not go to such extremes, and such turmoil was not noticed during its revolution. Singled out for my protection for being the kingdom's only province with minerals, which provides our Mint with the bars that are coined there, it was nevertheless plagued by the spirit of restlessness. Such was the case in its capital, the town of San Miguel Heredia, although the movement there was not meant to overthrow what the restless call the Spanish yoke, nor persecute the Europeans, nor aspire to Independence. It was directed mainly against the house of a neighbor, a son of the same province, Mr. Antonio Tranquilino Rosa, **subdelegado** of the royal treasury, who was almost universally despised because of his connections, his dominance and his arrogance.…

subdelegado: Official who assisted the intendant in governance.

Manifesto for the Mexican People by the Representatives of the Provinces of North America, Chilpancingo, 6 November 1813[16]

In late 1813, José María Morelos, the priest who had inherited Hidalgo's mantle as Mexico's rebel leader, organized a congress made up of delegates he had handpicked. It abolished slavery and opted for a presidential political system independent of Spain, based on the **separation of powers**. This manifesto, which doubled as declaration of independence, stressed the centuries of purported Spanish despotism in the colonies.

separation of powers: The division of government into separate executive, legislative, and judicial branches to prevent the concentration of power.

Fellow citizens: until the year 1810 a foreign domination trampled our rights; and the evils of arbitrary power, practiced in wrath by the cruelest conquistadors, did not even allow us to ascertain if liberty, whose articulation passed our lips as a criminal offense, meant the existence of something good, or if it was only a spell to charm the peoples' frivolity. Buried in the stupidity and dejection of servitude, all the nations with a social pact were strange and unknown to us, all feelings of happiness were far from our hearts, and the custom to obey that we inherited from our ancestors had been established as the only law that nobody dared to break. The court of our kings, more sacred as it was more distant from us, seemed to us to be the mansion of infallibility, from where the oracle made himself heard from time to time, and only to terrify us with the majestic thunder of his voice. Like the people of Athens, we adored *an unknown God*, and thus we did not suspect that there were other principles of government than the political fanaticism that blinded our reason.

---

16 Original title: *Manifiesto que hacen al pueblo mexicano los representantes de las provincias de la America Septentrional*, in J.E. Hernández y Davalos, ed., *Colección de documentos para la historia de la Guerra de Independencia de México de 1808 a 1821* (México, 1881), 5: 215–17.

DOCUMENT 26:

J.P. Robertson and W.P. Robertson, *Four Years in Paraguay: Comprising an Account of That Republic under the Government of the Dictator Francia,* ca. 1814–15[17]

In 1811 the Scottish-born merchant William Parish Robertson (1794–ca. 1850) moved to Buenos Aires in the wake of his brother John Parish. In that port city, he befriended José de San Martín. Two years later, he settled in Asunción, the capital of Paraguay, only to leave again in 1817 because of the country's growing isolation. The four years he spent in Paraguay coincided with the establishment of Dr. Francia's dictatorship, on which W.P. Robertson comments here in no uncertain terms.

I was now on a footing of greater or less intimacy with all the principal families and personages of the city and its vicinity. I appeared to be a welcome guest wherever I chose to visit. All jealousies of our mercantile character and operations had disappeared; and, indeed, so far from any feeling of that kind showing itself, the kind hearted inhabitants, by innumerable little acts of personal attention and courtesy, showed an evident desire to render agreeable to me my residence in the country.

As I intended to remain for a few years at **Assumption**, I sedulously cultivated, on my part, a kind and frank intercourse with all,—old Spaniards as well as Paraguayans; and by continuing in my dealings the liberality which my brother had always kept up in his, I repaid, as far as I could, the cordiality with which I was every where received.

There were two or three very agreeable families in the place, and some really well informed men, with whom I got something more intimate than with the mass. At the same time, the political surveillance which now every day penetrated more and more into the very bosom of domestic life, made it absolutely necessary that my intercourse with those about me should be of a general and open kind; such as to leave no room for suspicion that I mixed myself up, in the remotest way, with the fears and the jealousies, which were already entertained in many quarters, of the now all-powerful Doctor Francia.

This extraordinary man had been, from the very day of my arrival, the object of greatest interest to me, even in a place so full of interest to a stranger as was Paraguay. I had come straight from England, where an ancient monarchy is firmly established, to a country professing the purest

Assumption: Asunción.

---

17 Philadelphia: E.L. Carey & A. Hart, 1838, volume II (of two): 187–93.

republicanism. But the moment I began to look into Francia's government, many of my illusions about South American liberty were dispelled.

… In England we had monarchy, but happily based on free institutions. In Paraguay they boasted of a republican form of government, but the despotic will of one man ruled and enslaved the community at large.

With this despotic chief I was suddenly brought into terms of intimacy: my fortunes, to a certain extent, were to be placed in his hands; and, without compromising my own character, I was so to guide and govern my own conduct, as to maintain the good will, if not to win the favour, of the all-powerful consul.

I gradually fell into the same sort of intimacy with him which he had extended to my brother. It was a remarkable circumstance, that during our whole stay at Assumption we never could perceive that he allowed the least approach to familiarity on the part of any other respectable individual. Indeed I am sure he had (at that period) no intimacy but with ourselves. I never, in all my intercourse with him, met at his house a third party who was admitted to a *seat*, or to join in our conversation. Any interruption to our *tête-à-tête* was casual. The consul invited nobody merely to visit him (as far as I could learn) during my stay, except myself.

My own peculiar position, therefore, even more than simple curiosity, led me to investigate Francia's character as closely as I could. His public acts were before me; but I wanted, as much as possible, to get at the springs of action,—the impulses, passions, or principles, by which he was guided,—a knowledge of which could alone enable me to form a just or correct estimate of the man who, it became clearer to us day by day, was about to exercise whatever influence he pleased over the destinies of every living soul in Paraguay.

… Francia was vindictive, cruel, and relentless. These were the detestable but leading qualities of his character. But he not only never forgave an injury, real or supposed,—he gradually marked out all those whom he believed, in his own mind, to be secretly opposed to his tyranny, as his victims; and whenever these were doomed in the gloomy recesses of his jealous and suspicious heart, their destruction, sooner or later, invariably followed.

The owner of the house in which we lived, Don Pascual Echagüe, was a native of Santa Fé, but married to a Paraguayan lady of good family, and settled in Assumption. A pasquin on the Dictator was found one morning, stuck on the wall of the house in which our landlord resided with his family. To suppose that Echagüe himself had stuck it there was monstrous and absurd; yet that day he was thrown into prison and into chains. His unhappy wife, after her husband had languished in solitary confinement for some months, contrived to get an interview with the Dictator. She threw herself at his feet. Her tears and her sobs choked her utterance. "Woman," said the stern and immoveable tyrant, "what do you want here!" "Oh, my husband my husband!" was all that the unhappy lady could articulate. Francia then turned to his guard—"Order," he said, "another *barra de grillos* (heavy fetter) to be placed on Echagüe, and an additional one every time that this mad woman dares to approach me." The wretched husband, like many other victims, died in his prison, and in his chains.

Francia's word was a law more irrevocable than were ever the laws of the Medes and the Persians.

A shipwright of the name of Soloaga, a Buenos Ayrean, was busily engaged in building a small vessel for me. One evening, as I was examining the work going for Ward, an order from the Dictator came to Soloaga to look out for some half-dozen of planks, wanted for I don't know what government job. "I can do it in the morning," said Soloaga to me, for he was much interested at the moment in showing me all the fine points of the vessel. I recommended him to fulfil the Dictator's order on the instant, but he delayed.

Next morning early he was called up by the Dictator, and asked if he had picked out the wood wanted. Soloaga was just on his way, he said, to do it. "Sir" said the Dictator impatiently, "you are a useless member of society here, for you do not serve the Patria. Leave it therefore within twenty-four hours." The man had been married and established in the country for years, and was carrying on an extensive business. "Señor Excelentisimo," he began; but Francia stamped his foot, and sternly added, "Leave the Republic within twenty-four hours, and quit my presence this moment." Wife, children, work, property, all were abandoned; and in twenty-four hours Soloaga was on his way to Corrientes, never to return to Paraguay.

These domestic incidents will perhaps convey to you more distinctly than mere abstract delineation could do, the cruel, callous, pitiless nature of the man. His ambition was as unbounded as his cruelty. His natural talents were of a higher class than those which had been displayed by any one of his countrymen in either a public or private capacity. His education was the best which South America afforded; and he had much improved that education by his own desire to increase his general attainments. He possessed an exact knowledge of the character of the people of Paraguay. He knew them to be docile, simple, and ignorant, easily guided to good or to evil, and without moral or physical courage to resist oppression. He was sagacious, astute, patient, and persevering. No moral or religious principle was allowed to stand between him and his plans; his end was absolute imperious sway; and in using his means for attaining it, he was prepared to view the com-mission of crime without fear, and to inflict every suffering which human nature could endure without pity and without remorse.

Manuel Belgrano to José de San Martín, Santiago del Estero, 6 April 1814[18]

The secretary of the Buenos Aires merchant guild, Manuel Belgrano (1770–1820) was a member of the city's junta that seized power in 1810 from the viceroy. He then embarked on a career as one of Buenos Aires' chief military leaders. His battlefield record is a mixed one. He failed to subdue Paraguay, but victories in Upper Peru prevented future royalist threats from that region. After one of his defeats as commander of the Army of the North, the ruling second triumvirate of Buenos Aires replaced him with José de San Martín. The subsequent meeting of the two men was the start of a close friendship. In this letter, written three months later, Belgrano stresses that the war cannot just be won with arms. He also urges San Martín to raise the flag Belgrano had designed, which is still that of Argentina today.

My friend: I speak to you in keeping with my wishes for your success....

You have to wage the war there not only with weapons, but by means of opinion, always reinforcing it with natural, Christian, and religious virtues; for the enemies have done the same to us by calling us heretics, and only in that way have they attracted barbarous people to take up arms, telling them that we had attacked the religion.

Perhaps someone will laugh at me; but you should not be carried away by exotic opinions or ideas from men who don't know the country they are treading on; besides, in this way you will end up having a subservient army, since having been educated in the Catholic religion that we profess and its maxims, the men that make it up cannot be more conducive to order....

I have said enough to you; I would like to speak more to you, but I am afraid to take away your precious time, and my ills will not let me either; I will only add that you should raise the flag I left you and that you should fly it when the whole army has been formed. Do not stop imploring Our Lady of Mercy, always calling her our general, and don't forget to bring the **scapulars** to the troops; let them laugh, the effects will compensate you for the laughter of superficial fools.

Remember that you are an apostolic Christian Roman general; remember that you should never, not even in the most trivial conversations, show disrespect in what you say to our holy religion; keep in mind not only the

scapulars: Catholic garments that express the wearer's devotion to a Christian life.

---

18 In Comisión Nacional del Centenario, *Documentos del Archivo de San Martín*, 12 vols. (Buenos Aires: Imprenta de Coni Hermanos, 1910), III: 43–44.

generals of the people of Israel, but also the Gentiles and the great Julius Caesar who never ceased invoking the immortal gods....

Said to you by your true and loyal friend.

José Miguel Carrera, *Proclamation by the Restorative Army to Its Brothers in Concepción*, 1814[19]

The first leader of an independent Chile was José Miguel Carrera (1785–1821), who seized power in a coup d'état in 1811. After a failed royalist attempt to end his rule, Carrera appeals here to royalist soldiers to join the just cause. He singles out the "Araucanians," those living in the south whose Indigenous ancestors had defeated Spanish forces time and again. Later that year, the royalists would defeat Carrera's regime.

℮

SOLDIERS who moan under the banners of the tyrant: the government orders me to consider you as the victims of the perfidy of some evil men; and I have too much proof of the violence with which you defend your ranks. You, who were born in Arauco's soil and descend from the brave, who for three centuries resisted the colossal power of the Carloses and Felipes: you, who naked, undisciplined, without the benefit of firearms have shed more blood of the European tyrants than they have in their entire conquest from the Mississippi to Cape Horn; it is impossible that now that you are facing enslavement, no longer to a large empire, but to the miserable satellite of the Viceroy of Lima, you will give in to such a despicable yoke.

ARAUCANIANS: turn your eyes to yourselves and what you experience. What fate does Peru's head of state assign to you? In Europe, Spain will necessarily cease to exist. The Viceroy, whose all-consuming ambition has completely exhausted Lima's forces and resources, can impossibly survive without enslaving himself to a foreign power. You can already see that the legions of Buenos Aires penetrate by way of the **Desaguadero River** to protect the revolution of Arequipa and Cuzco, and that because the troops of Goyeneche have been entirely exterminated, not a single army corps can be seen that could resist up to Lima the victorious arms of the LIBERATORS OF THE FATHERLAND.

Desaguadero River: A river east of the Andes.

---

19 Original title: *Proclama del exercito restaurador a sus hermanos de Concepción*, John Carter Brown Library, Providence, RI.

PART 4

Fernando's Restoration, Continued Warfare, and Independence

DOCUMENT 29:

José Hipólito Unanue, *To the King, Our Lord. The Thinker of Peru*, 1815[1]

The Peruvian scientist José Hipólito Unanue (1755–1833) wrote this work upon his return to Peru after a stint as delegate to the Cortes of Cádiz. In the book, which praises Fernando VII, he presents a causal connection between the constitution that had been adopted in Cádiz and the recent revolts in Upper and Lower Peru (Cuzco, Arequipa, La Paz). What troubled him in particular was article 255 of the constitution, which said that "graft, bribery, and perversion of the course of justice on the part of magistrates and judges lead to popular action against the transgressors."

On 3 August last [1814], Cuzco waved the dark flag of insurrection, basing its execrable proceedings against the legitimate authorities on popular action as granted to the towns by article 255 of the constitution. Such an arbitrary and unjust inference could only be made by criminals who intend to cut, kill, steal and abandon themselves to all kinds of crimes under the first pretext that was offered to their imagination; but if we examine the events of all the stages of the American war without prejudice and without harboring illusions; if we take into account the maneuvers and impostures of many of their deputies in the Cortes, and finally, so as not to get bored, if we read the Madrid newspapers of the month of April … [we may wonder]: Is it not necessary to confess that the aforementioned popular action was granted to the people to shake off their legitimate domination? I wish that the viceroy, without risking universal upheaval, could have cast the fatal constitution into oblivion, so that we would have been spared the streams that have run with tears and blood!

---

1   Original title: *Al Rey, nuestro señor. El pensador del Perú* (Peru, 1815), 24–28, 33–35.

[With] every piece of mail that came from the Iberian Peninsula, the government had to suffer infinitely by having to render prompt obedience to yet another order that had been issued without any agreement or examination, and for whose reading alone it was necessary to spend most of the time; and when the government received a notoriously outlandish and ruinous order that could be drowned in silence, at least while explaining what bad consequences its introduction would have, it found itself outwitted by those who had dictated it, who had been careful to send many copies and duplicates through different channels to notify the *sovereign people*.... One example of this was the abolition of tribute, which has set back the good cause and produced enormous misfortunes, as time will tell....

It is astonishing to see the speed and goodwill with which the provinces of Puno, Guamanga, and Huancavelica adopted the wicked example of the **cuzqueños**. In less than sixty days all had been turned upside down, and in almost all of them the same scenes of execration and horror were repeated. La Paz, invaded at the end of September by the fierce **Pinelo y Torre** and the apostate priest **Muñecas**, was forced to welcome lascivious and blood-thirsty soldiers who burned, killed, and carried along ruin and desolation. The meritorious intendant, the Marquis of Valdehoyos, was killed by sticks, and then hanged in leather; and more than one hundred and seventy of the important residents of the city, without distinction between Europeans and Americans, showed their loyalty to Your Majesty through their final torments, being tortured in the cruelest ways. The same soldiers who that honorable and brave chief presented on the battlefield abandoned him in the heat of combat; and so it was no longer possible to avoid his unfortunate fate, and that of the city, victim of the debauchery and violence of the many revolutionaries who had gathered with those who came from Cuzco.

cuzqueños: Residents of the Peruvian city of Cuzco.

Pinelo y Torre: Juan Manuel Pinelo y Torre, a Peruvian native who had served in a royalist army that opposed Buenos Aires' designs on La Paz. He changed sides and headed to the Cuzco army sent in 1814 to Puno and Upper Peru.

Muñecas: Ildefonso de las Muñecas (1776–1816) was a priest who had turned guerrilla leader. He was executed two years later after a lost battle.

Simón Bolívar, letter from Jamaica, 6 September 1815[2]

In 1815, the independence movements seemed to have largely faltered. Spain's commander Pablo Morillo wrote in that year to the inhabitants of New Granada, reminding them that the world looked differently from the way it had during the previous seven years. Fernando VII ruled the Spanish empire, Napoleon had been carried off to his distant exile, Louis XVIII sat on the French throne, and England worked for a peaceful globe.[3] Earlier that month, Simón Bolívar had presented the situation as a temporary setback which would precede a certain insurgent victory. In an eloquent piece of propaganda written from his Jamaican exile, he explained the reasons for the revolts and sketched his idea of an independent future for America.

My dear Sir:

… Success will crown our efforts, because the destiny of America has been irrevocably decided; the tie that bound her to Spain has been severed. Only a concept maintained that tie and kept the parts of that immense monarchy together. That which formerly bound them now divides them. The hatred that the Peninsula has inspired in us is greater than the ocean between us. It would be easier to have the two continents meet than to reconcile the spirits of the two countries. The habit of obedience; a community of interest, of understanding, of religion; mutual goodwill; a tender regard for the birthplace and good name of our forefathers; in short, all that gave rise to our hopes, came to us from Spain. As a result there was born a principle of affinity that seemed eternal, notwithstanding the misbehavior of our rulers which weakened that sympathy, or, rather, that bond enforced by the domination of their rule. At present the contrary attitude persists: we are threatened with the fear of death, dishonor, and every harm; there is nothing we have not suffered at the hands of that unnatural step-mother—Spain. The veil has been torn asunder. We have already seen the light, and it is not our desire to be thrust back into darkness. The chains have been broken; we have been freed, and now our enemies seek to enslave us anew. For this

---

2 In Harold A. Bierck, Jr., ed., *Selected Writings of Bolívar*, compiled by Vicente Lecuna, 2 vols. (New York: The Colonial Press, 1951), 103–22.

3 Proclamation by Pablo Morillo to the inhabitants of New Granada, 23 September 1815, in Antonio Rodríguez Villa, ed., *El Teniente General Don Pablo Morillo, primer Conde de Cartagena, Marqués de la Puerte (1778–1837)*, 3 vols. (Madrid: Establecimiento Tipográfico de Fortanet, 1908), 2: 580.

reason America fights desperately, and seldom has desperation failed to achieve victory.

… What madness for our enemy to hope to reconquer America when she has no navy, no funds, and almost no soldiers! Those troops which she has are scarcely adequate to keep her own people in a state of forced obedience and to defend herself from her neighbors. On the other hand, can that nation carry on the exclusive commerce of one-half the world when it lacks manufactures, agricultural products, crafts and sciences, and even a policy? Assume that this mad venture were successful, and further assume that pacification ensued, would not the sons of the Americans of today, together with the sons of the European *reconquistadores* twenty years hence, conceive the same patriotic designs that are now being fought for?

… Every conjecture relative to America's future is, I feel, pure speculation. When mankind was in its infancy, steeped in uncertainty, ignorance, and error, was it possible to foresee what system it would adopt for its preservation? Who could venture to say that a certain nation would be a republic or a monarchy; this nation great, that nation small? To my way of thinking, that is our situation. We are a young people. We inhabit a world apart, separated by broad seas. We are young in the way of almost all the arts and sciences, although, in a certain manner, we are old in the ways of civilized society. I look upon the present state of America as similar to that of Rome after its fall. Each part of Rome adopted a political system conforming to its interest or situation or was led by the individual ambitions of certain chiefs, dynasties, or associations. But this important difference exists: those dispersed parts later re-established their ancient nations, subject to the changes imposed by circumstances or events. But we scarcely retain a vestige of what once was; we are, moreover, neither Indian nor European, but a species midway between the legitimate proprietors of this country and the Spanish usurpers. In short, though American by birth we derive our rights from Europe, and we have to assert these rights against the rights of the natives, and at the same time we must defend ourselves against the invaders. This places us in a most extraordinary and involved situation.

… Americans today, and perhaps to a greater extent than ever before, who live within the Spanish system occupy a position in society no better than that of serfs destined for labor, or at best they have no more status than that of mere consumers. Yet even this status is surrounded with galling restrictions, such as the prohibition to grow European crops, or to store products which are royal monopolies, or to establish factories of a type the Peninsula itself does not possess. To this add the exclusive trading privileges, even in articles of prime necessity, and the barriers between American provinces, designed to prevent the exchange of trade, traffic, and understanding. In short, do you wish to know what our future held? Simply the cultivation of the fields of indigo, grain, coffee, sugar cane, cacao, and cotton; cattle raising on the broad plains; hunting wild game in the jungles; digging in the earth to mine its gold—but even these limitations could never satisfy the greed of Spain.

So negative was our existence that I can find nothing comparable in any other civilized society, examine as I may the entire history of time and the politics of all nations. Is it not an outrage and a violation of human rights to expect a land so splendidly endowed, so vast, rich, and populous, to remain merely passive?

… More than anyone, I desire to see America fashioned into the greatest nation in the world, greatest not so much by virtue of her area and wealth as by her freedom and glory. Although I seek perfection for the government of my country, I cannot persuade myself that the New World can at the moment be organized as a great republic. Since it is impossible, I dare not desire it; yet much less do I desire to have all America a monarchy because that plan is not only impracticable but also impossible. Wrongs now existing could not be righted, and our emancipation would be fruitless. The American states need the care of parental governments to heal the sores and wounds of despotism and war. The parent country, for instance, might be Mexico, the only country fitted for the position by her intrinsic strength, and without such power there can be no parent country. Let us assume it were to be the Isthmus of Panamá, the most central point of this vast continent. Would not all parts continue in their lethargy and even in their present disorder? For a single government to infuse life into the New World; to put into use all the resources for public prosperity; to improve, educate, and perfect the New World, that government would have to possess the authority of a god, much less the knowledge and virtues of mankind.

… When success is not assured, when the state is weak, and when results are distantly seen, all men hesitate; opinion is divided, passions rage, and the enemy fans these passions in order to win an easy victory because of them. As soon as we are strong and under the guidance of a liberal nation which will lend us her protection, we will achieve accord in cultivating the virtues and talents that lead to glory. Then will we march majestically toward that great prosperity for which South America is destined. Then will those sciences and arts which, born in the East, have enlightened Europe, wing their way to a free Colombia,[4] which will cordially bid them welcome.

---

4   Earlier in the letter, Bolívar predicts that New Granada will unite with Venezuela, forming a nation that "should be called Colombia as a just and grateful tribute to the discoverer of our hemisphere."

Rafael Sevilla, *Memories of an Officer in the Spanish Army: Campaigns against Bolívar and the American Separatists,* 1815[5]

Captain Sevilla, a native of Andalusia in southern Spain, was part of Morillo's expeditionary army from embarkation in 1815 through at least the battle of Carabobo in 1821. He describes the siege of Cartagena, in which land forces enjoyed naval support, and the terrible condition of its population after the city's surrender.

ʊ

On the 29th [November 1815], **the general-in-chief** ordered me to reinforce the point called Cospique, on the edge of the bay, where there was only a company of **Morales'** blacks, belonging to the King's regiment, commanded by Captain D. José Baussá. There we kept observing the movements of the enemy, who was in possession of a fort or redoubt situated on the banks of the wharf, next to the arsenal. The castles at the mouth of the port were in the possession of our people, which gave us the advantage of being able to fire at the canoes crossing the bay.

> **the general-in-chief:** Pablo Morillo.
>
> **Morales:** Francisco Tomás Morales (1781–1845), a royalist officer.

On 2 December, the general-in-chief arrived there, followed by **General Enrile**, commander of **Irauli engineers**, the assistants, about twenty Hussars under **Captain Santander**, and many other gunners, led by Officer Ortega. We were trying to establish the headquarters there in order to protect the ships, which did their best to force open the port, in order to make their gunfire on the stronghold more effective. But an enemy movement made the accomplishment of this project unnecessary. At seven o'clock in the morning of the 4th, we noticed that 80 or 90 insurgents, no doubt in an attempt to get food, as they were starving, came out of the redoubt in front of us and went into the mangrove.

> **General Enrile:** Pascual Enrile y Alcedo (1772–1836), who would later become the lieutenant governor of the Philippines.
>
> **Irauli engineers:** The literature is silent on these men.
>
> **Captain Santander:** Francisco de Paula Santander (1792–1840), later vice-president of Colombia.

We were on the roof of a house in Cospique drinking coffee with the general-in-chief, when he was notified of the enemy's advance. My uncle Enrile recognized them with his spyglass and said they were not over a hundred men. "Then you go and beat them, Sevilla, with your company," said Morillo. "It is necessary to make them pull back in every dangerous situation. Santander and Ortega have to mount their horses and get ready with their people to protect the operation in case their support is necessary." Without wasting a minute, I put my cup on the table, saluted, and ran downstairs. The brave second lieutenant García, alarmed by the news, had

---

5   Original title: *Memorias de un oficial del ejército español: Campañas contra Bolívar y los separatistas de América* (Madrid: Editorial América, 1916), 66–69.

already formed the company. "Company," I said, "the whole headquarters is watching us; today is a day of glory for us if we know how to behave with courage, or a day of blemish and derision if we do not proceed as worthy and dedicated champions of the Spanish cause." "There is not one here who is not willing to let himself be shattered before reappearing before his general," said the first sergeant, who was an olive-skinned veteran with big mustaches and a suntan....

Then I gave the word of command and we rushed like dogs of prey for those impassable mangroves. The enemy, deployed as guerrillas, stood firm and fired massively at us and with precision, which left one soldier dead and a sergeant wounded. "Draw your bayonets and go at them!" I said without stopping to pick up those who had fallen.

When the insurgents saw that we came down at full speed with a determined spirit to engage in a hand-to-hand fight, they left the ambush and began to make a retreat towards the fort, while we stayed within reach and exchanged fire with them. However, they did not penetrate the redoubt from where they had left but continued towards the stronghold.

Our soldiers, blind with enthusiasm, tried to do the same. "Stop," I shouted, "it is a trap: they try to bring us closer to a point where entire battalions will be hidden to destroy us. No one goes beyond the fort. Eight men will go to reconnoiter it with one in command." The man with the whiskers called eight of the most intrepid by their names and boldly approached the fort and entered it ... "Barbarians!" the ensign said in my ear, "they have gotten into the lion's den; they are going to tear them apart."

But to our surprise, we saw five minutes later the one in command peeking through a high embrasure, beckoning us to approach. We trotted, entered, and convinced ourselves that there was not a single defender of use left in the fort; We only found about twenty bruised and emaciated men lying in their beds, who were about to expire from misery.

When General Morillo saw that we had taken over the stronghold, he sent the Hussars at full speed, which, passing like a lightning bolt ahead of us, reached the enemy guerrillas, who were retreating, and they harassed and decimated them until reaching the frontline.... One quarter of an hour later, the aide-de-camp Navas presented himself to me with 40 reinforcement troops, commanded by a royal black officer, giving me the general's order that we should stand firm there and that in any difficult situation we should maintain our position, whatever the number of those who attacked us. I arranged for several eavesdroppers to be ensconced, half-buried in the sand and hidden by the foliage on the side of the besieged city.

The general withdrew to the lines, and when it got dark he sent us a portion of salted meat, biscuit and cheese from Flanders, which we devoured, because we had not eaten all day, and we offered some pieces to those sick enemies who could swallow, of whom there were few, and of these some died when trying their first bite.

[After the final victory on 5 December,] Morillo sent his staff officers to prevent all army chiefs from doing harm or that any resident who did not offer resistance was mistreated; they should only demand the delivery of weapons under penalty of death.

This threat was not necessary to force the surrender of Cartagena's insurgents, because they could not; they were not men, but skeletons: men and women, living portraits of death, clung to the walls in order to walk without falling, such was the horrible hunger they had suffered.

For twenty-two days, they had eaten nothing but leather soaked in tannery tanks. Women who had been rich and beautiful, men who belonged to the pick of that once opulent mercantile center of both worlds, all those, regardless of sexes or classes, who could move, rushed, pushing and running over our soldiers, not to fight them, but to search their backpacks for a crust of bread or some biscuit.

Before that terrifying spectacle, all our compatriots forgot that those were the murderers of their companions, and not only gave them however many items of food they had, which those unfortunates eagerly ate, many of them dropping dead as soon as they had swallowed a few pieces of biscuit, but they also improvised a communal meal for everyone and soup for those who could not come get it themselves. Indescribable was the state in which we found the rich town of Cartagena de Indias. The bad smell was unbearable, as there were many houses full of rotting corpses.

The first thing that General Morillo ordered, once he was inside the stronghold, was that a large ditch be dug by the troops and the few civilians who could work, and that those piles of corpses that infested the population were buried in it. Many bodies were removed from the houses in carts and deposited in the mass grave. But no matter how large the ditch was made, it could not contain them all, and many had to be carried off in canoes, with stones tied around their necks, to be cast into the sea.

DOCUMENT 32:

Simón Bolívar, decree regarding the emancipation of enslaved people, Carúpano, Venezuela, 2 June 1816[6]

> After the defeat of the second Venezuelan republic, Simón Bolívar and scores
> of other revolutionaries went into exile in Les Cayes, Haiti. With support
> of Alexandre Pétion, president of the Republic of Haiti, they organized two
> attempts to topple the royalist regime in Caracas. The first attempt began
> with the arrival of Bolivar and his men on 1 June 1816 at the small port of
> Carúpano, which he found to be deserted. The next day, in keeping with his
> promise to Pétion to abolish slavery in exchange for Haitian support, Bolívar
> issued a decree that emancipated the enslaved Africans, albeit on certain
> conditions.

To the inhabitants of Río Caribe, Carúpano y Cariaco.

… I decree the complete freedom of the slaves who have groaned under
the Spanish yoke in the past three centuries. Considering that the Republic
needs the services of all its sons, we must impose the following conditions
on the new citizens:

First article: Each robust man between the ages of fourteen and sixty will
present himself in his district's parish to enlist under the colors of Venezuela
twenty-four hours after the publication of the present decree.

Second article: The elderly, women, children, and invalids will remain forever
exempt from military service, as they will be from domestic and rural service in which they were formerly employed for the benefit of their masters.

Third article: The new citizen who refuses to take up arms to fulfill the
sacred duty to defend his freedom will remain subject to servitude, not
only he himself but also his children under the age of fourteen, his wife,
and his elderly parents.

Fourth article: The relatives of soldiers employed in the liberating army
will enjoy the rights of citizens and the complete freedom that this decree
grants them in the name of the Republic of Venezuela.…

----

6   In Simón Bolívar, *Obras Completas*, ed. Vicente Lecuna, 2nd ed., 3 vols. (Habana: Editorial Lex,
     1950), I: 55.

Brigadier Francisco Tomás Morales to Pablo Morillo, Ocumare, 15 July 1816[7]

Hearing about an imminent royalist attack on Carúpano by land and sea, Bolívar embarked his men after one month. His fourteen vessels sailed to the port of Ocumare, located closer to Caracas. Carlos Soublette took the rebel soldiers inland, captured the town of Maracay, but was defeated by the royalist troops, even though these were outnumbered. Led by Francisco Tomás Morales and his second Manuel Bauzá, the royalists went on to beat Bolívar, who arrived at the front later. Disorder ensued as the independence fighters fled the enemy, exacerbated by the flight of the *Libertador*, who sailed away, leaving his men exposed to Morales' army. Perhaps distracted by the presence of his mistress, Bolívar lost much prestige, which took long to restore.

At midnight on the 13th, I left with 700 men, assigning lieutenant colonel Manuel Bauza, sergeant major of the first army group to form the vanguard with 350 men, made up of two companies of the regiment of the Union and two of the King. I followed him with the rest of the second group, some volunteers, and the cavalry of this land, warning this commander in advance not to fire a shot before reaching forward-deployed enemy troops. Indeed, at half past five in the morning the rebels were in sight, placed in groups on top of a steep hill which was extraordinarily difficult to access, so that if I hadn't completely trusted the rank and file, and the commanders and officers that led them, I would have had some doubt about a good outcome; but since there is no obstacle that could resist courage, I believed I could surely achieve victory. At six the vanguard's advanced detachments opened fire, and within moments shots were fired everywhere. At seven we had already conquered more than half of the mountain, but the fatigue from the very arduous climb made it necessary to reinforce the army with reserve troops, and from that moment on the fighting became more horrific and stubborn.

Directed by their worthy officers, our soldiers at times advanced to the top, and although firing increased from the insurgents, who were led from afar by the outlaw Simón Bolívar, they got there by half past nine. These unfortunate men abandoned their unassailable positions and as they fled, wandered in all directions, ditching rifles, ammunition, and even the clothes

---

7   In Antonio Rodríguez Villa, ed., *El Teniente General Don Pablo Morillo, primer Conde de Cartagena, Marqués de la Puerte (1778–1837)*, 3 vols. (Madrid: Establecimiento Tipográfico de Fortanet, 1908), 3: 82–83.

that hindered them from running freely; so that in little time the phony expedition ended, [and with it] the efforts of more than six months of calculating and planning, supplies, provisions, baggage, opinions and hopes on the part of a horde of felons who, vexed by their crimes, live as fugitives tormenting good folks and casting dishonor on humanity.

The cowardly and weak Bolívar left the battlefield in advance as usual, and imitating his example, so did his followers, leaving all over the road to Ocumare compelling signs of the panic and fear in which they fled, abandoning some of their wounded, who were relieved of their pain and groans in due course.

… The spectacle presented all the way until this port [Ocumare] is certainly horrifying: wounded men, cadavers, and horses thrown over a cliff, rifles and leather straps [worn by soldiers] spread out, barrels with supplies and a thousand other results of their indecent plunder are seen littered in the forests on either side.…

This gang of felons who came to the beach of Ocumare thinking that they were totally in possession of Venezuela, who proudly and disorderedly penetrated as far as Maracay, without keeping in mind that the King's arms would punish their offenses, have gone up in smoke, and the innocent towns have been freed of past horrors, which have already disappeared under the sweet influence of the wise government of an adored King.

The rebels have lost 300 to 400 men, who were either killed or wounded; among the former is counted colonel Vicente Landaeta, son of loyal Valencia, and a French captain in his service, and among the latter four officers; we seized more than 1,000 new, untouched and still packaged rifles and over 300 that they threw away in their flight; more than 60,000 gun cartridges, six hundredweight of gunpowder in bulk, 32,000 gun-flints, a crate of rifle bullets, five bronze molds to make these, three *pedreros* and three *esmeriles* of the same metal; fifteen lances, … one complete printing machine, nineteen drawers of letters for the same … as well as two carronades, which have been found in a boat that they left anchored in port. They also abandoned the sacred vessels and pieces of silver used in the sacked churches …

pedreros: Short-barreled cannons.

esmeriles: Small cannons, six feet in length.

DOCUMENT 34:

Proclamation by Javier Mina, Explaining the Motives for His Expedition, Galveston, 22 February 1817[8]

In his native Navarra (Spain), Francisco Javier Mina (1789–1817) formed a guerrilla movement that fought the French invaders. He was captured and spent four years in a French prison. Released in 1814 after Napoleon's first rule as emperor ended, Mina joined a group of men who wanted to start a revolt against Fernando VII in Mexico, from where the revolution was to be spread across the empire, including Spain. The expedition that he announces here would eventually be fatal for him.

The healthy and sensible part of Spain is today well-convinced that it is not only impossible to conquer America again, but impolitic and contrary to well-understood interests: in dispensing with the unquestionable justice that assists the Americans, what would be the advantages they would derive from subjugating it again? Who would be the ones who would benefit from such a sizable iniquity, if it were possible? Two kinds of people are those that only and exclusively take advantage of the enslavement of the Americans: the king and the monopolists: the first to sustain his absolutist empire and oppress us at his discretion; the second to gain riches to support despotism and keep the people reduced to penury.

They are Fernando's most active agents and America's fiercest enemies. The courtiers and the monopolists would like to eternalize the state of pupilage in which they have placed the nation, in order to elevate their fortune and that of their descendants above their ruins. Spain, they say, cannot exist without our Americas.

It is clear that these gentlemen understand Spain to mean their own small group along with their relatives and people close to them. Because once America is emancipated, there will be no more exclusive favors, nor sales of governorships, intendancies and other jobs of the Indies for their children. Because when American ports are opened to foreign nations, Spanish trade will end up in the hands of a more numerous and enlightened class. Because, in short, a free America will undoubtedly revive the national industry, sacrificed presently to the despicable interests of a few men.

---

8   Original title: *Proclama de Javier Mina, explicando los motivos de su expedición*, in *Colección de documentos relativos a la época de la independencia de México* (Guanajuato: A. Chagoyan, 1870), 242–44.

If seen from this angle, the emancipation of Americans is useful and advantageous for most of the Spanish people, it is much more so for its certain tendency to definitively establish liberal governments throughout the old monarchy. Without destroying the colossus of despotism, sustained by fanatics and monopolists, we can never recover our dignity everywhere.

For this undertaking it is indispensable that all the towns where Spanish is spoken, learn to be free and to know and practice their rights. The moment that a single section of the Americas secures its independence, we can flatter ourselves that liberal principles sooner or later will extend their blessings to the rest.

British Foreign Office, "Confidential Memorandum"[9]

Because the British government helped Spain wage the Peninsular War against Napoleonic France, it could not recognize the independent states that emerged in Spanish America. While pursuing neutrality, Britain did get involved in mediation between the two warring sides. Here, on behalf of George Prince Regent—who reigned on behalf of his incapacitated father, King George II—the condition are listed that Spain must fulfill in order to allow Britain to act as mediator.

Although the Prince Regent has felt it his duty to observe a strict neutrality throughout the contest which has agitated the South American Provinces, **H.R.H.** has never ceased to entertain an anxious desire that that great Continent might be restored to tranquility under the ancient sovereignties of the Crowns of Spain and Portugal. The Prince Regent has looked to this object with the more earnestness from the regret with which H.R.H. has seen ancient authorities subverted, from the peculiar interest which he feels in whatever may concern the dignity and welfare of the illustrious families whose possessions are thereby endangered, and from a firm persuasion that the Continent of South America must long remain a prey to its own internal convulsions, before it can assume any separate form of regular Government capable of providing for the happiness of its own inhabitants, or of adequately maintaining relations of peace and amity with other States.

It is, however, the opinion of the Prince Regent that this desirable object can alone be obtained by a speedy settlement of all existing differences, and by the restoration of a perfect understanding between the Crowns of Their Catholick and Most Faithful Majesties, and further by each determining to adopt a system of government within their respective dominions favourable to the interest and congenial to the feelings of the natives of those countries, it being obvious that, whatever may have been the original policy of the Colonial system of either Crown, it has become in the progress of time inapplicable to countries of such extent and population.

… That such have uniformly been the Prince Regent's sentiments upon this subject will appear from the enclosed Despatch and Instruction which contain the basis upon which H.R.H. was willing, in the year 1812, to undertake a Mediation between the Crown of Spain and its Provinces in South

H.R.H.: His Royal Highness.

---

9 In Charles Kingsley Webster, ed., *Britain and the Independence of Latin America 1812–1830: Select Documents from the Foreign Office Archives* (London: Oxford UP, 1938), I: 352–58.

America. It is much to be lamented that the Spanish Government did not at that time either avail itself of H.R.H.'s good offices, or take some step on its own part for proclaiming its determination to act in future on principles suited to the Government of a great Continent. There is much reason to apprehend that the interval which has elapsed has tended materially to aggravate the difficulties of restoring the authority of His Catholic Majesty. The destructive warfare which has been carried on has tended to widen the breach between the contending parties. Beyond all question, the alienation of the Colonies from the Parent State has progressively increased, and yet the progress towards the establishing of any adequate form of Government in South America has been so inconsiderable, that a large proportion of the population may be presumed to be desirous to place themselves again under the protection of some regular Government and established order of things.

Under these circumstances, were Spain now, however late, to change her policy and avowedly to adopt towards her South American subjects a more liberal system of government, a reasonable hope might still be entertained that the Spanish Colonies would return to their allegiance, and the great Continent of South America be thus rescued from the scene of self-desolation into which it has been so long plunged.

It appears to the British Government that the probability of such a result might be considerably improved, were Spain frankly to come to a distinct understanding with the principal Powers of Europe as to the system she meant hereafter to pursue, and were the people of South America to be convinced that those Powers not only favoured the restoration of the lawful sovereignty, but that their influence with the Court of Madrid might be considered as affording to that people a pledge for the faithful observance on the part of the Spanish Government of the basis of any pacification that might be effected under their sanction.

… Should such a measure as above described be determined upon, the Prince Regent would be most willing, under satisfactory arrangements as to the mode of carrying the same into execution, cordially to lend himself to an endeavor to serve the interests of his Ally the King of Spain. He is moreover desirous of being perfectly explicit with the other Mediating Powers, as he has already been with His Catholic Majesty, with respect to the principles upon which alone he could undertake to charge himself with such a Mediation,—which principles are as follows:—

First, that Spain shall have previously entered into satisfactory engagements for the Abolition of the Slave Trade, it being inconsistent with the principles upon which H.R.H. has declared his determination to act, to employ his influence to re-establish a governing Power in that quarter of the globe, whose laws shall permit a traffick in slaves which has been very generally abolished by the local authorities now existing.

… Secondly, that a general amnesty shall be proclaimed for all past offences; an armistice to be established under suitable regulations during the period which may be necessary for carrying on explanations in furtherance of the Mediation.

Thirdly, that such a community of privileges and admissibility to employment may be granted by the Mother Country as may place the South Americans upon the footing of Spanish subjects in conformity to the principles already solemnly recognized by the late **Cortez**.

And fourthly, that the people of South America shall have secured to them free commercial intercourse with all nations, Spain enjoying, as the Parent State, a fair preference in the intercourse with this portion of her dominions.

Cortez: The Cortes of Cádiz, which had been dissolved by King Fernando VII upon his return to power in 1814.

Bernardo O'Higgins to José de San Martín, Concepción, 30 July 1817[10]

The Battle of Chacabuco (12 February 1817) marked the start of the return to rule of the revolutionaries in Chile. But not until the Battle of Maipu (5 April 1818) was their position secure. In the interim, royalist forces who had escaped after Chacabuco posed a danger. And as this document shows, the insurgent leaders feared alliances between these Spaniards and Indigenous groups.

The enemy would undoubtedly have succeeded in rousing the provinces to revolt if I had not placed active lieutenant governors and committed patriots there. In the vicinity of the mouth of the Itata, thirty men from Talcahuano disembarked with some arms and ammunition to beef up the forts and scattered to Quirigue, Chillán, Caucenes, murdering, robbing, etc. The lieutenant governors were alerted, and each of them proceeded smartly against the bandits. In Chillán, the two sides battled for two hours in the interior of a forest until the bandits dispersed, and in Caucenes ten were apprehended, whom I have ordered to be hanged and whose heads will be placed on the spots where they committed their excesses, and here I have ordered two to be hanged who were arrested on the coast at Tomé. In this way things have quieted down in the interior.

Forty of the Spaniards who were defeated in Arauco are there as well, and they have frightened the coastal Indians, making them believe that those from Buenos Aires were coming to take their lands and their wives. These Indians, who are used to believing what the **Recollects** tell them, are still alarmed and form a threat to the Arauco stronghold, where there are 150 men, and I am sure they will never be able to overthrow it.

[The bandits] also communicated their messages to the plains and hillside Indians on this side of the mountain range and those on the way to Valdivia. They didn't end up frightening them because as a precaution I had dispatched envoys with some presents to the chief governors of the land; these have answered me by assuring me of the old friendship which they have always professed.

Recollects: A French reform branch of the Franciscan missionary order.

---

10 In Comisión Nacional del Centenario, ed., *Documentos del archivo de San Martín*, 12 vols. (Buenos Aires: Imprenta de Coni Hermanos, 1910), V: 388.

H.M. Brackenridge, *Voyage to South America, Performed by Order of the American Government, in the Years 1817 and 1818, in the Frigate* Congress[11]

In 1817, the US government appointed the lawyer and journalist Henry Marie Brackenridge (1786–1871) secretary of a diplomatic mission to South America. As part of that mission, Brackenridge spoke extensively with politicians in Buenos Aires. In this passage, Brackenridge describes the viewpoint of one of those men, who argues that Buenos Aires should enjoy the power it seeks vis-à-vis the interior provinces of the Río de la Plata in order to carry out its goal of helping South America put an end to Spanish rule.

In a familiar conversation with one of their [Buenos Aires'] most intelligent men, but entirely friendly to the present administration, I ventured to ask him what was the nature of the complaints of the provinces against the capital, and whether it was really true that there had been an abuse of power towards them. He admitted that there had been causes of complaint, both on account of the acts of the government, and of its agents; but, said he, was it to be expected that every cause of dissatisfaction could be prevented? There are local demagogues enough to aggravate and magnify these complaints, and thus exasperate a people not accustomed, heretofore, to think for themselves on public affairs; and, therefore, easily led astray. Here, said he, is one of the great difficulties we have to struggle with in our contest for independence. Each province, or government, as well as each petty district of such province, although zealous in the common cause, wishes to pursue its own course. It, therefore, becomes necessary for the capital to exert itself continually to bring them to unite their efforts. To this salutary end, compulsion and coercion are, sometimes, unavoidable; but they can never give pleasure to those who feel them. Here is the true reason for the dislike to Buenos Ayres; and yet, such is the inconsistency of the human passions, should the contest terminate happily, she will be regarded as the common benefactress. We were not inattentive spectators, said he, of your late contest with Great Britain, and we observed that your confederative system opposed great obstacles to your carrying on the war with efficiency; several of your states almost refusing to join, and your general government appeared to want power to coerce a union of your strength and resources. From this, you can readily conceive the difficulty of coercing a people who have formed the most extravagant ideas of independence, and who, enjoying

---

11 Baltimore: Published by the Author, 1819, volume II (of 2): 37–41.

a momentary security from Spain through the very means taken by Buenos Ayres, are, notwithstanding, desirous of placing themselves beyond her control. And what, sir, would be the result should every province and petty district follow the example of Artigas? Buenos Ayres would not be able to raise those armies which have kept the Spanish power in check in the upper provinces, and which, like the stone of Sisyphus, threatens to roll down and crush those below. Salta, Tucuman, Cordova, Mendoza, and the rest, each acting in its own way, would separately fall an easy conquest to the army of Lima; which now requires the combined forces of all to resist. The capital would be reduced to very narrow limits, its resources would be cut off, its commerce with the interior destroyed; and, although we should make a brave resistance, we would probably be subdued at last, and this flourishing city, like Monte Video, Caraccas, Cumana and Barcelona of Venezuela, would exhibit only a heap of ruins, instead of being what it is now, *the most formidable enemy to the Spanish power in America.* The re-conquest of Chili, which has filled the Spaniards with despair, would not have taken place; Paraguay, which hugs herself in her inglorious security, purchased by the blood and treasure of Buenos Ayres, could not resist the Spanish army descending from Peru, or ascending the Parana; and as to Artigas, although he might for a time enjoy his wild independence, in consequence of having no fixed habitation, yet this would not be the case with the inhabitants of towns and those engaged in the pursuit of agriculture, should Spain resolve to adopt the plan of extermination which has been followed by Morillo. The war in Peru could not be continued a single moment without the aid of Buenos Ayres; for what ultimate object could be gained by mere bands of guerillas, unsupported by a regular army? Buenos Ayres has introduced a regular system, the want of which, has given such advantages to the Spaniards in other parts of America, and she has been the nursery of officers, regularly instructed in the newest and best principles of the military art. This is no time to be over scrupulous about form, when we are endeavoring to save the state from threatened destruction.

Decree issued by Bernardo O'Higgins, Santiago de Chile, 3 June 1818[12]

In the same way that Morelos wanted to abolish ethnic distinctions in Mexico by proposing to call all its inhabitants "Americans," Chile's Supreme Director Bernardo O'Higgins (1778–1842) decreed that everyone born in Chile could call themselves Chileans, irrespective of their backgrounds.

After the glorious proclamation of our Independence, which was secured with the blood of its defenders, it would be shameful to allow the use of formulas invented by the colonial system. One of them is to call Spaniards those who, because of their rank, are not mixed with those other races which in the past were called bad. Since we no longer depend on Spain, we should not call ourselves Spaniards, but Chileans. Consequently, I order that in all types of judicial documents—whether in criminal cases, **cases regarding blood purity**, in case of the proclamation of marriages, baptismal registers, in confirmations, and funerals, the phrase "Spaniard, native of so and so" be replaced by "Chilean, native of so and so." … It must be understood that no distinction should be made with the Indians, who must be called Chileans.…

Transcribe this law for the governor of the bishopric, so that he can circulate it to the courts of justice, entrusting it with the task of its observance and its circulation to those corporations and state judges …

cases regarding blood purity: Legal cases about the question of whether somebody had African or Indigenous (or Jewish) ancestors.

---

12 In José Antonio Váras, ed., *Recopilacion de leyes i decretos supremos concernientes al ejército, desde abril de 1812 a abril de 1839*, 7 vols. (Santiago de Chile: Imprenta Nacional, 1866–88), I: 45.

Pablo Morillo to Spain's Ministry of War, Montalbán, 4 July 1818[13]

The use of enslaved black people to fill military ranks was an option that insurgent leaders in Venezuela and New Granada had chosen from the earliest days of the independence wars. Royalist commander Pablo Morillo explains here why he has decided *against* raising a battalion of enslaved blacks.

❧

His Excellency—Appreciating the great advantages for Royal service, and for the pacification of these provinces, I devised a plan, which I have reported to you, to raise a battalion of brown slaves, a plan that ripened due to general approval until the poorly understood interest of some owners began to suffocate the voice of reason, and set in motion the intrigues that are common in these lands …

I disregard the need to prevent in all possible ways that the insurgents' army increases its forces with blacks who are discontented with their condition, as I ignore the outstanding attitude of this caste of men in the face of war fatigue in unhealthy countries, and the readiness derived from their actual condition to receive military discipline, and also the useful and important services that have been provided and are still being provided by over two thousand men of like kind who are currently found in our armies in both the provinces and the **kingdom of Santa Fe**, although I cannot but remind **Y.E.** of what I have presented to you before about the very violent state in which the slaves of these lands find themselves since the revolutionaries with their lauded equality built momentum for the natural seeds of the desire for liberty, in spite of the peace and subjection in which they are supposedly kept by their masters, who, obsessed by greed, have succeeded in blowing the minds of the others, without being bothered by how implausible the slaves' supposed apathy is, among both those who for some time have enjoyed the sweet satisfaction of being free as well as those who because of close contact and conversations with the former are comparing their present state to freedom. But in this matter, it has proven true what generally happens when the spirit of opposition, far from analyzing the facts, compels one to fall into the most classic contradictions. On the one hand, it is asserted that the slaves are calm and submissive, and that there is

kingdom of Santa Fe: Morillo probably means the audiencia of Santa Fe (Bogotá).

Y.E.: Your Excellency.

---

13   In Antonio Rodríguez Villa, ed., *El Teniente General Don Pablo Morillo, primer Conde de Cartagena, Marqués de la Puerte (1778–1837)*, 3 vols. (Madrid: Establecimiento Tipográfico de Fortanet, 1908), 3: 493–95.

no need to be afraid that they try to flee to the enemy armies, while on the other hand, those of the opposition party threaten us with a general uprising of the slaves if some of these are allowed to join the new planned battalion under the King's flags. As an example of that, the interim captain-general refers to what happened on a hacienda in the environs of Victoria, whose slaves (as is claimed) have refused work, clamoring that they want to serve in our armies. But having gathered information in the very locations mentioned in this story, I found out that the hacienda in Caña named Figuire, belonging to the heirs of Dr. José Domingo Blanco, has been disputed for more than ten years and therefore without a master to subdue the slaves; I also learned that a large part of the males have served in our armies, and that on the same day that the new foreman tried to bring to heel a few men who already craved the military life, these men clamored to be restored to their former state. And that confirms once more, Y.E., my earlier assertion that it is morally impossible for a man who has enjoyed liberty to live peacefully and quietly in slavery, and that his calm is that of volcanoes that are quiet while the material is being put together that one day must trigger the most horrifying explosion.

Pablo Morillo to Spain's Minister of War, Caracas, 20 September 1818[14]

Three years into his mission and increasingly short on soldiers, Morillo
realized that he could not win the war by military means alone. In this letter,
he advocates the dispatch of priests, whose presence will improve the morality
of the inhabitants, who will thereby become attached to the royalist cause.

On several occasions, I have stated to His Majesty that one of the most
sensible measures to be taken in order to consolidate the peace and calm
of these provinces is to send missions there of members of various religious
orders, who would be spread among the towns to preach and teach the
[Christian] doctrine to the inhabitants, seeing to it that they are enticed
and instructed, and laying the foundations for the affection, respect and
submission that they must have towards the King, our lord, and his just and
fatherly government. In the current circumstances in which evil has grown
and hardships have increased, I don't hesitate to assure Your Excellency that
forty or fifty members of the orders and as many secular clergymen serving
as priests in the towns would have more effect on public opinion and would
contribute more to the pacification of these lands than a good division of
choice soldiers, assuming that these priests will display the exemplary virtue
that distinguishes their sacred ministry, because in the Indies, more than
any other part of the world, clergymen must be exemplary and virtuous. I
have just traveled around these provinces to review the army divisions, and
by careful examination, I have noticed the state of neglect and disorder in
which these inhabitants live. Almost all towns have no parish priest, and if
they are so fortunate to find one of average ability, he is responsible for an
immense number of parishioners to whom he cannot attend. The residents
live like wild tribes, scattered across woods and mountains, without priest
or church, receiving no sacraments and having lost any idea of religion and
society. One frequently sees youths of both sexes, twelve to fourteen years
of age, who have not been baptized, heard Mass or ever seen a priest; and
that is how they get married and propagate like Indian natives before the
conquest, except that they are descendants of Spaniards, mixed with indigenous races and people of color, whose customs and love for the savage life
they have adopted. This deplorable situation has been and still is the logical

---

14 In Antonio Rodríguez Villa, ed., *El Teniente General Don Pablo Morillo, primer Conde de Cartagena,
Marqués de la Puerte (1778–1837)*, 3 vols. (Madrid: Establecimiento Tipográfico de Fortanet, 1908), 3:
607–09.

consequence of the devastating war that these lands have experienced since the start of their revolt, in which the revolutionaries have put an end to pious institutions, leveled towns, wiping out the priests, and physically and morally doing away with their writings, their example, and their works, because these can convince one of the truth of our holy religion and the respect and submission owed to the sovereign. Living in fields and deserted areas, without judges or other authorities, they form bands of robbers … and commit all kinds of excesses and create all kinds of disturbances. In addition to the principles cited, this anarchy and the dissolution of government and society is also rooted in the indolence and ignorance of the ***tenientes justicias mayores***, the magistrates that govern the towns here … who are elected without examination or care, and who only attend to matters that can gain them one hundred pesos, the price that it costs them to use their title. Most of them can barely read or write, and their positions often end up in the hands of characters that support the independent party or men with a very bad reputation.

tenientes justicias mayores: Their position was somewhat comparable to that of a sheriff.

Nicolás Cabrera to the militia of free blacks and mulattoes, Buenos Aires, 16 February 1819[15]

In 1819, the government of Buenos Aires ordered the militia of free blacks and mulattoes to be garrisoned. An overwhelming majority of the militia men refused to follow this order, since it meant that they could no longer reside in their own homes, and because they associated the confinement with slavery. They accused the government of trampling over their rights and suggested that the government ignored the contribution of their armed service to the fatherland. At this juncture, their commander, **Nicolás Cabrera** gave this speech to calm down spirits. Eventually, the protest fizzled out after the government allowed militiamen to return to their homes.[16]

Nicolás Cabrera: (1780–1832), a free man of color born in Córdoba province, moved to Buenos Aires, where he rose to the rank of captain of the black militia. He was appointed commander of the free black militia in 1815 and in 1819 to lieutenant colonel of regulars.

ↄ

Speech to the civic regiment of blacks and mulattoes by their commander.

Comrades, I have no other expression than those of my heart to convey the cruel pain I have felt in the past days because of the bitter events that have occurred in our regiment due to the misconduct of some ill-advised individuals. The confidence that the Supreme Government, the authorities, the chiefs and all the citizens of the country had in our loyalty, and their trust that we would be the most determined defenders of the freedom of the country and of the established order; the confidence that we had known how to inspire with our conduct, with our services and even with our blood; that confidence that served us as a reward and satisfaction in seeing us honored and loved by the members of other classes, all that trust became uncertain in the bitter moments that I do not want to recall. Who doesn't get wrapped up in his grief when he remembers those moments? However, we must remember that it is in our power to remedy the evil without doing anything other than refraining from provoking our own ruin with new offences. Let respect for the authorities, love of order, and adherence to the public cause be clear even from our own countenances; let us close our ears to the perverse suggestions of those who wish to disturb the tranquility without facing the consequences; let us always trust more in the word of a government that has been constantly good to us than in the slanders and

---

15 Schomburg Center for Research in Black Culture, Manuscripts, Archives and Rare Books Division, The New York Public Library, "Black Troops—Infantry Regiment of Blacks and Mulattoes," New York Public Library Digital Collections, accessed 22 June 2020.

16 See, for this episode, Gabriel di Meglio, "Soldados de la Revolución. Las tropas porteñas en la Guerra de Independencia (1810–1820)," *Anuario IEHS* 18 (2003), 39–65: 60–64.

false promises of those who seek only their own advantage at the expense of the country and ourselves. By behaving in this way, comrades and friends, be assured that we will be more beloved and considered than we were before by the Supreme Government, by the authorities and officers, and by all the citizens who have regarded us for a few moments with distrust. The country demands our services, and we are going to present them; once we are no longer needed, we will return to our homes happier and with more glory; but as long as we are needed, we are sure that we will not leave the capital because the government of the country wants to keep us in its vicinity so that, united with the other regiments, we can defend freedom and order if they are attacked. Nothing is done, nor has anything been done involving us that is not a distinction and an honor given to us; let us justify, friends, the feelings that favor us, and let us wipe away the outrage in which some of our own comrades wanted to cover us; let us obey the legitimate powers as subjects; let us fight as free people against the enemies of order and of the country, only in that way will we salvage the confidence and appreciation of good people that we could otherwise lose. Nicolas Cabrera, Buenos Aires, 16 February 1819.

PART 5

Imperial Defeat and Construction of New Regimes

DOCUMENT 42:

J.R. Rengger and M. Longchamp, *Historical Essay on the Revolution of Paraguay and the Dictatorial Government of Dr. Francia. Part of the Voyage to Paraguay,* 1819[1]

> On their research trip to South America, the biologist Johann Rudolf Rengger (1795–1832) and his fellow Swiss scientist, the biologist Marcellin Longchamp, arrived in the Paraguayan capital Asunción in July 1819. During the following six years, they witnessed the workings of Dr. Francia's dictatorship. One method he used to shape public opinion was to curb the power of the clergy, which he suspected of royalist sympathies.

‿

Around this time, the dictator made an addition to the troops of the line and also gave the militia better facilities, either to protect himself against his neighbors or because he feared domestic civil unrest. To give quarters to a new levy of 600 men, he seized the Franciscan monastery and told the monks to look for lodgings at [the convent of] the **barefooted monks**. Then a Spaniard, known for his fanaticism and encouraged by the false rumor of a Russian expedition against South America, ventured to say: "The Franciscans may have departed, but soon it will be Francia's turn to leave." When the dictator received this speech, he had the Spaniard brought before him and told him: "When I will leave is unknown to me, but I know that you will leave before me." He had him shot the next morning and confiscated his assets, so that his widow and his children, though creoles, were reduced to beggary. That is how the horror government in Paraguay began. Dr. Francia saw himself and the state as one, and declared that anyone who dared to resist his will, or even just to criticize his actions, was a traitor of the fatherland.

barefooted monks: They belonged to a so-called discalced congregation (perhaps Carmelites), which meant that they went barefoot or wore sandals.

---

1   Original title: *Historischer Versuch über die Revolution von Paraguay und die Dictatorial-Regierung von Dr. Francia. Ein Abschnitt der Reise nach Paraguay* (Stuttgart and Tübingen: J.G. Cotta, 1827), 34–36.

Also, a few days later another Spaniard was punished with the death penalty for saying something similar.

For these executions, as in all subsequent ones, the dictator himself produced the necessary cartridges; for his mistrust prevented him from entrusting these to the troops, except for those at the most important posts such as the prisons and the powder magazine. At the same time, he was so stingy with the ammunition that he ordered only three men to go to each execution, so that the victims had to be killed more than once by bayonet stabs. And yet he witnessed these atrocities, as the executions always took place under his windows, often in his presence. The death of the two Spaniards spread consternation among all who threw a glance at the future. It was different with the common herd, who liked to see it as a guarantee of the dictator's intentions. Until then, the general opinion had been that he had only sought the supreme power to become the **monk** of Paraguay, and to hand it over one day to King Fernando. Now the strictness applied to Spaniards had to completely invalidate this opinion. It had spread because the dictator did not imitate his neighbors, who persecuted the Spaniards often out of sheer greed. The Spaniards had not suffered more in Paraguay than the creoles, if anything less, because they lived more secluded. Only the carelessness of the two who were executed led him to proceed differently. The interference with religious order had embittered them, and it was chiefly this impression that he wanted to cover up by means of terror. Knowing the influence which the Spanish monks, more than the other ones, had on the people, and foreseeing that they would use it on that occasion, he locked the Franciscans and the barefooted monks up in the monastery, and declared them unfit to hear confession, and forbade their compatriots to visit them.

monk: It is unclear what the authors mean.

Testimony of Juan José García before Antonio Fominaya, governor of Socorro, Socorro (New Granada), 12 March 1819[2]

In addition to the armies of San Martín and Bolívar, numerous small groups of fighters engaged in the struggle for independence. One guerrilla group based in Zapatoca, New Granada (present-day Colombia) was led by Ignacio Calvo, a rebel leader who had previously been exiled but escaped, and who was much feared by the royalists. His group apparently used the man testifying here, Juan José García, as a spy. It is puzzling, though, that Calvo is still mentioned here as an active guerrillero, because according to other documents he had been executed on 1 January 1819. However, Spanish sources also mentioned him as one of the guerrilla chiefs occupying Socorro in July 1819.[3]

ev

In the town of Socorro, on the twelfth day of March 1819, at 9 p.m., my clerk Victor Losada brought to me a man he had met in the street and whom he had known beforehand. The man had called him and told him that he came as a spy. Accompanied by his brother, Losada led him to my lodgings…. He said his name was José García, that he was born in Socorro and that he was a farmer by profession, and that he has been with Calvo's band for two years in the mountains of Favita; Calvo gave him twelve reales and ordered him to go to this town of Socorro in order to find out about the troops there and then return.

Asked where Calvo lives, how many there are in his company, and what kind of weapons he has, he said that he lives in Castame in the mountains of Favita on the river bank, where they have their quarters, and his force is made up of two hundred and seven men.

Asked what kind of weapons and ammunition they have, he said that they have firearms—both rifles and shotguns—and that each man has his own. They also have thirty machetes, and as for ammunition, he doesn't know the amount because each man has his own in his bag.

Asked what conversations he has heard, he said that he has heard that they are waiting for orders from **the Llanos** to attack, that he doesn't know where, but that they did order him here to examine the forces.

the Llanos: The grassy plains.

---

2   In Ernesto Restrepo Tirado, ed., *Archivo Santander III* (Bogotá: Aguila Negra Editorial, 1914), 192–95.

3   Oswaldo Díaz Díaz, *Historia extensa de Colombia, Volumen VI: La reconquista española, Tomo 2* (Bogotá: Ediciones Lerner, 1967), 207.

Asked what caused him to absent himself from his native region, he said that the motive was … that they took him to **the forces** three years ago now, before the royal army entered this town.

Asked which other residents of this town or surrounding towns found themselves with the rebels and what motivates them, he said that those who find themselves there are Ignacio Calvo, who is the commander of them all, and N. Segura, his second, in whom he has put all his trust; that the latter goes out with a small detachment, robbing and killing, and that he makes a soldier of anybody he imprisons, and that all his conversations are directed against the monarchical government, and that their motivation is to enter the Kingdom [of New Granada] and lay it waste.

Asked how many times he has come to this area and with what goal, he said, twice, the first time during **the week of Saint Barbara** with the objective of finding out the size of the forces that occupy this town, and the second time yesterday. Both times he was ordered to come by the traitor Calvo, and the first time, when the armed forces were strong, he went back, and now he met with the forementioned clerk whom he ended up telling that he had come to be presented to the judge.

Asked if apart from the two hundred and seven men that he mentions there are other bands or divisions next to the place where Calvo is, and if they frequently communicate with each other, he said that there is no band of rebel troops in that area, and that the bulk of the bands are about a two days' hike away on the banks of the Meta, with whom Calvo communicates.

Asked why he says that they try to enter the Kingdom when they have no more than two hundred and seven men, as he mentioned, when it is impossible to attack with those alone, and from which does he infer that there are more forces for the task, he said that he has not seen nor does he know that there are more troops than he mentioned.

Asked if all two hundred men that he mentioned are foot soldiers or if some of them are mounted, he said that all are foot soldiers and that when the opportunity presents itself for a detachment to go out, they seize beasts and ride without a saddle.

Asked for what reason the first time that he was ordered to go to this town, he didn't give himself away but instead returned to give notice to Commander Calvo of the troops and weapons that he had seen, whereby he showed his devotion to the rebel band; at the same time, with what goal he made himself known tonight to the witness, he said that the first time he did so out of fear because they told him at the market that Mr. Governor killed those [enemies] who presented themselves, and he doesn't know the woman who told him; and that this time he met the clerk whom he told that he came so that he could present himself.

Since he says that he didn't come forward the first time out of fear, whereas that should have been the same now, leaving the question why he was afraid the first time … it is clear that he presented himself now because of the weakness of the rebel forces, and because he is fearful that he will be killed in action.

J.P. Robertson and W.P. Robertson, *Letters on South America; Comprising Travels on the Paraná and Rio de La Plata*, 1819–20[4]

After leaving Paraguay in 1817 (see Document 26), the Scottish merchant William Parish Robertson moved back to Buenos Aires, where he would live until 1820. In these years, he was present at the annual festivities to celebrate the local start of the independence movement on 25 May 1810.

Public entertainments of every kind in South America go by the generic name of "*funciones.*" There were theatrical funciones, funciones de Iglesia, or church processions, government funciones, or public processions, and, above all, *las funciones mayas*, the annual celebration, on the 25th of May, of the independence of the country. On this latter occasion the square was tastefully fitted up with a moveable boarding which constituted a continuous archway on the four sides, leading into the centre. This boarding was painted and decorated so as to produce a scenic display as viewed from within, the arches being hung with festooned garlands, and the panels covered with emblematic designs, which formed an agreeable vista during the day, and which were illuminated during the night. The rejoicings continued generally for three days. They commenced on the eve of the 25th with music and an illumination of the town, dancing, and a general promenade in the great square; at sunrise the following morning, a salute was fired from the guns of the fort; and the children of the various schools, all neatly dressed, assembled in the *plaza*, where they were formed round the "Pyramid," a not very handsome obelisk, which, standing in the centre, had been erected in commemoration of the Revolution, and on which were inscribed the names of those heroes who had been the leaders in the emancipation of the country. Here the children sung the national hymn…. Which may be closely if not literally translated thus:

> Hear mortals hear! the ever sacred cry,
> Which through the air resounds—'tis liberty!
> Behold the broken chains 'neath which we've groaned;
> And see equality on high enthroned!
>
> With all a mother's anxious throes, the earth
> Gives to a young and glorious nation birth;

---

4   London: John Murray, 1843, volume III of 3: 125–29.

With laurel leaves its brow is circled round,
And at its feet a **lion** bites the ground.

Chorus

Green may the laurels ever be
Which we have gathered from on high!
Oh let us live but to be free!
Or, crowned with glory, let us die!

The hymn having been sung, and the children having retired, the square gradually filled during the forenoon with well dressed people. The troops appeared in new uniforms; and a grand procession of the public bodies, including the governor, his staff, the corps diplomatique, and all the field officers, proceeded from the fort or government house to the cathedral, where high mass, with Te Deum, was celebrated. In the afternoon and during the whole evening bands of military music played popular airs on the balcony of the cabildo or town hall; the inhabitants in gay attire crowded the streets, as well as the plaza mayor or great square, and here a grand display of fire-works took place at nine o'clock, when several thousands assembled to witness them; the night closing in with **tertulias** given by many of the principal families, and with patriotic assemblages in all the principal cafes of the city. It was for several years remarked, during the fervid course of the revolution, that the 25th of May always brought good news; and these creating an enthusiasm which animated all classes, and throwing down for the moment the dikes of classism, it was wonderful to see what general hilarity distinguished the "Fiestas mayas" throughout.

Richard Longfield Vowell, *Campaigns and Cruises, in Venezuela and New Grenada, and in the Pacific Ocean; from 1817–1830*[5]

Richard Longfield Vowell (1795–ca. 1837) was one of the 6,000 foreign mercenaries serving in Bolívar's armies during the wars of independence. He later also fought in Chile. After he returned to England, he wrote in great detail about his experiences. Here he comments on the social consequences of the wars on display in New Granada in 1821.

Quilichao is the first town on the road which rises from the valley to the ancient city of Popayan. In the neighborhood are extensive gold mines, which, in time of peace, used to be the source of wealth, not only to the owners, but also to the inhabitants at large, by means of the commerce introduced, on their account, into the country. In consequence of the war, the slaves and hired peons, who used to work these mines, had all been pressed into the armies of one party or another. We saw, still lingering about the deserted works, some wretchedly poor women and children, clothed in strange grotesque dresses, which were evidently the remains of the former gaudy clothing they used to take pride in, during the time of their prosperity, when the mines were worked. They all wore on their heads caps of a conical shape, striped with various colors; and had the appearance of some unearthly beings, as they issued, cowering and dejectedly, from their miserable hovels, built in the deep excavations, from which the sand containing gold had been dug. Some of them produced vultures' quills, filled with small quantities of gold grain, which they had collected; and bartered it, with the soldiers, for the heads and offal of the bullocks slaughtered for the army. The soil appears like a coarse red ochre; and contains, here and there, veins of a heavy black sand, in which the gold grain is found.

---

5   London: Longman and Co., 1831, I: 209–10.

Law adopted by Colombia to confiscate the possessions of Spaniards, 1821[6]

> Sooner or later during the independence period, the day of reckoning came for Spanish natives. In some parts of Spanish America, all of them were expelled, while some form of discrimination was introduced almost everywhere. The Congress of Colombia decided soon after its inception to confiscate the possessions of all Spanish natives.

๛

The GENERAL CONGRESS of COLOMBIA has come to decree and decrees the following.

Art. 1. Having been liberated by the weapons of the Republic, all property in each and every province, town, or place must be sequestered and confiscated that belongs to the Spanish government.

Art. 2. Included in this confiscation will be all movable and immovable property of all kinds, all credits, assets, and titles that belong to Spaniards who emigrate from a land that is under threat or attack by the troops of the Republic.

Art. 3. Excepted from this punishment are the Americans who within a time span of three months have returned to the same land from which they emigrated or those who are free inside the territory of the Republic.

Art. 4. Also excepted are the goods of each individual, whether American or Spanish, who by joining the Republic's troops in a liberated land, presents himself to its leaders and embraces the system of independence.

Art. 5. The personal and matrimonial property of women, and of the children of those who emigrated, provided they remain inside free territory, will be excepted from the confiscation of goods.

Art. 6. From all those who emigrated with an heir-apparent, only one-third to one-fifth of their goods will be confiscated.

---

6   John Carter Brown Library, Providence, RI.

Art. 7. Exempt from the punishment of confiscation are those under 21 years of age, even if they have emigrated, provided they don't engage in any kind of service against the Republic, and as long as one year after reaching that age, they **present themselves to enter the free territory**. In the interim, their goods will fall under the same regulations as in the case of minors or absentees.

Art. 8. All property confiscated from Colombians by the Spanish government because of its hatred of independence will be administered at the expense of the state until the legitimate party concerned presents itself to reclaim it.

Issued in the general palace in Rosario de Cúcuta, 16 October 1821. To be implemented—**Francisco de Paula Santander**.

present themselves to enter the free territory: Their possessions would not be seized if they entered Colombian soil within a year after turning 21.

Francisco de Paula Santander: Santander (1792–1840) was Colombia's vice-president.

Lionel Hervey to the Marquis of Londonderry, Madrid, 27 May 1822[7]

Although the odds of preserving their rule in mainland America were no longer in their favor, authorities in Spain remained optimistic. Lionel Hervey (1784–1843), the secretary to the British embassy in Madrid, asserts that Spanish politicians continue to rely on rosy reports from the American colonies.

❧

Martinez de la Rosa: Francisco Martínez de la Rosa (1787–1862), a university professor who was elected to the Cortes of Cádiz and served as Spain's first prime minister, was appointed as secretary of state in 1822.

Bardaxi: The diplomat, lawyer, and politician Eusebio Bardají Azara (1776–1842) was Spain's secretary of state in 1821–22.

I find that M. **Martinez de la Rosa** has adopted the sentiments of his predecessor, M. de **Bardaxi**, upon the subject of Mexico, and the other South American Provinces, and that the accounts which he has received from Mexico and Peru induce him to believe that those countries are not yet irretrievably lost to Spain, and that it will be impossible for the revolutionists to establish an independent Government. I did not think myself at liberty to enter into any discussion of this question, but I ventured to observe, that the Spanish Government had always been deceived in the reports which they had received from America, and that the system of procrastination, and the refusal to accept of the offers of the Americans, might force them to make overtures to some other Powers or to establish a republican form of Government.

---

7   In Charles Kingsley Webster, *Britain and the Independence of Latin America, 1812–1830: Select Documents from Foreign Office Archives* (London: Oxford UP, 1938), 386.

Basil Hall, *Extracts from a Journal, Written on the Coasts of Chili, Peru, and Mexico, in the Years 1820, 1821, 1822*[8]

Serving as a captain in the British Royal Navy, the well-traveled Scot Basil
Hall (1788–1844) came upon a group of enslaved blacks in Panama in 1822.
As he observes, the presumed freedom struggle that was being concluded in
South America had largely bypassed those held in servitude.

As I had been kept out of bed for two nights, attending to the pilotage of
the ship, I was glad to retire at an early hour; but I could get no sleep for
the noise in the Plaza, or great square, before the windows of my room.
After some time spent in vain endeavours to disregard the clamour, I rose
and sat at the window, to discover if I could see what was going on. It was
a bright moon-light night, and the grass which had been allowed to grow
up in the centre of the square was covered with parties of negro slaves,
some seated and others dancing in great circles, to the sound of rude music
made by striking a cocoa-nut shell with a short stick; while the whole party,
dancers as well as sitters, joined in a song with very loud but not discordant
voices. It appeared to be some festival of their own, which had assembled
to celebrate in this way.

I was half disappointed, at discovering nothing appropriate or plain-
tive about the music; on the contrary, it was extremely lively, and seemed
the result of light-hearted mirth. Many of the groups were singing, not
without taste and spirit, in a patriotic song of the day, long well known in
the independent states of the south, but only recently imported into the
isthmus. The burden of the song was Libertad! Libertad! Libertad! but I
conceive not one of these wretches attached the slightest meaning to the
words, but repeated them merely from their accordance with the music.
While listening, however, to these slaves, singing in praise of freedom, it
was difficult not to believe that some portion of the sentiment must go
along with the music: yet I believe it was quite otherwise, and that the
animation with which they sung, was due entirely to the lively character of
the song itself, and its happening to be the fashionable air of the day. There
was something discordant to the feelings in all this; and it was painful to
hear these poor people singing in praise of that liberty acquired by their
masters, from whose thoughts nothing certainly was farther removed than
any idea of extending the same boon to their slaves.

---

8   Edinburgh: Archibald, Constable and Co., 1824, volume II of 2: 152.

Francisco María Roca, *Friend of the Country or Essays about the Happiness of This Province*, 1822[9]

> Bolívar's plan to have the *presidencia* of Quito (whose area corresponded more or less to that of today's Ecuador) join Venezuela and New Granada in forming the new country of Colombia was not supported by many of its inhabitants. One reason for the port city of Guayaquil to remain outside Colombia, as explained here by one of the leading local revolutionaries, Francisco María Roca (1786–1846), was that its natural economic ties were with its southern neighbor of Peru, not Colombia.

PROPOSITION I

Let us examine whether it is in Guayaquil's interest to join a society with which it is linked commercially and if its interests will be damaged by joining another one.

It will seem excusable to wait with proving this assertion, because when a farming town is connected to a mercantile town by nature and its own interest, the other one being big, strong and rich, no one can present a reason for them to be separated; but if anyone is persuaded that the incorporation of the province [into another realm] will not at all influence its commerce, we will prove that he is deceived.

… Peru forms an inseparable unit with Guayaquil because of the mutual purchase of products, the capital that sustains shipping, and the precious metals that facilitate all exchanges. When we are united in name with another state that does not need or cannot consume our production, we will still absolutely depend on Peru, where our goods will be regarded as those of another people, and duties will necessarily be imposed on them in the places where they are consumed, while our government will impose similar duties on those who export here, viewing them as strangers. This attitude will make Peru look for the goods that we provide in our own country and elsewhere.

… Maybe they will tell me that once our ports are open to all the nations of Europe, they will rush from everywhere to bring us rich cargoes; but this can only be argued to those who neither know the country nor have any idea of our trade. Because what is the product that will draw Europeans to our ports instead of those of Peru? … Of all products, the Europeans may

---

9 Original title: *Amigo del país ó Ensayos sobre la Felicidad de esta provincia,* John Carter Brown Library, Providence, RI.

only look for cocoa, and then in limited amounts. And what will we do with the surplus and with the other products? We will lose them and ruin our agriculture as a direct consequence of such an unequal trade....

PROPOSITION II

We have proven that the province [of Guayaquil] has and will always derive all its advantages from Peru, and that any obstacle that must necessarily arise from belonging to another state will hamper and slow down its progress. But we must impartially examine whether a union with Colombia can be a happy one under the plan adopted by that Republic, whether in peacetime or during the turmoil of war.

... Some have tried to persuade us that the Republic [of Colombia] has an imprescriptible right to be joined by Guayaquil, and they are generous enough to allow us to impose some conditions on the union. They base themselves on the following reasons: 1. the constitution of the Republic, which seems to comprise this province, since it used to be within the boundaries of the Viceroyalty of New Granada; 2. our local situation; and 3. the protection it has given us against the enemies. Others mention the liberality of their institutions, and the fainthearted fear that their force will overrun everything and incorporate us without letting us make sure that they don't treat us as slaves....

Despite this, free and impartial men assure us that the Republic has no more rights than the King of Persia to demand we join it. The constitution, which contains a solemn act to unite the provinces of Venezuela and Cundinamarca, agreed upon by their representatives, is certainly a great and respectable work of politics, because it presents these peoples to the face of the world with a dignified character and a focused plan; but once they proceed to make that agreement a compulsory law that forces people who did not gather to establish it, who collaborate with another state, and who have shaken off the Spanish yoke by themselves, their behavior can only be classified as an infringement on the rights of man, or as an abuse of power similar in every way to that which has made us groan for three hundred years ...; because just as no man has or can have the right to command another against his will, even if it is to make him happy, neither does any society have that right over another one, without renewing the barbarism of the sixteenth century and the laughable decisions of Alexander VI.[10]

---

10 A reference to the Spanish conquest of America, enabled by the papal bull *Inter caetera* (1493), issued by Pope Alexander VI, which granted all lands of a line west and south of the Azores and Cape Verde Islands to Spain's Catholic Isabela and Fernando.

It is proven in politics and confirmed by experience, how towns that are deprived of their laws, customs and peculiar governments, lose the spirit peculiar to them that generates their energy; and if the incorporation of the province brings us these deprivations, we cannot find in it the happiness we seek. It may be argued that America has had the same laws and the same kind of government, and that consequently no town has to suffer the effects of those alterations. But this is not true, because in the Spanish system, America had neither laws nor government, and left to the whims of their despots, the towns were tyrannized more or less according to the disposition of the one who dominated them....

What good will the best laws and institutions of Colombia do for us? They cannot be adaptable to our character and will be incapable of making us happy because of the distance. In the brilliant era of their republican greatness, the Romans ... were despots of the peoples with whom they were united. A proconsul was a small tyrant who in no way differed from the Spanish viceroys or governors, and in no way from the intendant or governor that we have.

The constitution divides the Republic into departments, governments of provinces and cantons. Does it give us any advantage to form a department on our territory, which is divided into governments and these again into cantons? The president of the Republic will give the administrative jobs to the military, and that is the way it has to be because of the close links between the army command and the world of politics; and it is absolutely justified that men who have sealed with their blood the freedom of the Republic earn the distinction of being appointed to senior posts. But this system, which will make the Colombians happy, will not lead those of Guayaquil to happiness, for whom it would make no difference to receive officials from Colombia or Europe: we would thereby not have our own representative popular government, and our condition would not have improved.

Antonio José de Sucre to Simón Bolívar, Yungay, Peru, 25 February 1824[11]

Despite San Martín's declaration of independence of Peru, many areas of the former viceroyalty remained in royalist hands in the early 1820s. The hopes of revolutionaries received a serious blow when the rebel garrison in Callao mutinied in February 1824 after having suffered numerous deprivations. It forced the insurgent commander to abandon Lima and enabled royalist troops to move into the capital. The Colombians, however, remained committed to a war of liberation. Colombia's congress responded by naming Bolívar dictator of Peru. His chances of success in reversing the situation in Peru seemed slim, as becomes clear in this letter written by Antonio José de Sucre, Bolívar's right-hand man. Just ten months later, Sucre would lead the revolutionaries to victory at Ayacucho, an event that seemed inconceivable at this stage.

I must speak to you now about what matters most. If events force us to retreat to Colombia, it is necessary to do it by ship. Over land we would lose the army. The Venezuelans and New Granadans, who are not very enthusiastic about going to Quito, will stay behind sick or will fall behind, while the people from Quito will leave when they arrive in their country. The mules we have are detestable and bad for such an arduous march; the horses are the same and we lose most of them. Of those that **Molina** brings from Lima, only 60 are usable and the others need to get fat, or better, get exchanged on the coast if there are means to do so. **Santa María** inspected the Vargas battalion, and I suggested to him to notify you of its condition; it cannot do ten marches in a row. The Peruvian recruits all get sick, as recruits in general do, but these recruits have the opportunity to run away, even when they are dying in the hospital. Count therefore on the transportation of a large hospital. The Peruvian army takes off like pigeons when it hears retreat; the only way to transport it safely is to drive it to the shore and embark it. We need to ponder much on this operation to leave the country, focused on the bare facts; you will have done that with the most careful reflection.

I will allow myself to give you my opinion. If you try to abandon this territory, it is better to do so using the advantages that we have; I think that the Spaniards would not disdain to enter into an armistice of 12 to 20

Molina: Sucre's aide-de-camp Ramón Molina.

Santa María: Genaro Santa María, a Colombian aide-de-camp of Bolívar who later turned against him. He also attended the meeting of a group of conspirators who decided to assassinate Sucre in 1830.

---

11 In Simon B. O'Leary, ed., *Memorias del General O'Leary*, 32 vols. (Caracas: Imprenta de la "Gazeta Oficial," 1879), I: 130–33.

months to **wait for the results of European affairs,** if we offer to evacuate
Peru. Then we could carry out this evacuation with calm and order and return
our 7,000 men to Colombia with whom we could defend ourselves well,
and more if we decide to bring four thousand from the South to Venezuela,
while also bringing as many Venezuelans. With a foundation of 6,000 men
from New Granada and Venezuela, we would have 10,000 for any need; and
this [arrangement] could be organized for those 12 to 18 months. What I do
not know is how to maintain and support such a strong force in the South.
You know those departments in order to judge their resources.

In this year we should see the dénouement of Europe, which will more
than anything decide [the fate of] America. Every Colombian must now
keep one eye on Peru and another on the Holy Alliance. This damned
coalition of Europe's kings makes me fear the continued existence of our
institutions; I cannot deny to you that I am more concerned about them
than about the Spanish from Peru, because the latter would at most take
Quito from us, but the Europeans can destroy us all.... There is already talk
of a division of America in favor of the sovereigns of the Holy Alliance,
leaving Mexico for Spain. I don't doubt it because Fernando, in exchange
for keeping something, will give up the rest, and we have seen how these
sovereigns have behaved vis-à-vis their [own] peoples. Against us they will
be crueler and more shameless, since they still believe we are Indians.

Maybe these Spaniards from Peru will oppose this project, and I do not
think much of tempting them. I was desperate to talk to you to indicate my
views about a negotiation that could perhaps take place to save our honor,
and maybe our existence, which if that project is real, we may not be able
to. We have arrived at the most terrible crisis of the revolution....

The Spaniards lost everything because they wanted to support their constitution at all costs, and although we must all die rather than be colonists
or belong to Spain, we do not have the means for such a solution.... It was
rumored that France wants to appropriate Colombia during this breakup of
America, and death is worth more than being French colonists and being
governed by the Bourbons.[12] We are in for a great conflict, from which I
expect very little relief provided by the commissioners from England in
Bogotá. The English government is more generous than the others, but it
will not be so generous as to engage in a war for our support. I am aware of
its conduct with respect to Spain, to which it also spoke much of protection
to maintain its liberties, and I don't want to deceive myself with vain hope.
We will be delivered to our fate, and we must use all means and measures

---

12 The vice-president of Colombia, Francisco de Paula Santander, expressed his fear of French
     invasion in a letter to Bolívar around the same time. Rumors about such an event, fueled by the
     French invasion of Spain in 1823, were still floating around one year later.

to avoid wasting so many efforts, hardships, and sacrifices to achieve our independence.

Goodbye, my General, I wish more than anything to talk to you, because I would shed a thousand doubts and be satisfied after hearing your opinions; for now I only want to add that if our affairs have to miscarry, it is better to escape our fate here in a battle, in which we will decide if we have enough means to oppose all mankind, in case people want to reduce us to servitude.

Manuel Antonio López, *Historical Memories of Colonel Manuel Antonio López, Deputy to the General Staff of the Liberating Army: Colombia and Peru, 1819–1826*[13]

Just before the battle of Ayacucho (9 December 1824), two generals on either side allowed the royalists who had relatives or friends in the republican camp to fraternize. The long embrace of two sets of brothers recounted here underscores that the independence fight was often a civil war.

❧

Everything began to take on a martial character. The forces in both camps were inspected by their commanders, and … prepared to make breakfast. At eight o'clock **General Monet**, a well-built, dashing figure with a cinnamon-colored beard, came down to the patriot side, called **Córdova**, a friend and acquaintance since the previous day, and told him that there were several officers in the Spanish camp who had brothers, relatives, and friends in the republican camp. He wanted to know if they could see each other before the battle. General Córdova replied that in his opinion there was no objection to this and that the General-in-Chief would undoubtedly consent to it; and having communicated it to General Sucre, he immediately gave permission to anyone who wanted to speak to his friends to go to the line, and he did so with great pleasure, since he was as versed in humanity and courtesy as he was in warfare. We were more than fifty, predominantly Peruvians such as Lieutenant-Colonel Pedro Blanco, and *numantinos* or members of the Colombian Battalion of Numancia … among them the sergeant-majors from Granada Rafael Cuervo, Antonio Zornoza and Pedro Torres, and the Venezuelans Pedro Guás from Guanare and Antonio Guerra from Maracaibo.

Many came along more out of curiosity than interest. We left the swords within our line, and we met in the neutral zone that was separate from the Spanish camp; Monet and about forty commanders and officers were there; he and Córdova, the two line generals that day, began to talk to each other a little to our left; after those from the other camp had respectfully saluted General Monet, Major Cuervo, and other *numantinos* and Peruvians whom they knew, we moved forward … to release youthful cordiality, like students do when they hear the school bell ring; but surpassing us in speed was Spanish Brigadier Antonio Tur, an interesting young man of great

General Monet: Juan Antonio Monet (1782–1837), a Spanish general who had earlier taken part in the battle of Junín.

Córdova: The Colombian general José María Córdova (1799–1829).

---

13 Original title: *Recuerdos Históricos del coronel Manuel Antonio López ayudante del Estado Mayor Jeneral Libertador: Colombia i Perú 1819–1826* (Bogotá: J.B. Gaitan, 1878), 143–44.

height and about 34 years of age, who had perhaps been the one to ask for this meeting. He rushed to us, looking for Lieutenant-Colonel Vicente Tur of Peru's general staff, who was his brother and about six years his junior.

Finding him right away, he addressed him in a sharp tone: "Oh! My little brother, how sorry I am to see you covered in shame!" Vicente replied: "I did not come here to be insulted by you, and if that is the case, I'm leaving." Antonio ran after him and embraced him, and they cried in each other's arms for a long time. This scene, but without reproaches, was then repeated between Pedro Blanco, commander of a squadron of Hussars of Junín, and his brother, commander of a Spanish cavalry force, both natives of Upper Peru.

DOCUMENT 52:

Gaceta del Gobierno de Lima, 1 January 1825

> Three weeks after the decisive battle of Ayacucho, the official government newspaper of republican Peru was elated about the defeat of the royalists and grateful to the victorious army. The future seemed bright.

Peru, at last free and independent, presents itself in the new year worthy of its great destinies. It triumphed over its oppressors, declared the rights of man, and guarantees, all at once, the freedom of all America. There is no army anymore anywhere in this continent; hardly a handful of insignificant men are left who in Callao resist the sanctity of the most solemn surrender of their legitimate commanders. A single campaign, a single engagement sufficed to destroy those who had been victorious for fourteen years; they begged for our clemency; it has all been defeated, and the echo of peace resounds everywhere. At Junín began the dawn of so much glory; in Ayacucho, the sun shone, and the dense clouds that covered the Peruvian horizon have vanished for good.... Glory to our brave warriors! Glory to the virtuous Colombians! Eternal glory and boundless gratitude to the immortal SUCRE, LIBERATOR OF PERU. Order has succeeded anarchy, virtue egoism, liberty oppression, and happiness has supplanted misfortune.... While it lay dying, Peru stretched out its hands to BOLIVAR; he pulled it from the grave and restored its honor and life. Europe may arm itself to harm us, the whole world may conspire against us, but a united America is not afraid of such threats as long as Bolívar presides over its destinies.

Law issued by Peru's Governing Council, forcing enslaved people to return to work, *Gaceta del Gobierno de Lima*, 22 September 1825

Peru's independence in 1821 was immediately followed by the adoption of a law that freed all enslaved people born in the future and the gradual emancipation of those who were still enslaved. The slave trade was forbidden. Nevertheless, enslaved people still had to work until their emancipation, although more than a few men had run away, usually to fight in an army. The Peruvian government decided to force them to return to work.

As a consequence of the war and the invasions that this capital has suffered, many slaves, calling themselves free, have abandoned their houses, and have renounced the obligation to acknowledge their masters, under the pretext of having enrolled in an army corps. Neither the nation uses these workers nor can the land, to the cultivation of which most of them are assigned, be prepared and fertilized. It was bound to happen this way; but it is also necessary for the government to prevent in time the disorders of the wandering and vagabond life to which they are committed. For this purpose, it decrees:

1. Within the set term of twenty days, starting on the date of publication of this measure, all masters will give their slaves printed tickets that certify their ownership. This will be supervised by the inspectors of the neighborhood or valley where they reside, and approved by those of the district.

2. When the term mentioned in the previous article has expired, night watchmen, patrols, and commissions from the countryside and the city will apprehend those found without slave tickets and those enlisted in some regiment or battalion, bring them to the nearest police station, and report to the prefect so that he can arrange for them to be handed over to the masters who claim them, after they pay the prisoner's expenses. Otherwise, the slaves will be made to work the land or their skills will be applied otherwise.

3. He who under any pretext associates with the slaves to insult their masters or impedes the execution of the provisions of the previous articles will be put in **jail**, and the prefect, notified of what has occurred, will arrange for a judge to start a trial so that the correct punishment will be applied according to the law.

jail: It soon turned out, however, that there were too few jails in the city.

4. The conduct of the slaves, their devotion to their work, and the respect and subordination that they show towards their masters, are qualities they need to have to enter the **manumission lotteries**, as set out in the decree of the provisional government of 21 September 1821.

5. The masters, on their part, shall take care to minister to their slaves adequate food and clothing, and treat them with great humanity, especially the elderly, who shall not be assigned to work in the fields or tasks beyond their strength, and the correctional punishments that are applied must be moderate. In case of serious offences, the inspectors will intervene as ordered.

6. The inspectors are responsible to the government for the legality of the ticket they sign, it being understood that those tickets should be renewed the first day of each month to avoid any fraud.

7. This decree will be observed in the entire territory of the republic, and the prefects, intendants, and governors will be charged with its punctual fulfillment.

8. The Ministry of State in the Department of Government and Foreign Affairs is responsible for the execution of this decree.

Print, publish and circulate. Issued at the Government Palace in Lima, 19 September 1825, year six of independence and 4 of the Republic. **Hipólito Unanue**, **Juan Salazar**, and **José de Larrea y Loredo**. By the order of **H.E.** and Minister Manuel Lino Ruiz de Pancorbo.

Constitution of Bolivia, 22 November 1826[14]

When Upper Peru declared itself an independent new state in 1825 and named itself for *El Libertador*, it lacked a constitution. Upon the request of its politicians, Bolívar wrote it the next year. His plan for a constitution was adopted with only minor changes by the country's constituent congress.

Article 11. Bolivians are

1. All those born in the territory of the Republic.
2. The children of a Bolivian father or mother born outside the territory, when they legally express their wish to take up residence in Bolivia.
3. Those who fought for liberty in Junín or Ayacucho.
4. Foreigners that obtain naturalization papers or have lived in the territory of the Republic for three years.
5. All those who until today have been slaves are hence rendered free when this Constitution is published, but they cannot leave the house of their former masters, except in a way that a special law will determine.[15]

Article 12. The duties of every Bolivian are

1. To be subject to the Constitution and the laws.
2. To respect and obey the constituted authorities.
3. To contribute to public expenditures.
4. To sacrifice his goods, and his own life, when the health of the Republic requires it.
5. To watch over the preservation of the public freedoms.

Article 13. The Bolivians who are denied the exercise of electoral power will enjoy all civil rights granted to citizens.

---

14 In J.R. Gutiérrez, ed., *Las constituciones políticas que ha tenido la República Boliviana (1826–1868)* (Santiago: Imprenta de "El Independiente," 1869), 4–5.

15 Bolívar's proposal had not mentioned that formerly enslaved people could not abandon the house of their former masters, merely stating "A special law will determine the compensation to be made to their former owners."

Article 14. To be a citizen it is necessary

1. To be a Bolivian.
2. To be married or older than twenty-one years of age.
3. To be able to read and write, although this qualification shall be
    required only after the year 1836.
4. To have some form of employment or trade, or to practice some science
    or art, without subjection to another person as a domestic servant.

Article 15. Citizens are

1. Those who fought for liberty in Junín or Ayacucho.
2. Foreigners who have obtained citizenship papers.
3. Foreigners married to a Bolivian woman who fulfills conditions 3
    and 4 of article 14.
4. Single foreigners who have lived in the Republic for four years and
    fulfill the same conditions.

Article 16. The citizens of the nations of what formerly was Spanish America
will enjoy citizenship rights in Bolivia according to the treaties signed with these.

Article 17. Only those who are citizens exercising citizenship can obtain
employment and offices in public service.

Article 18. The exercise of citizenship is suspended

1. In case of madness.
2. For the blemish of being a fraudulent debtor.
3. For being criminally prosecuted.
4. For being a notorious drunk, gambler or beggar.
5. For buying or selling votes in the elections or disturbing the peace
    during the elections.

Article 19. Citizenship rights are forfeited

1. For betrayal of the public cause.
2. For naturalization in a foreign country.
3. For having suffered infamous or corporeal punishment by virtue of
    a judicial sentence, and not having obtained a restitution of rights
    from the legislature.
4. For accepting employments, honors, or emoluments from another
    government, without the consent of the **Chamber of Censors**.

GLOSSARY

Abascal y Sousa, José: Viceroy of Peru (1806–16) whose determination helped maintain Spanish rule in Peru for several years.

Angostura, Congress of: Congress convened by Bolívar that met from 1819 to 1821. Its delegates created the republic of Colombia, uniting New Granada, Venezuela, and Quito.

Artigas, José Gervasio: Leader of rural workers and vagrants in the Banda Oriental who conducted a guerrilla war against royalist forces in Montevideo and later republicans from Buenos Aires. He also tried to introduce land reform.

Ayacucho, Battle of: Decisive battle in the South American wars between royalists and independence fighters, fought on 9 December 1824 near the Peruvian town of Ayacucho.

Azurduy, Juana: A mestiza native of Upper Peru who commanded an all-male army that engaged royalists in 16 battles.

Banda Oriental: Easternmost territory of the viceroyalty of the Río de la Plata.

Bayonne: Town in southwestern France, where Napoleon forced Spanish King Fernando VII and his father to relinquish their claims to the Spanish throne in 1808.

Bogotá: Capital of the viceroyalty of New Granada, then of independent Cundinamarca (1813–15) and Colombia (1819–30).

Bolívar, Simón Antonio José: Chief leader of the independence movement in northern South America who served as Colombia's president (1819–30), dictator of Peru (1824–27), and president of Bolivia (1825).

Bonaparte, Joseph: King of Naples who was named King of Spain by his brother Napoleon in 1808.

Boves, José Tomás: Spanish native who became the leader of an army of *llaneros* in Venezuela. Helped the royalist cause and was feared for his cruelty.

Boyacá, Battle of: Encounter in which Bolívar's forces defeated the royalists and thereby laid the foundation for the independence of New Granada.

Buenos Aires: Capital of the viceroyalty of the Río de la Plata. Formally part of an independent republic by 1816, it was never occupied by royalists during the wars of independence.

Caracas: Capital of the first two independent Venezuelan republics (1811–12 and 1813–14).

Cartagena de Indias: Port city in New Granada that declared independence in 1811, after which it was engaged in a war with royalist forces that led to a siege in which thousands died.

castas: Mixed-race people of African descent and any other ethnicity.

Chacabuco, Battle of: Military encounter on 12 February 1817 in which the Chilean revolutionaries led by O'Higgins defeated their royalist enemies.

Cochrane, Thomas, Lord: Scotsman who as commander-in-chief of the Chilean navy helped reduce Spanish naval power in the Pacific.

Comisión de Reemplazos: Committee in Spain that financed and organized armed expeditions to South America.

Cortes of Cádiz: Spain's first parliament, made up of delegates from both sides of the Atlantic, which adopted a progressive constitution in 1812.

Council of Regency: Body established in 1810 to rule over Spain and the "Indies," which organized the Cortes of Cádiz.

creole: White person born in the Americas.

Cry of Dolores: Hidalgo's call for a revolt against Napoleon's France.

Cundinamarca: Area around Bogotá that rebelled against Spanish rule and declared its independence in 1813. Conquered by Morillo's troops two years later.

Elío, Francisco Javier de: Royalist governor of Montevideo (1807–09) and viceroy of the Río de la Plata (1810–12).

Fernando VII: Spain's King who was overthrown by Napoleon, but returned to the throne in 1813, when he installed a reactionary regime that only considered a military solution to the conflicts in the Americas.

Francia, José Gaspar Rodríguez de: Leader of Paraguay's independence.

freedom of the womb: Freedom enjoyed at birth by children of enslaved mothers, as decreed by various independent countries.

Guanajuato: Mexican mining town sacked by Hidalgo's army, which made members of the middle and upper classes turn against his movement.

Hidalgo, Miguel: Leader of a massive Mexican insurrection against Spanish rule, in which mostly Indigenous people and *castas* took part.

Huaqui, Battle of: Military encounter on 20 June 1811 in which royalist troops from Peru defeated those from Buenos Aires.

Iturbide, Agustín de: Royalist commander who authored the Plan of Iguala and became the emperor of independent New Spain in 1821. His brief rule ended in his abdication and execution.

Iturrigaray, José de: Viceroy of New Spain who was ousted in a *coup d'état* by *peninsulares* in 1808.

Junín, Battle of: Battle in Peru in which Bolívar's troops defeated their royalist enemies on 6 August 1824. Prelude to the Battle of Ayacucho.

La Laguna, Battle of: Battle fought in Upper Peru on 13 September 1816, in which the royalists won, killing 700 of their enemies.

Lima: Capital of Peru's Viceroyalty.

Liniers, Santiago de: French native who led the defeat of British invaders in 1806 and 1807. Ousted and executed by royalists during his tenure as interim viceroy of the Río de la Plata.

llaneros: Residents of the Venezuelan *Llanos* (the tropical grassland plain home to a vast cattle industry) who initially fought on the royalist side but switched their allegiance to the revolutionaries in 1817.

Maipú, Battle of: Battle of 5 April 1818, in which San Martín's forces defeated the royalists, securing republican rule in Chile.

Mexico City: Capital of the Viceroyalty of New Spain.

Miranda, Francisco: Precursor of the independence movements who served as dictator of Venezuela during that country's first republic (1811–12). Betrayed by fellow insurgents.

Montevideo: City in the east of the Río de la Plata, which was in royalist hands until 1814. An insurgent victory in that year was followed by many years of turmoil.

Morelos, José María: Parish priest who took over as leader of the Mexican insurrection after Hidalgo's death. Organized a congress that issued a constitution.

Morillo, Pablo: Spanish Field Marshal whose army restored royalist rule in much of northern South America before the tide turned against him.

Napoleon Bonaparte: France's emperor who replaced Fernando VII as Spain's King in 1808 with his own brother Joseph.

Nariño, Antonio: Native of Bogotá accused of conspiring against Spanish rule in 1794. Worked as a pro-republican journalist during the independence struggle.

New Granada: Viceroyalty consisting of today's Colombia, Ecuador, and Panama.

New Spain: Viceroyalty made up of Mexico, Central America, the Spanish Caribbean.

O'Donojú, Juan: Spain's last captain general in New Spain, who recognized its independence.

O'Higgins, Bernardo: Insurgent army commander who became Supreme Director of Chile.

pardo: Mulatto.

peninsular: A white person born in Spain.

Peru: Viceroyalty.

Pétion, Alexandre: President of the republic of Haiti who helped Bolívar and his men gain a foothold in Venezuela in 1816 on the condition that slavery be abolished.

Pezuela, Joaquín de la: Viceroy of Peru (1816–21), whom army officers forced to resign because of his handling of the war.

Piar, Manuel: Born in Curaçao, this *pardo* general among the fighters for Venezuelan independence was arrested on Bolívar's orders and executed for allegedly inciting race war.

Plan of Iguala: Devised by Iturbide and issued in 1821, this document proposed to declare New Spain's independence as a constitutional monarchy.

porteño: Resident of Buenos Aires.

Quito: A *presidencia* (a small administrative unit) under Spanish rule, this area was incorporated into Colombia in 1819 without input from its inhabitants.

Riego, Rafael: Major in the Spanish army whose call to restore the Constitution of Cádiz found wide acceptance in 1820 and prevented a large fleet from trying to reconquer Buenos Aires.

Río de la Plata: Viceroyalty, comprising today's Argentina, Bolivia, Chile, Paraguay, and Uruguay.

San Martín, José de: After a military career in Spain, this native of today's Uruguay became the chief leader of the armed struggle against the royalists in southern South America.

Sobremonte, Rafael, marquis de: Viceroy of the Río de la Plata (1804–07).

Someruelos, Salvador: Captain-General and Governor of Cuba (1799–1812).

Talaveras: The Royal Regiment of Talavera de la Reina, which arrived in Chile in 1810, helped to defeat the independence fighters at Rancagua in 1814, but lost to them at Chacabuco in 1817.

Tucumán: Town in present-day Argentina where the government of Buenos Aires convened a congress in 1816 that declared "the independence of the United Provinces of South America."

Túpac Amaru: Peruvian leader of the largest anti-Spanish revolt before the independence wars, in which he was supported by tens of thousands of men.

Upper Peru: Region in interior South America that was transferred in 1776 from Peru to the new viceroyalty of the Río de la Plata. It became Bolivia upon gaining independence.

SELECT BIBLIOGRAPHY

Adelman, Jeremy. *Sovereignty and Revolution in the Iberian Atlantic.* Princeton: Princeton UP, 2006.

Anna, Timothy E. *Spain and the Loss of America.* Lincoln: U of Nebraska P, 1983.

Blanchard, Peter. *Under the Flags of Freedom: Slave Soldiers and the Wars of Independence in Spanish South America.* Pittsburgh: U of Pittsburgh P, 2008.

Collier, Simon. *Ideas and Politics of Chilean Independence, 1808–1833.* Cambridge: Cambridge UP, 1967.

Costeloe, Michael P. *Response to Revolution: Imperial Spain and the Spanish American Revolutions, 1810–1840.* New York: Cambridge UP, 1986.

Demélas, Marie-Danielle. *Nacimiento de la guerra de guerrilla: El diario de José Santos Vargas (1810–1825).* La Paz: Plural Editores; Lima: Institut français d'études andines, 2007.

Di Meglio, Gabriel. *¡Viva el bajo pueblo! La plebe urbana de Buenos Aires y la política entre la Revolución de Mayo y el rosismo.* Buenos Aires: Prometeo, 2006.

Echeverri, Marcela. *Indian and Slave Royalists in the Age of Revolution: Reform, Revolution, and Royalism in the Northern Andes, 1780–1825.* New York: Cambridge UP, 2016.

Ferrer, Ada. *Freedom's Mirror: Cuba and Haiti in the Age of Revolution.* New York: Cambridge UP, 2014.

Hamnett, Brian R. *The End of Iberian Rule on the American Continent, 1770–1830.* New York: Cambridge UP, 2017.

Helg, Aline. *Liberty and Equality in Caribbean Colombia, 1770–1835.* Chapel Hill: U of North Carolina P, 2004.

Johnson, Lyman L. *Workshop of Revolution: Plebeian Buenos Aires and the Atlantic World, 1776–1810.* Durham, NC: Duke UP, 2011.

Lucena Giraldo, Manuel. *Naciones de rebeldes: Las revoluciones de independencia latinoamericanas.* Madrid: Taurus, 2010.

McFarlane, Anthony. *War and Independence in Spanish America.* London: Routledge, 2014.

Morales, Edgardo Perez. *No Limits to Their Sway: Cartagena's Privateers and the Masterless Caribbean in the Age of Revolutions.* Nashville: Vanderbilt UP, 2018.

Múnera, Alfonso. *El fracaso de la nación: Región, clase y raza en el Caribe colombiano (1717–1810).* Bogotá: Banco de la República/El Áncora Editores, 1998.

Ossa Santa Cruz, Juan Luis. *Armies, Politics and Revolution: Chile, 1808–1826.* Liverpool: Liverpool UP, 2014.

Rieu-Millán, Marie Laure. *Los diputados americanos en las Cortes de Cádiz (Igualdad o independencia).* Madrid: Consejo Superior de Investigaciones Científicas, 1990.

Rodríguez O., Jaime E. *"We Are Now the True Spaniards": Sovereignty, Revolution, Independence, and the Emergence of the Federal Republic of Mexico, 1808–1824.* Stanford: Stanford UP, 2012.

Soriano, Cristina. *Tides of Revolution: Information, Insurgencies, and the Crisis of Colonial Rule in Venezuela.* Albuquerque: U of New Mexico P, 2018.

Stein, Barbara H. and Stanley J. Stein. *Crisis in an Atlantic Empire: Spain and New Spain, 1808–1810*. Baltimore: Johns Hopkins UP, 2014.

Thibaud, Clément. *Repúblicas en armas: Los ejércitos bolivarianos en la Guerra de Independencia en Colombia y Venezuela*. Bogotá: Planeta, 2003.

Van Young, Eric. *The Other Rebellion: Popular Violence, Ideology, and the Mexican Struggle for Independence, 1810–1821*. Stanford: Stanford UP, 2001.

Walker, Charles F. *The Tupac Amaru Rebellion*. Cambridge, MA: The Belknap Press of Harvard UP, 2014.

Mexico City, 3, 15, 34, 35
Mina, Francisco Javier
    Proclamation by Javier Mina, Explaining the Motives for His Expedition, 141–42
Miranda, Francisco, 27–28, 29–30, 52, 72
Molina, Ramón, 171
monarchism, 49
Monet, Juan Antonio, 174
Monteagudo, Bernardo de, 116
Monteverde, Domingo, 29, 30
Montevideo, 19, 20, 24, 26, 113
Morales, Francisco Tomás
    letter to Morillo on Bolívar's failed invasion of Venezuela, 139–40
    mention by Sevilla, 135
Morelos, José María
    about, 18
    Campillo's letter to, 105–07
    Manifesto for the Mexican People by the Representatives of the Provinces of North America, 123
Morillo, Pablo
    on dispatching priests to improve morality, 152–53
    mentions of, 135, 136–37, 148
    Morales's letter to on Bolívar's failed invasion of Venezuela, 139–40
    on not drafting enslaved people into army, 150–51
    reconquest of New Granada and Venezuela for Spain, 36–37, 39, 132
mulattoes, 3, 7. *See also* black people
Muñecas, Ildefonso de las, 131
Murat, Joachim, 75–77

Napoleon Bonaparte
    conquest of Spain, 7–9, 35
    letters to Murat on Spanish America, 75–77
    religious freedom and, 13
    Spanish American reactions to, 10, 28
Nariño, Antonio, 6, 33
navy, 41–42
New Granada
    about, 1

Cádiz constitution and citizenship debate, 35
Comuneros revolt, 5, 68
Fernando VII's military expedition against, 36–37
García, testimony of, 158–60
independence movement, 31–32, 38–39
maps, *2, 27*
Ortiz, interrogation of, 68–69
religion, appeals to, 34
revolt fears, 6
soldier demographics, 45
union with Venezuela, 39
Vowell on social consequences of war, 163
    See also Bogotá; Caracas; Cartagena de Indias; Colombia; Quito; Venezuela
New Spain, 1, *2, 16. See also* Central America; Mexico
newspapers (freedom of the press), 12, 33, 34–35, 88
Nicaragua, 47, 121–22
North America, map, *48*

Ocumare (Venezuela), 30, 139–40
O'Donojú, Juan, 46, 47
O'Higgins, Bernardo
    Chile, liberation of, and, 27, 40
    decree on race, 149
    letter to San Martín, 146
    Peru, liberation of, and, 42
Ortiz, José, interrogation of, 68–69
Osorio, Mariano, 27

Padilla, Manuel, 23
Panama, 167
Pancorbo, Manuel Lino Ruiz de, 178
Paraguay
    Artigas and, 26
    Brackenridge's *Voyage to South America*, 148
    independence movement, 23–24
    Rengger and Longchamp's *Historical Essay on the Revolution of Paraguay and the Dictatorial Government of Dr. Francia*, 156–57
    Robertson's *Four Years in Paraguay*, 124–26

From the Publisher

A name never says it all, but the word "Broadview" expresses a good deal of the philosophy behind our company. We are open to a broad range of academic approaches and political viewpoints. We pay attention to the broad impact book publishing and book printing has in the wider world; for some years now we have used 100% recycled paper for most titles. Our publishing program is internationally oriented and broad-ranging. Our individual titles often appeal to a broad readership too; many are of interest as much to general readers as to academics and students.

Founded in 1985, Broadview remains a fully independent company owned by its shareholders—not an imprint or subsidiary of a larger multinational.

For the most accurate information on our books (including information on pricing, editions, and formats) please visit our website at www.broadviewpress.com. Our print books and ebooks are available for sale on our site.

broadview press
www.broadviewpress.com